Mable's Girl

Becka,

I hope you enjoy my book.

God bless you.

Cherie A. Dryden

Mable's Girl

Cherie Ann Dupler

TATE PUBLISHING
AND ENTERPRISES, LLC

Published by Tate Publishing & Enterprises, LLC
127 E. Trade Center Terrace | Mustang, Oklahoma 73064 USA
1.888.361.9473 | www.tatepublishing.com

Tate Publishing is committed to excellence in the publishing industry. The company reflects the philosophy established by the founders, based on Psalm 68:11,
"The Lord gave the word and great was the company of those who published it."

Book design copyright © 2013 by Tate Publishing, LLC. All rights reserved.

Published in the United States of America

ISBN: 978-1-62994-404-3
1. Biography & Autobiography / Personal Memoirs And
2. Biography & Autobiography / Historical
13.10.01

Dedication:

When I was less than two years old my mom and my grandma taught me my first song, a chorus. It has been and continues to be the foundation of my life. What a wonderful gift they gave me.

"At the cross, at the cross,

Where I first saw the light:

And the burdens of my heart rolled away;

It was there by faith, I received my sight,

And now I am happy all the day."

To my wonderful grandmother, Mae, who taught me about Jesus and also about the joy of worship; and to my equally wonderful mother, Mable, who read Bible stories to me and told me to "always tell the truth." To these two women, I thank you. I love you both.

Herein lays the truth.

Table of Contents

Introduction

Introduction

I decided to write about some of my family history, as well as some of my life not on some whim, but because I felt that I may have something worthwhile to say, and also because I felt compelled to share it. Perhaps it may serve to assist someone who may go through similar times or situations. I think and I hope that it will also entertain from time to time.

I share my life growing up so you may see the family I thought I knew very well. Perhaps they are similar to yours. I think you will be able to identify. Finally, I share my life as a young mother and more. Most Moms will be able to empathize with much of this. Certainly for those of us who are part of the Baby Boom Generation, your story is likely similar to my own at least in most respects, such as historical references and the cultural outlook of that time period. For others, maybe it will enlighten and provide insight to a world, timeframe and experiences different from your own. Regardless of the time, my story is your story. Though you may not know me yet, by the time you finish this book, you will. Know that on every page I have you in my thoughts, my prayers. Perhaps within these pages, you may glean something valuable for your life. I sincerely hope so.

Names of all living people have been changed in respect to their privacy. Any references I have used here are to tell what happened, simple *facts,* how I felt about it, what I knew at the time or now, how I observed, perceived and learned others responded or felt, and are by no means to be considered some academic, historical, spiritual, theological *final word* on any given subject. I do not claim to be an authority, nor have I written with the intent to offend or to start a debate with anyone.

Historical and other general references were obtained from Internet, unless otherwise noted.

These following verses, among others, have not only given me much comfort in times of need, they have proven to be truth. Perhaps they will be both for you as well.

A man's heart plans his way; But the LORD directs his steps.
Proverbs 16:9

For I know the thoughts that I think toward you, says the LORD, thoughts of peace and not of evil, to give you a future and a hope. Jeremiah 29:11 NKJV

No weapon forged to be used against you will succeed; you will refute everyone who tries to accuse you. [1] This is what the LORD will do for his servants – I will vindicate them," [2] says the LORD.

Isaiah 54:17 NET Bible

Prologue

I take walks in the wooded park near my house, both for exercise and for leisure, appreciating the green serenity, the wind whispering through lush foliage of the trees and brush, the quiet ripple of the small waterfall as it rushes under the foot bridge. The sky on a summer day in my park is like no other, white cumulus clouds against the brilliant blue backdrop.

Today's walk was different though. The day was as shiny as usual; the sounds and smells were the same. ...

But today, my mother died.

She was old and getting more feeble, but is this really ever "expected?"

I passed a woman I knew who was walking her dog, aptly named Chili Dog, for his spicy personality and constant slobbery grin. She greeted me warmly. I returned her smile.

"How ya doing?" she said.

I responded, "My mother died this morning."

Not knowing how to respond, her face filled with sympathy and wonder that I was here, in the park, walking ... so normal.

Sometimes the familiar helps to ground us, when something happens that is too large to absorb at once. It is time afforded for processing information, which we refuse to process. Somehow, if we refuse to admit what happened, then maybe it didn't; maybe we can unmake the happening.

But no. It happened. I began my trek around the shimmering lake.

Hi Mom...

I felt her presence, almost as though she was physically beside me.

"Hi! I can see why you like it here so much. It is beautiful," she smiled.

Mom and I walked together, observing everything with poignancy. There was no need for conversation. The communion between the two of us and with nature did not require words.

Memories flooded in, so many happy times together intermingled with regret, which I apologized for as soon as it surfaced in my mind.

She smiled again, knowing I was sorry. It wasn't necessary to apologize. We were together.

I rounded the crest of a hill on one of the grassy walking trails. I felt her presence keenly. She looked at me, so pleasant, so full of love. I knew this not because I saw it, but because I felt it.

She spoke, "I love you..." It was so sincere, so heartfelt, and so amiss? Wrong? Her assurance made me think I was going to *need* that assurance somehow. The dawning snowballed.

"Mom..." my voice wavered, knowing there was some *thing*, "WHAT did you do?"

She heard me. She watched and she loved, but she didn't smile and she didn't speak; she had warned me.

I closed up. My only thought was "I will know soon enough." I left the park, her lingering presence still, real. I was sad yet prepared, but for what?

Chapter 1

The beginning…

I am an illegitimate child, by the factual definition of the word, as well as an adoptee. My dad was not my natural father. I didn't find any of this out until I was in my fifties after my mother's death. How things like this, you know, things that rock your whole world affect you, no matter what time of life it happens is entirely dependent on how much you allow them to affect you. For awhile, I let it affect me big time. I was devastated. I felt robbed. Rather than get ahead of myself, let me start at the beginning, not only my childhood, but Mom's young life before me, all the stories I heard, and all the things I believed and held dear.

When I was growing up my aunt, mom, sister and I often gathered around the kitchen table to sing together or compare our physical features or just chat, while the men conversed quietly in the living room. I remember we once tried to wiggle our ears, all watching closely as we each in turn failed. However, I could move my eyebrows one by one up and down, a talent not everyone has acquired. We laughed so hard at the littlest things. For example, Mom always kept a bottle of scotch under the kitchen sink to use as a remedy for coughing when Dede, my younger sister, and I were children. I hated the taste. However, Aunt Rene (pronounced like "teen," short for Floriene) didn't. When she visited, we got one of the three shot glasses we owned out of the cupboard. Dede and I sat at the kitchen table and watched wide-eyed as Rene poured the vile tasting stuff into the shot glass. With much preparation on her part (a performance for the benefit of her young audience), she grimaced, moaned, and raised the glass to her lips. I watched in fascination as she quickly downed the burning liquid, lowered the glass, letting air out of her mouth with a *whoosh* noise followed by a scary squeal as though her insides were on fire. Her face turned red, so for all Dede and I knew, they were. But we knew Rene would likely live till next time she visited and entertained us with this never tiresome show. Mom always watched her sister with bemusement.

As I moved from child to adulthood, we continued these antics but our conversations *may* have gained more depth. After my mother died, I missed our times together, our talks. I missed Mom's joy in her grandchildren, my own dear little ones, made more poignant since my sister never married nor had children.

Mom was so smart. She had gotten straight A's in school. Often, she shared how one of her teachers had her show the rest of the class how things were "supposed to be done," even in math! I was impressed since my math skills were *nil*. I remember her saying she was the fastest in her typing class. She was the first of her family, out of five siblings, to earn a high school diploma. Back then high school was considered the ultimate education since only the very well off was able to attend college. It would be a long time before the educational system would be accused of "dumbing down" anything, so obtaining a high school diploma was a true achievement.

When Mom graduated from high school in 1936, the Great Depression was in full force. A local boy from Cleveland, Ohio, Jesse Owens, won four gold medals at the Berlin Olympics. President Roosevelt was reelected.

Both Mom and Aunt Rene told me that though so many were hungry and jobless during the Depression, they always had jobs, plus everything was dirt-cheap. It didn't really matter what price anything was since most didn't have the money regardless of the cost. After high school, Mom obtained a job at the same place Grandma and Rene worked, the DWG cigar factory.

Grandma had a pretty name, Sophia Mae, but the way they pronounced it then, (i.e. So-fie-ah rather than So-fee-ah), was not so pretty. Most people just called her Mae.

When many were going without, my mother's family always had enough food, enough money to pay bills and enough to do some fun things too. Though Grandpa, (nicknamed "Putter" by friends since his surname was Putman), worked as a full time switchman for Nickel Plate Railroad, he didn't contribute to the budget very often, unless he thought to bring some candy home to his children. Most times, he spent his cash on other women and alcohol. Grandpa's mother had money, or so I was told. She may have helped them out some. Regardless, Grandma, my aunt and my mom were hard workers and their family was not in want.

I was told that one time at the cigar factory, a female worker came up to my grandmother's machine and said to her "Oh look Mae! This bracelet is from Putter. He is just SO generous to me, such a generous man!" She sauntered away grinning at the pain she caused. Grandma slid off her stool and headed to the women's restroom to compose herself. Grandpa's paycheck went for what he wanted, his women, and an occasional gift for his children. Grandma's paycheck supported the family. When Mom and Rene started working, they purchased a house for the family for $10,000. It was a three bedroom, two-story house, with a full basement, room enough for all. Since it was purchased during the depression, this was quite a deal. I am not sure how they paid for it, but knowing them, I would imagine they saved their money in a savings account and paid cash for it.

Mom was the youngest of five children, so she was home most when the older children were absent. Grandma shared things with her that adults normally would not share with a child. Mom said that Grandma was so sad with all Grandpa's wild ways that she cried a lot. Mom listened and sympathized. Telling children things normally reserved for a good friend may have caused lasting negative impressions, but Grandma was overwhelmed and had nobody to talk with, not even with her own sister, who also once had an affair with Grandpa.

Mom's childhood was not without any fun, however. She told of a time when she was about eight years old. Her cousins were to come that day for a visit. She found a cow pie (for those who may not know, this is a pile of cow feces) in the lane to their house, and she covered it with much sand. When her cousins arrived she generously invited them to come play in her sand pile. They did.

Other children that Mom and Rene knew would talk about what fun Grandpa was when they came over. He was good at being *IT* when they played *Tag* or *Hide and Seek.* Mom said that she wanted to shout at them that he wasn't that nice! Grandpa came home drunk late at night. Mom and Aunt Rene helped him get clean, handed him soap and towels as he stood at the bathroom sink or over the toilet, and scratched his back if he asked.

When Mom and Rene got older, they asked Grandma why she just didn't leave Putter. Even though he was their father, they did not call him "dad" often, but called him by his nickname as others did. Grandma said she couldn't. No matter what, he was their father and she loved him. They never understood, but didn't push Grandma. Mom later learned that she was 14 years old when Grandpa made things official by getting married to Grandma. Grandma had been a *common law* wife all that time. They had intended to get married at the beginning, but fate seemed to intervene. When Grandma and Grandpa were going to get married, they were very young and didn't have much money. Their buggy broke down and they didn't have time to fix the buggy and get married and back to work on time. Mom often thought maybe this was one of the ways Grandpa justified what he was doing with other women, since he and Grandma were not "really" married. But even after he made their marriage official, Grandpa still played around with other women and he also got drunk frequently.

Grandma also told my Mom and Rene about their brother William, who died when he was five, of polio. The doctor told her to make hot poultices and put on his arms. She heated them by placing them on the open oven door. Grandma went crazy with grief as she watched her little son die in so much pain. Grandpa was never mentioned. I think Mom and Rene assumed he was out drinking with someone. Through it all, Mom *learned* that men could not be trusted and that they caused much pain.

Mom and Rene's oldest sister, Bonnie, married young and had her own home in Indiana by the time the two of them were in their teens and had been on to Grandpas shenanigans for some time. I liked to entertain myself as a child by repeating my Aunt Bonnie's full name, Bonnie Catherine Imogene Putman. Imagine having so many names! Their oldest brother, Uncle Clifford, was on his own and lived out of town, as did their brother, Uncle Roy, who got a Catholic girl pregnant, married her and moved out. I always heard how nice and sweet Clifford was, and what a womanizer Roy was, just like Putter. Clifford never had any children of his own, but Roy and Marge had five.

It was reported that when Aunt Marge was in labor (long before I was born), Roy was with, or knew, another woman, in the *Biblical* sense of the word. Aunt Marge grew tired of her husband's philandering and invited his current "woman" to move in with them for a while. Her idea paid off. After a time, the extra woman ceased to hold any appeal for Roy. I suppose Uncle Roy preferred mystery to the reality. The "extra" moved out. Aunt Marge loved my grandma, her mother-in-law. I have often wondered if Grandma gave her tips about how to handle her son. She had, after all, been dealing with his father for years. Grandma was a wise woman in so many ways.

One time Marge went to Grandma to ask for her assistance. Roy was too amorous, in her opinion. She said he was coming home in the middle of the day to have his way with her and then expected the same again that night, every night. Since she had children, as well housework, she was understandably tired. Maybe it was Grandpa who spoke to Roy about it. I was never sure of this. Roy was more than a little upset with his wife's tattle, so he retaliated by paying her no attention whatsoever in the boudoir. It wasn't long till she came to him for some much needed attention. He thoroughly enjoyed repeating this to his parents. Nothing was ever said further.

Aunt Rene used to tell of when Grandpa's brother Earl came to visit. He made wonderful lasagna for them. Earl had traveled and came across this then exotic dish. Nobody else in the neighborhood had ever eaten lasagna.

But Earl was also an alcoholic and ended up in jail for embezzling money. He lost all of his money and Grandpa's money earned in the oil industry. I used to look at Mom's black and white pictures of various oil wells, some with Earl posed in front of them. I remember once, when I was quite small, being taken to one of them and watching it pump. I had to stand way back from it so I would not get soiled when the oil came up. I used to think, *wow; if it weren't for my great uncle Earl, we might be rich.*

Mom was my source for my family history, as was Aunt Rene, but when Mom died, Rene was the only one left.

"Oh Cherie! I remember it so well, the day the war ended!" Rene's face was wreathed in wrinkles as she smiled, remembering the festive day. "The town square was full of people laughing and dancing and skipping and they were grabbing each other and hugging. It was wonderful! Don't you remember? Did you go?" Rene sometimes got me or my sister confused with our mother. She had memory lapses, forgivable.

The world was simply a different place back then.

Chapter 2

1940 something...

It was the time of Rosie the Riveter, human ingenuity, we-can-do-it, "for the boys," for freedom. Why do humans seem to need a reason to do "good"? And today, it seems to be more of *what little can I get by with in order to get the other guy or the government to do for me.*

Not all did "good" then, however.

Mom told me about men who worked at the factory. Most of the men were away at war so women made up the majority of the staff, but there were a few male foremen. Though these men were all married, it didn't stop them from being inappropriate with the women workers. One would take hold of mom's upper arm, for example, in a seemingly innocent way, but he always managed to get his hand between her arm and her breast, gently brushing her breast as he removed his hand. She tried to avoid him. What else could she do? She needed the job. There was no human resources department then to report sexual harassment. He, and those like him, probably felt an additional need to assert their manhood since they were not away fighting in the war. Regardless, it served to reinforce her notion that all men were not to be trusted.

The unions were another example of not "good" things back then. The union organizers came to the cigar factory and got everyone angry, and they were scowling all the time. If a worker didn't want to join the union, the other workers who chose to join shunned her. Some workers who had cars received slit tires. Others had their hair pulled or other practical jokes, like tacks showing up in a chair just as she was sitting down or lewd signs taped to her back. Everybody knew it *wasn't* a joke. How far would it go? My Aunt Rene was afraid. Crowds of angry workers were waiting for *holdouts* to get off work. Some of them were not workers, but strangers from out of state. Word had spread that the "criminal" element had arrived on the train from Chicago, and that Communists were behind much of the increasingly violent acts, such as when a rear window was busted on a car when a worker tried to leave. Physical harm seemed the logical next step. Putter told Rene that when she got off work he would pick her up. He told her, "Rene, come straight to the car. And if anybody tries to hurt you, I will handle it." Rene was relieved to see her dad kept his word for once.

There was a crowd of union workers milling about outside the red brick factory building when she got off work. They watched, staring, and started to move in her direction as she neared her dad's car. Putter opened his door as she quickly slid in the passenger side. He stood and glared back at the crowd, pulling a steel bar from his pant leg. The crowd stopped their ambling advance. He quickly got behind the wheel, and the crowd watched as they drove off.

Rene sat near her father as he drove. His face was rigid. His hands gripped the steering wheel. He said nothing. Neither did she. She couldn't remember ever feeling protected with him before. It was a good feeling. She never spoke of it much, nor did Putter. It was the only time she remembered feeling something positive with Putter. It was the only time she understood why her mom had liked him to start with. She speculated maybe something had happened to Putter to make him a womanizer. Maybe his dad had done the same thing. One kind act, however, would not remove years of abuse. Rene recounted how, for example, when she was a young girl, Putter would send her to pay a bill knowing the creditor wouldn't say anything to her about his being late.

Eager to leave the cigar factory, when there was an ad in the paper for workers at a large automotive factory, Mom and Rene stood in line along with the others for several hours waiting to get in. They were going to hire many people. This job would pay very well so as they neared the front of the line their excitement grew.

Finally they entered the huge building. There was a table set up where the applications were being taken. The man handing out the applications looked at Mom and Rene, up and down, then shook his head.

"You are too fat to work here. We only hire thin people."

Aside from the obvious prejudice and the less likely ability to get away with this type of *obvious* discrimination today, neither Mom nor Rene were anything close to morbidly obese. They were overweight, as are many who are good workers.

Chapter 3

Revelations…

After my mom died, and after I *saw* her in the park and got the sense that something was wrong, that there was a secret, I had so many unanswered questions. *Why* did Mom take this secret to her grave? Did it matter? She was my mother and I loved her. It is just that this seemed *so obvious* to anyone who had *any* sense of what is *right*, that you don't keep deeply personal secrets from your children when they deserve answers as their birthright. Certainly my mother exemplified what I considered to be virtuous behavior. She was a person of kindness and generosity. That is why this secret didn't fit with the picture of the mother I had known. She was smart. She was beautiful. She wouldn't hide things from me.

I remember once in third grade when Mom came to my class to visit. It was prior to Thanksgiving and we were doing an art craft project, a turkey made with pinecones with a colorful tail of construction paper pasted to the end of the pinecone. I remember being so proud of her sitting there. A couple of the girls in my class told me later that my mom was pretty. She did look so pretty and smart. She wore her gold-rimmed tortoise shell glasses and had make up on. She always wore *Tangee Natural* lipstick, made to bring out your natural beauty. It looked orange in the tube, which fascinated me since it turned color on your lips. The ads said something like "the lipstick that goes on clear and gradually transforms into the perfect shade for you. Ideal for women who want to look beautiful without looking artificial." My mom never looked "artificial." Mom smelled good too, wearing her staple *White Shoulders* perfume. This was the woman I thought was "Mom."

One afternoon, I was chatting on the phone with my Aunt Rene, who was then 89 years old. Mom had passed away three years before.

Though she had difficulty understanding things at times, her mind was still fairly sharp. She was also in her own home and still did her own yard work. She lived in Lima.

I had just asked her a question about Mom and Dad.

She said, "Well, if Harry was your father, …" or a similar statement, and it grabbed my attention. She attempted to continue talking as though she had not said it the way it came out. Maybe she didn't notice or maybe she just didn't want me to notice. Then again, maybe she did.

"Is Harry Dupler my father or not?"

Silence.

"Rene?" I laughed nervously and repeated, "Is Harry my natural father?"

"No."

I was more than stunned. Shattered. I wasn't in the present time.

I floated somewhere.

I knew I was still me, but who was I? Who was Mom?

She had always preached never to lie. She had always told me how much she loved me and that I could *always* trust her.

She said, "Nobody ever loves you like your mother."

All this virtuous "reality" vanished in a second.

Gone. I reeled.

Where was I? Who was I?

No wonder Harry had always seemed to favor Dede. In that moment, although so many loose ends were no longer loose, many more had been created. *Mom was dead. Dad was dead. I could not confront her, or ask her the questions that I had to have answered.*

Why did she do this? How could she say she loved me and not explain this precious secret? How? Who was she? Did I ever really know her?

What do I do? God help!

I didn't want my panic and need for answers to upset Rene, but of course I knew I had to press for more. "Rene, do you know who my natural father is?" I said. "His name?"

"Yes," she said.

Questioning her was awful. She was frail. Would my questions be too much for her? I didn't have a choice. She was the only one left who could give me any answers. Why didn't she tell me years earlier?

Betrayal. *Everyone* has betrayed me. The people who always said they loved me were the ones who kept the most from me.

How does the world work? I could not remember.

It was as though my slate was blank and I had just been born, had no grounding, no information and had to start learning and inventing, growing all over again on my own, from square one.

Calm down.

"What is his name?" I asked.

"Hubert … He died a few years ago. I saw his obituary in the paper. I thought to myself, 'Well, it's finally over.'"

It wasn't over for me.

I wondered if Rene could be lying or remembering something wrong, something that didn't pertain to me.

"Are you sure?" I said.

"Yes!" She sounded less hesitant this time, and went on to explain the whole story, part of which I had heard many times.

I knew how much Mom wanted a baby and how she used to go to Gregg's Department Store and look at baby dresses and dream. The part I never heard until now was how Mom planned her pregnancy, sought a man out that she thought would make a cute baby girl, and approached him. He was a widower who had a little red-haired son.

Rene also told me again of how she and Mom went out on the town when they were young women. I had heard about this many times before.

No new information, no apology. I had to escape.

Hang up! Hang up.

Breathe.

Don't upset Rene. Why not! How could she keep this from me?

But now she told me. Don't upset Rene.

I hung up the phone. I cried. I emailed my much older cousin, Phil, in California to see if he knew any of this.

Does the name Hubert ... mean anything to you? If it does, what do you know?

He emailed back almost immediately.

*"Yes. Rene told you? He was your father. Mable didn't want you to know. I emailed Mara [*my cousin and his older sister] *as to what to say to you. She told me that it should have come out long ago. Tell her."*

Phil was able to give me more information. He was a genealogy buff who had access to websites that I did not. He emailed the news clipping about Hubert and his earning the Silver Star. It had been in the Lima News. He also talked to Hubert's second wife and widow. He gave me her number. He had already talked to her. He told her he was doing research and thought perhaps he may have a relative that was also her relative. He didn't tell her the relative was me and he didn't tell her he suspected her husband had an unknown daughter. Phil charmed her for information and got what he needed. Her entire family was coming to her house soon for Thanksgiving. She was laughing as she told him all he wanted to know, so excited about the party.

I called her and explained what I had just learned about my mother and Hubert. It did not go well.

"I don't believe you," she said. "He wasn't that kind of a man."

"My mother was a very attractive woman," I answered.

Silence.

"If he had known about you, the kind of good man he was, he would have followed you. ..."

"Mom didn't want him," I said. "She only wanted a baby."

"What kind of woman was she!" she said. Since this same thought had also crossed my mind but as more of a sincere question than an accusation, I said nothing.

Our call ended quickly and unpleasantly, but she said she would let her two grown children know. My father's first wife had died in childbirth. I told her I would get back with her.

I called her a couple weeks later.

She said, "I let my kids know, and you have really upset things. ... My kids are all successful people."

"I want nothing," I said. "They are family."

"Uh huh. That is up to them," she said, "we are Christian people."

"So am I," I said.

"Anybody who might have cared is dead," she said.

I knew she did not believe me, did not want to believe me.

It is so frustrating to be doubted when you are telling the truth. It made me angry then and it makes me angry now.

I was able to find my older brother (Hubert's little red-haired boy who was 8 when I was born). We had both been born and raised in Lima, 60 miles away. I was shocked to discover he now lived a couple miles from my house. I drove by his house, and I saw him several times from afar. We emailed. He was very helpful, given the circumstance.

He wrote, "I can understand how shocking this is for you. It is to us as well. I am emailing several pictures of my dad to satisfy your curiosity. I hope it helps."

I emailed him several pictures of myself that he said he would forward to our brother and sister. I downloaded my father's picture. As it downloaded on my computer screen, I began to cry. There was a man staring at me with my own eyes. He looked so familiar I felt I *should* know him. The pictures my brother sent of himself and our younger brother looked less like our father than I do. No DNA test would be necessary to prove I was his daughter. My brother did not wish to have any meeting. He and his wife moved a year later. I believe my father's widow had enough negative impact on my brother and her own two children that perhaps they did not want to meet me. I emailed him that if ever any of them needed anything medically, to please let me know. I would try to help them, if there was a match, if they needed a blood donation. Occasionally, I send my brother a greeting email card on the 4th of July and other special occasions. I have nieces and nephews on that side. My siblings have relations on my side. My children would love to know their relatives, as I would, but these things are out of my control.

It must have been as much of a shock for them to find out their husband and father had another daughter and a sister as it was for me to find out about my mother, and also what appeared to be a conspiracy by my whole extended family. The man they loved and respected and thought they knew had a secret he never shared. Perhaps my mother and he had agreed it was to be kept. Perhaps he thought it *best* never to share it, not even with his wife. I can only imagine from a wife's perspective how shocking this news was. It would be almost as shocking as it was for me.

Our *heroes, my mom, their dad (also my dad)* had clay feet. They were not the people we thought that they were, who they had both led us to believe. They were human. They made grave errors. We love them anyway. We forgive anyway. Maybe someday, we can breach the divide. Like it or not, we are and always will be tied by blood. If we are Christian, we believe nothing is really any coincidence.

Later, when visiting my aunt, I asked her what Grandma did or thought when Mom got pregnant. Grandma had always seemed so mild-mannered to me.

Rene said, "She walked to where Hubert was living. He wasn't there. Either his mom or his aunt was though and when she came to the door, she asked her, 'what are you going to do about this? What is he going to do about this?'

The woman told her she knew nothing about it.

And your mom didn't want him! She didn't love him. She was done."

I guess Grandma had a lot more spunk than I thought.

I imagined a conversation Rene may have had with Mom. She had often told how she tried to talk to Mom about her decision. She said Mom scared off guys they went out with because all she talked about was wanting to have a baby and hinting that they could help her to do that. She also told me how Mom got out of the factory and got her new job.

"Mable! Mable! Wait up! Boy you walk fast!" Rene said. She and Mable were walking to Bishops corner store on 4th street to pick up a few items. It was always hard to keep up with my mom. "I heard you left the factory," Rene continued.

"Rene, I told you I was looking for another job," said Mable. "Commercial Motorfreight is perfect. Better conditions, work I enjoy, and I have contact with truckers that have to check in at the window between the office and the loading dock, right by my desk."

Mable glanced at Rene, smiled, and then continued walking. "I saw the ad in the newspaper. I was hired on the spot. I like my boss, and his wife, Patty, works there too as a secretary. She types faster than me! I really like her too. And, one of the truckers and I have gone out a few times," Mable paused to allow this to sink in.

"He's tall, dark and handsome, though a little on the thin side. He is a widower with a little red-haired boy. He seems nice enough and acts interested. We could make a cute baby I think," said Mable. For some reason whenever she'd told some of the other guys what she wanted, they backed off.

"I think Hubert may be the guy I have been looking for to father my daughter."

Rene stopped and faced her sister. She hadn't been concerned with her sister's plan before, but now Mable made it sound like this man might agree to her request. "Mable, are you sure?"

Mom was lost in thought as she had again been to Gregg's Department Store, the best one in town, that very afternoon. She meandered through the baby clothes department. The little dresses all looked so sweet. She allowed herself to finger one tiny cotton pale pink dress with smocking at the bodice. It was soft just like the baby girl who would wear it. She checked the size, *6 months*. She had started to come to Gregg's regularly and had already bought perhaps 15 or 16 adorable outfits in various sizes from newborn to 24 months. It took a nice chunk of her paycheck to come to this particular store, but nothing was too good for her baby. She had managed to dress herself in the latest fashions, and her baby would be dressed equally well.

Rene tugged at her sleeve. "Mable, are you listening? This is the *real* thing, a no turning back thing!"

Mable clenched her jaw as she began what she hoped would be a *final* word on the matter. What was so darned difficult to understand about a 29-year-old woman wanting a baby? Rene already had one abortion. Rene's married boyfriend, Miller, had taken Rene to Ft. Wayne to a doctor there who was willing to perform abortions for those willing to pay for them. Miller accompanied her, which Rene found "sweet" and he paid for the procedure. Mom helped her through afterwards, when it seemed the bleeding wouldn't stop. "Rene, I have my mind made up. I *want* a baby. Whether I end up married or not, I am *going* to be the mother of a baby girl. Not having a child would be a wasted life."

When Mom's mind was made up, nobody could stop her. I observed her, that resolve, as I grew up. From what Aunt Rene told me, Mom had been even more adamant when she was younger. Nobody could change her mind about anything. Societal norms and taboos of the time notwithstanding, Mom *did* get pregnant. She dated Hubert just long enough to achieve that. Rene told me they went to the *picture show* a few times, but Mom wasn't in love. She wanted what she wanted and since she was clear with Hubert from the beginning about her desire to have a baby and he was the *chosen one;* she held no remorse.

Ironically, when I was a child, Mom told me that I was bull-headed when I dug my heels in and would not do something she wanted me to do. She said Grandpa was bull headed too.

Chapter 4

Baby Girl...

"PUSH! PUSH! Boy, you sure don't look like you're having a baby! Never saw a woman come into this hospital in labor wearing make-up and long earrings," the nurses joked with Mom. It was a short first labor, only four hours. This was the labor story she told. What Mom didn't tell me was that her brother was the one who took her to the hospital because she was not married. Later when I was told the story of my birth, I assumed my uncle took her because Dad was out of town on a business trip. That is what she told me. He took many of those while I was growing up.

Ether was administered to her, but Mom tried not to breathe much of it because her baby was about born. What was the point? But the hospital had rules, and doctors gave their orders, and the nurses would not tolerate anything else. Mom took a deep breath and was out.

"Five pounds, six ounces! You had a girl!" Mom told me she could hear their voices dimly.

"What?" She tried to answer, but she wasn't sure if she did or if she just thought it.

"Mable, wake up! You have a baby girl!"

"I got my girl! I got my girl!" Happiness beyond description flooded Mom at the same time she caught a wave of nausea from the ether. The latter won out and the nurse rushed to give her the bean-shaped emesis basin.

But Mom had more to be concerned about than her upset stomach. A single woman giving birth at this time would have been shunned by people at church, but Mom didn't go to one. Society in general was not accepting of single mothers, and Mom would have been the target of gossip, at the least.

There were no birth announcements in the newspaper for single women. There were no visitors allowed on the maternity floor except for the husband or the grandparents. Mom was in the hospital the normal stay of about two weeks. Other women on the floor must have talked about her, but I doubt that Mom cared. She had her girl.

Her baby had brown fluffy fuzz on her head. She had all her fingers and toes. Mom tried to breast feed, but was told she had "inverted nipples" and couldn't do it. She would learn years later this was not true. The hospital staff encouraged formula over breast milk, suggesting it was better for the baby. There was no La Leche League at that time to assist women with breast-feeding. There was only encouragement to bottle-feed. This was also the society that thought smoking was good for your lungs just a decade or so prior. Before Mom left the hospital, my weight dipped to just under five pounds, but that small weight loss is normal. The birth certificate read: "Child's Name: Cheri Ann Putman. Mother of Child: Mable I. Putman."

When I was six she changed the spelling of my name to Chérie. She liked the looks of it better and wanted the accent since that was the way it was pronounced.

Margaret Putman, Roy's wife, was listed as the "informant."

Under "Father of the Child" it was left blank, just the way Mom wanted it.

To be a single mom at this time was particularly precarious, not only due to stricter social mores. If Mom had lived in Memphis, Tennessee, for example, she may have run into a woman named Georgia Tann, but I am sure there were likely people running similar, perhaps less prominent operations at other locations, including Ohio.

According to the book The Baby Thief, by Barbara Bisantz Raymond (2007), Georgia Tann separated more than 5000 children from their families from 1924 to 1950. Many of the victims were single moms. Others were simply poor. Ms. Tann would have them declared unfit through a judge who was in cahoots with her in order to steal babies and adopt them into rich families. It was at this time *closed adoptions* were legalized, with officials claiming it would save adoptees from dealing with the social stigma of being illegitimate. Tann was applauded for her work and made her personal fortune by selling children to wealthy people, such as actors June Allyson, Dick Powell and Joan Crawford. Not only did many adopted families abuse the children, but also Georgia Tann sexually abused many.

Since his first wife died in childbirth, Hubert had been alone. It wasn't easy raising a child on his own, even though he lived with his mom and she helped care for his son. Maybe, he thought my mom would be the answer to his prayers. Sure she wanted a baby. He didn't have a problem with that. Maybe she would grow to love him. Even if she didn't, what woman when faced with the raising a child wouldn't want the father involved?

I tried to see this from Mom's perspective. It seemed logical to me as well to prefer to have the father involved. However, I wasn't raised with Putter as a father.

Hubert underestimated my mother's resourcefulness. Through knowing her and having a child with her, Hubert learned more about women (one woman, in particular) along with realizing his own skewed thinking. There was no way to correct this once the deed was done and I was born. Mable liked him enough to pick him to father her child, enough to want him to see the latest pictures of his daughter, enough to bring his daughter to the office for a visit so he could catch a glimpse of her on a few occasions, but she had her cute baby and that was as far as she wanted it.

Mom knew Hubert had more integrity than most men. He had a Silver Star, after all, earned from saving others at his own peril when he was in Italy during the war. He was a skilled trucker, and at the time that was a respected, honest, and lucrative profession, more so than now. He was a good man and Mom must have known he wanted her. She knew he loved her and would be a good father, but she wanted her baby to herself and she didn't want to share her child with anyone. Even if she married later, this baby was hers and hers alone. There was logic to her thinking. Mom never had a father who cared for her mother. She likely figured that if she let a man in her life, even a man like Hubert who seemed kind, he could still hurt her and thereby hurt her child. He could still be like Putter. She could not take any chances.

Perhaps Hubert was hurt when he realized my mothers resolve. I would like to think so and I believe it to be so based on all I heard from his widow and my brother about his character, that he was a "good man."

He saw his child (by age two) several times, though Mable would not allow a direct "Hi there. I am your dad," meeting. This was to be hidden from the child *forever.* Mable had been clear on this point, but Hubert had been certain she would change her mind. He loved the pictures of his little girl on Mable's desk. She was obviously loved and well cared for. He didn't understand why my mother wouldn't accept his help, (other than the expensive leather baby carriage she allowed him to purchase).

He considered pursuing it, forcing her to allow him to see the child. But it would affect his son, his family if he decided to attempt something legal, as well as his little girl. In the interest of all concerned, Hubert decided to lay the matter to rest, go on with his life and try to forget he had a daughter who didn't know him, would probably never know him. Judging by the reaction of his second wife, his widow, if her husband "had known" he had a little girl, he was "the type of man who would have followed" her, loved her and have embraced her. Perhaps he would have, if my mother had given him the chance.

I remember one visit to Mom's office. Grandma took me across the street to the city bus stop. She knew the driver by name. I was told to sit near him, and he would watch over me until we got to the town square where Mom would find me. I felt big riding on the bus alone, but scared at the same time. I was two years old. I was wearing the latest in toddler wear from Gregg's.

As the bus pulled into the square, I could see Mom standing at the curb, waiting. I was relieved and excited to see her. She looked so pretty, all dressed up in her suit and heels. She smiled up at me as I stood at the top of the bus steps, and reached to lift me off and took me to her office. She told me that we were going to go get our picture taken later.

I liked all the desks at Mom's office. I was being carried so I could see the tops of them. Most were neat, though they had papers on them. There were lamps in the office, not just ceiling lights. Patty, the boss's wife, was there. I had met her before and she was nice. Mom put me down and then squatted so she was face to face with me. "I need to go out for a few minutes, but I will be right back. Patty is going to watch you." I shook my head. Mom always told the truth. She loved me. She would be right back. I looked around. But, I stood still. I knew that standing still and being quiet was being good.

I heard something and looked up. There was a man at the window where the truckers came to talk to the office people. I knew that trucks were back there. The man had dark hair and he was tall. He was smiling at me. He had a beautiful smile. He stared for a long time and then looked over at Patty who was working at the bulletin board.

He asked, "Is that her?"

Patty said, "Yes."

He looked back at me and stared longer, smiling. I didn't know him, so I didn't smile. I looked back at him. I wondered why he was staring at me. I waited for him to say something. He didn't. I thought about saying something and was just about to do so. But then he turned and walked back to where the trucks were in that other room. I watched his back get smaller as he walked.

I was curious. "Who was zat?" I asked Patty.

"A trucker," she answered.

Mom returned. I didn't know it then, but I had seen my father.

Later that day, Mom and I had our portrait taken together. I treasure that picture, now sitting in a pretty frame hanging on a wall in my living room.

I remember the photographer telling me to put my arm around Mom's shoulders. I was placed on a tall prop of some sort and I felt afraid due to the height, but with Mom right there and my arm around her shoulders and her arm around my bottom I felt safer. I can still feel the rough material of her business suit and the soft touch of her hair on my arm and I can smell her White Shoulders perfume. My Mommy. I can even picture "Daddy" standing on the other side of me. He *should* have been. There are so many of those, *shoulds*.

Chapter 5

"Harry"

Harry and Mable were married in a small ceremony. She met this balding, attractive man, nine years her senior, on the bus on her way home from work. It was evening and the inside bus lights were on. She caught him staring at her legs reflected in the window of the bus. This soft-spoken man amused her. It was she who initiated their friendly exchange. She doubted that he would have said anything otherwise, though she could tell he wanted talk to her.

Harry worked for a local, business owner of a steel factory. He had started as a lab technician. No war hero status for Harry, no Silver Stars like Hubert earned. Steel, however, was a valuable commodity for the military, both in weaponry and in tanks. This was his wartime contribution. Harry was closer to who Mable thought she had been searching. He was handsome, also a widower, and had *no* children. Perfect. No extra responsibility for her to deal with and no sibling rivalries for her baby girl. It was only a short while till she was able to "suggest" to Harry that he should move out of his deceased wife's mother's home where he was dutifully, though perhaps misguidedly, caring for her. She had blood relatives who could see to that job.

Harry was more than willing to accept Mable and Hubert's daughter as his own. Adding Harry to the blank "Father of the Child" birth certificate space was not a problem after the formal adoption. Mable had, at long last, succeeded in eliminating Hubert from the picture, the one man who may have *competed* with her in her daughter's life. Harry would *never* be any competition for that. The adoption would be forever closed. Chéri Ann Putman was erased at the flick of a pen and her more honest identity with it. Her last name was now Harry's surname. Mable hadn't intended for Hubert to be hurt. She had, after all, told him exactly what she wanted. He got what *he* wanted. His "contribution," *or perhaps fate*, was sealed the moment she knew she was pregnant. She couldn't help it if he decided he wanted more than she intended to give. She hoped he found happiness with someone. She hoped many things. But, she would not back down on her decisions. She couldn't.

"I am married now and we are the family," she thought. "My girl will never know the difference." Harry didn't know how to act around children or how to talk to them. He was never around small children much, but my mother assumed he would catch on.

To the amusement of the adults present for the momentous introduction of Cheri to her new father, Cheri, (now age three), had reacted within *her own* budding personality. She reacted with *total* indifference, glancing briefly at him and then going back to her play, unimpressed.

I remember that day.   I was playing in Grandma and Grandpas dining room. They were there, along with and Mom and Harry.

Grandpa said, "This is your dad." I looked up. Harry was standing a few feet away looking down at me with his big Hollywood smile. I had heard what was said. I took it in. I took him in. I felt nothing.

Where was he? Where had he been?   I knew what a dad was.

"He was away on a business trip." I was told that day, a "justified" lie and a source of amusement, I am sure, for the adults. I still don't think it was funny. Playing fast and loose with another persons birthright as though there is any viable reason for playing God, is not my idea of anything remotely resembling anything funny. It is indeed the opposite.

"OK."

I erased the inexplicable *nothing* feeling on purpose, as I went back to my play. I didn't know what I was "supposed" to think or to feel. I heard the adult's intake of breath and then laughter.

Had I done something wrong? I didn't mean to! I looked around to see. No, it was OK. They weren't mad.

"To thine own self be true," was Mom's motto, even if that is the only one to whom you *are* true. Harry agreed to keep the secret. In Mable's mind, if anything was "wrong" about all this, Harry's agreement must have made it somehow "right," like

when you are on a diet and somebody else, who is on one too, cheats on a hot fudge sundae with you. In fact, the whole family kept her secret. She knew they would. People didn't talk about family skeletons or air dirty laundry in public back then as more people are inclined to do so now.

She knew they better not say anything.

But Rene sometimes posed some "problems."

Secrets have a way of emerging from the shadows.

It usually isn't pretty.

It is speculation, of course, but perhaps Hubert *asked* Mom not to reveal anything to me and he would, in turn, not reveal anything to his family. However, Mom seemed to be the one deciding things right from the onset.

Hubert married his second wife one year after Harry and Mable got married. They had two children besides Hubert's little red haired boy from his first marriage.

Chapter 6

Mable's Little Girl

I liked trains, especially the little red caboose at the end. I remember standing on the front seat of the car watching a train pass in front of us. I said, "There it is! The booka booka booka booka boose!" The number of "bookas" varied as to when I could break free of my verbal loop. I was two.

I had a child size chair to make me higher on the car seat so I could see out better. There were no car seats for safety back then. I remember climbing into the car and sitting on it. Mommy always took a Mason jar with milk in it when we traveled in case I got thirsty and she also had a little painted metal potty, (child-size "chamber pot"), in case I needed that.

It was at this age I discovered *relationships*. I was somewhat precocious, I was told. I remember thinking about when a man and woman love each other and how I thought that would be, and when I thought I had it figured out, I said to Mom, "If a man loves a woman and a woman loves him back then if another woman or man love them, it doesn't matter cause they already love each other."

Mom nodded her head.

I remember thinking about that for several more moments before things became blurry to me again.

We moved from Grandpa and Grandma's house to a new house on Ewing Avenue, across town. Mom told me that Grandpa told her that I would cry to come back, but I didn't.

"Mommy, daddy doesn't love me. He loves Dede but he doesn't love me." Mom and I had this conversation a lot. "Oh, Chéri, Daddy loves you," she said. "It is just that he doesn't really know how to act around children. Dede is the baby so she just gets more attention. Babies always get more attention."

I became convinced by age six that this was something Mom truly believed, but that she was wrong. Since I knew her answer would not vary, I became resigned and stopped bringing it up. I was convinced that Daddy loved Dede and not me, for a variety of reasons. When Dede, for example, was in her playpen and she saw me playing with one of my own toys and decided she wanted it, she would reach out to me and demand "Mine!" She repeated it knowing her daddy would glare and yell "Give it to her!" I relinquished the toy quickly when he used that gruff tone.

Dede was named after a movie star who was popular when she was born, and she learned early on that Daddy was her personal lackey. She had blonde hair, blue eyes, and smiled like her daddy. He played with her, read to her, and laughed with pleasure at her antics. I thought she was cute sometimes, but she was too little for me to play with.

I liked to watch Mom boil Dede's formula filled baby bottles in the steamer. It smelled good.

I had a round, air-filled wading pool. Mom set it up and then took a picture of me trying to get Dede to sit down in it with me. I held on to her. She didn't like the water very much. She wore a green and white horizontal striped bathing suit. Her hair looked almost white in the sun.

I played in my room a lot or outside with other neighborhood children. I liked my pink mouse night-light on the dresser. I could just reach the light's push button switch on the base. I would turn it on and stare at its pink glow making shadows on my bedroom wall. Grandpa bought that night-light.

One time when I was sick with stomach flu in winter, Dad picked me up to carry me to bed. I was wearing my red and white striped flannel pajamas. He jostled me up and down a little, trying to be happy and making silly sounds so I'd feel better. I didn't want to interrupt him because I knew he was trying to help, but the jostling made me feel sicker. I knew I was going to throw up but tried to hold it in for his sake. I didn't want to hurt his feelings. As soon as he put me down, I ran for the bathroom. I made it just in time. How different life was after we moved out of Grandma and Grandpa's house.

Gone were the days when Mom and Rene took me on the bus to Kresge's or Woolworth's for lunch and then to the show. I loved going out with them and we went often. They always dressed up. They always looked pretty with their make-up and jewelry. Mom wore her Tangee Natural lipstick, but Rene liked dark red lipstick. I think I liked the dark red better. It looked good with her dark hair. Mom and Rene both got small samples of lipstick in tiny lipstick tubes they gave me for my very own. Rene even gave me some of her rouge. I loved playing make up. I loved going to the picture show. I was dressed up too, but I had to wear little girl dresses. Someday, I wanted to be an actress in the movies, a movie star. They were beautiful.

I didn't just go out with Mom and Aunt Rene. Sometimes Grandpa took me with him to Cussins and Fern, a store where you bought shovels and other tools. One time he took me to a neat little store with tall stools. I was only two. Grandpa lifted me to the top of the stool. It had a counter with a man standing behind it. The man was nice. I looked around. I told the man, "You have a cute little store here." He and Grandpa laughed. The man said "thank you." I told Mom about the *little store* when we got back.

Grandpa had taken me to a bar. I am sure he was a regular customer there and he did it to show me off.

My sixth year summer birthday party was a party not like earlier ones; those were just family picnics in Grandmas' backyard. This year, however, was my first just children's party. I remember thinking about the change a lot. I also remember thinking about the difference between living at Grandma's house and living in our own home. My life modeled my mother's secure mainstream life. She was no longer a single mom. She was a typical 1950's housewife. She wore housedresses all the time, not business suits and not shorts. At my birthday party, she was the perfect hostess for several well dressed children. My party dress was pale blue and sleeveless.

Last year we had watermelon and my birthday cake with 5 candles and we had ice cream. My cousin Roger came too. He is almost a grownup. Mommy said grandma is sick, but she doesn't really look sick. There are things she is not supposed to eat and

*anything with salt in it is not allowed. I can tell Grandma doesn't
like that. She says her food is tasteless without salt.*

*I miss living at grandma's house. I had a bunny named
Sammy there, in a cage. I fed him carrots. Grandpa played with
me a lot.*

*I miss my bridal gown grandma made for me. It was for
the weddings Grandpa and I had on the stairs. He was both the
preacher and my groom. While he sat on the steps with me, he
talked like a preacher would talk at a wedding and we said our "I
dos" and at the "kiss the bride" part we would kiss. One time
though, grandpa had a little spit on his lip. I didn't want to kiss
him after that.*

*I liked the way the dancers on TV looked when the men
dancers would lift them up in the air and twirl them. Grandpa
would lift me up like that and pretend with me that we were on TV
dancing.*

*Grandpa also played "bank" with me at the dining room
chairs. He would turn the chair back around for me. I was the
teller just like at the big tall teller places in the big marble bank I
went to with Mom and Rene. Our shoes clacked on the floor of the
bank and it echoed. Grandpa would come to my "window" and I
would give him his money. It was very professional. Grandpa
was a good customer and he always smiled at me. Daddy saved
his smiles for Dede.*

*This year my birthday party was at our new house on
Ewing Avenue. My friends from the neighborhood came. They are
Dorothy, who is 8, Sandy who is 4, Patty, from across the street,
who is the same age as me and is not really my friend; she is only
nice to me to get to come to my party and Mommy said we had to
invite her. Her Mom's name is Rosie. Rosie has a gravely voice
and yells a lot. She smokes. Gary, my next-door neighbor, who is
5, came, and my cousin Becky who lives down the street was there.
She is 5. Dede was there too. Mommy took a picture of all of us
out in the front yard with all my gifts. The party was in the
basement and Mommy decorated it with balloons and streamers
and we played games like Pin the Tail on the Donkey, and a game
where we had to balance beans in a spoon. I could play the games*

but I couldn't win since it was my party. The prizes were just for my guests. For gifts I got Mr. Potato Head, a doll, and paper dolls, a block game, and a merry-go-round you have to pump with your feet, from Mommy. Only two people can ride it at the same time. Patty really wanted to ride with Dorothy cause she is older. I got mad about that. Patty had to ride with me. I rode it so much I threw up after the party. Everybody had fun.

One thing I loved to do when we lived on Ewing Avenue was to watch for the milk wagon. It was a horse drawn wagon with a refrigeration unit inside filled with glass milk bottles. Some people had milk boxes on their porch but if not, then the milk was just placed on the porch replacing the empty ones the woman of the house left there, with full bottles. Once a week, Mom paid the milkman. He had two horses and you could hear the clop clop clop of the horse's hooves and an occasional snort from the horses ahead of time as well as the metal part of the harnesses bumping together. Sometimes I watched as the horse defecated on the stone covered street. It was the first time I had seen anything like that up close. It was so big.

I asked Mom why the horses had the square black things on their eyes. She said those were blinders and it is so the cars won't scare the horse. I couldn't understand how a car could scare a horse.

Although everything in my family's world seemed to be secure and mainstream, it may have not been so for everyone. Years later Mom told me that the very pretty next-door neighbor, Gloria, was having an affair with a married man down the block. She had a little girl younger than me named Charlene, who liked to splash in her cute plastic air-blown round swimming pool, which they kept on their tar-lined driveway. Gloria's husband was not around much. Mom and dad would entertain themselves by watching from their bedroom window, as Gloria and the man down the block would sneak behind the houses to meet late at night. I learned that adults lived way different than I had ever suspected. I had always enjoyed watching Gloria with little Charlene and thinking how cute they were together and how pretty Gloria was. Gloria smoked, wore short shorts, halter tops, and was tan. She was a little less "mainstream" than my family.

The next year we moved back to Grandma and Grandpas. Grandma was feeling sicker and Mom and Dad wanted to do something nice for her. She wanted to move and was having a hard time selling the house so Mom and Dad bought the old house and Grandma and Grandpa built a new one on the lot behind them. I was apparently destined to grow up in the same house that my Mom and Aunt Rene had purchased after the two of them started working at the factory. I was going to enter second grade in the fall at my new school, Jefferson Elementary. My much older cousin, Mara, Roy's oldest daughter and the one I got my middle name, Ann, from, had the same teacher in second grade as I did. Miss Crist remembered Mara. Mara was a very smart student. I always heard about that. Miss Crist had a nice old lady smile. Her hair was gray and she had curls.

There were a few unique words used by our family that I didn't know were unique until I encountered people who didn't know what I was talking about when I used the words. This usually happened in school in the most embarrassing way, but not always.

If I was whining, for example, about something or crying and not wanting to do something Mom wanted me to do, she would tell me "Now, don't be *bucky*." When I would tell my friends I got in trouble because I was being *bucky*, they would ask, "What's that?" Likewise, if I was at their house and asked where their bathroom was so I could make a *noise* or do a *bunch*, they had no clue that I was referring to urination or defecation. I imagine Mom used these unrecognizable terms since children have a way of announcing such functions at potentially embarrassing times.

Another word was "pined," (pronounced with a long "i," as in *pine* tree). This referred to the genital area. When I was very small and heading to the bathroom to make a *noise*, she would say, "be sure to wipe your pined." If I was doing a *bunch*, it was particularly important and obvious even to me to wipe my *pined*. Most of the other children did understand it when they were told to "*redd* up your room" as I was by both my grandma and Mom. It meant we were to pick up the mess, put toys away and get the room in order. I have since learned that this was likely rooted in my grandmother's Pennsylvania Dutch/German ancestry.

When I realized that not everyone used these terms, (usually accomplished when an adult or a child would look at me confused and as though I had suddenly grown a third eye and said, "what's that?" that I knew I had been duped), I resolved NEVER to do this to my children. When I had those children, I chose *tinkle* and *stinky*, much more obvious and thus, to my mind, *superior* descriptive terms than *noise* and *bunch*. I did stick to more clinical or at least recognizable terms in other ways though, such as *bottom*, *penis*, and *clean up your room*.

Mom took this picture of Dad, me and Dede at a barbeque Grandma and Grandpa held for the whole family. The dress I am wearing was the pale blue one that I wore for my sixth birthday party.

I remember that summer day. The barbeque pit was an elaborate one made of brick and Grandpa kept it neatly painted red and the cement between the layers of brick he painstakingly painted white. It had a chimney that rose up about ten feet. The stove area was probably three square feet. On the end was a metal door, which was opened so the fire could be stoked. Grandpa did roasting ears of corn, and various meats. The women all brought various other picnic type food and pies and cakes, all homemade.

I loved playing with Barry, my cousin who was closest to my age but even he was almost three years older. That is his leg in the picture. He was posing like a muscle man would and since Mom thought he was being overly, well, "male," and she was not amused, so she cut him out of the picture. When I asked her why she cut him out, she retorted, "he is not my kid." I never understood this part of my mother. I thought he was funny.

If the picture was panoramic, you would be able to see a crowd of people. My teenage cousin, Mara, always came to these large family gatherings in a swimsuit. She was leaning on the white picket fence in front of Grandma's yard. The swimsuit was sometimes a two-piece and much shorter than short shorts. The bra was tied with strings. I always wondered why she dressed that way. I asked Mom once and she answered, "She wants to be comfortable." I was sure that was true, but wondered why nobody else wanted that *comfort* then. I know now I also assumed that all families had a *Mara*.

Mom would never have said anything too negative about Mara. She loved her. She and my aunt had taken care of Mara for years when she lived with them and Grandma. Roy and Marge had been having financial difficulties and allowed Mara to move in at age nine months. Though they had other children after Mara, they allowed her to stay with Mom and Rene till she was nine years old. Roy got upset with Grandpa over something and took her back home. It devastated Mara as well as Mom and Aunt Rene. Roy didn't care that this was the only home Mara knew. When Mom visited them, Mara would beg her to take her home with her. Mom never told me what Roy got so upset over.

Perhaps this event made Mom even more resolved to have her own little girl, one that couldn't be taken away. I have been told that when I was born, Mara was jealous, even though she had adjusted to living at her own home and loved her parents.

Chapter 7

Our House

Grandma's house, now our house, was the sort where you knew that it had been truly lived in. Love was there. Deceit was there. Good food was always there. Arguing was there. All else that makes a family interesting was there. I have always felt that houses have their own character and that living in them affects the people who live there, as well as the house. I have heard some say that houses and their contents say a lot about the people who live there. I am not sure what ours said to others.

There was a familiar, soft, comforting creak as you ascended the stairs to the second story and reached the hall at the top, and the shiny, varnished banister was so smooth to the touch when you ascended or descended. Grandpa was always careful about keeping it varnished to a high shine. Well, the creak of the stairs was comforting unless you were trying to quietly make your way down the hall to lay at the top of the stairs to try to hear what the adults below were talking about in the evening when you were supposed to be in bed. That tell tale creak could be overheard downstairs if Mom was on her toes. On those occasions, she yelled, "Get back to bed!" If the forthcoming return to your bedroom creak wasn't heard, she would pursue further. It was useless to balk once she heard you.

There was a convenient landing at the bottom of the stairs and the coat closet was there, along with a smaller window, on the right, facing the backyard. This landing was perfect for children who liked to slide down the steps like on a playground and break at the landing. Three more steps down to the left brought you into the typical, spacious living room of most houses built in the 1930's.

This house, though similar to others in the tree-lined neighborhood, was not the clone that became the norm in the post WW2 and 1950's housing developments. Each house in our neighborhood had its own character. Ours sat on a corner and it had a large side porch off the living room that issued a perfect invitation on a warm summer night to sit outside. From there, one could stare at the fireflies or people watch and chat with neighbors who chose to take evening walks. There was no fear of gang's back then, or drive by shootings as there are in cities today. The front of the house faced St. John's Avenue. The side porch faced Hope Street. When I was little, before our move to Ewing, I had an imaginary playmate I named "A Johns." I liked the name St. Johns, so I used it.

The north wall of the living room embraced a wood mantled fireplace, which Mom decorated with various family photos and knick-knacks. At Christmas, our stockings and greeting cards were hung there and also along the dining room alcove, which was to the right of the fireplace. Though this was a formal dining room, it never looked austere, but warm and inviting with it's softly flowered pale green wallpaper.

The kitchen was off the dining room. Other than the holidays or Sunday dinner, we ate in the kitchen. The kitchen décor was nothing spectacular but by cooking and warmth it was immeasurable. Mom and Dad replaced the two smaller original kitchen windows over the sink with a much larger picture style window. Mom hung cheery kitchen curtains there. I can still see Dad standing at the sink washing dishes. He chose to wash dishes most times since Mom had cooked the meal. He was a man before his time in that regard and Aunt Rene and Uncle John viewed this as women's work and that he shouldn't be doing it. He ignored the comments.

The black, rotary dial telephone was on the counter beside the kitchen sink, with a couple phone books underneath it. Dede and I used to run for it when it rang to see who could answer it first. By the time I was 12 and in junior high school, if it was in the evening, it was usually for me. I still remember the phone number, CA5-7406. The CA stood for CApital although when the phone company first brought out the letters prefix they said it was CAtherine.

The wooden cupboards in the kitchen were painted white and were lined with colorful strips of shelf liner as were the drawers below the counter and the bottom cupboards beneath the drawers. The back door was beside the cupboards. Originally there had been an enclosed back porch. Grandma kept all sorts of things out there when she owned the house. She cooled baked goods out there on her table and stored things there. Later, my parents had the back porch removed and the back door then opened directly into the newly constructed carport.

On the other side of the back door, in the kitchen, was the door to the basement. That was where Grandma had stored canned goods, that she had canned herself, neatly on the shelves. Mom kept all sorts of Campbell soup cans in that same area or any other canned food she bought. She also had her washing machine down there and her rinse tubs. The old coal furnace and coal bin my grandparents had, were replaced with a new furnace and the wooden walls to the coal bin were removed. Mom also strung rope to hang clothes on in winter or when the weather was bad and she couldn't hang them outside.

On the other side of the basement door in the kitchen was the refrigerator and then the stove. Above the refrigerator was a cat clock. It was pink with bejeweled slanted green cat eyes and its tail moved back and forth as though it was slowly wagging it to mark the time.

Sometimes when Dad got things from the refrigerator, he would knock over a pop bottle. There was no harm done. It was sealed well with the cap or the rubber cap we placed on it for continued potency, if it had already been opened. He still allowed himself to get upset. My usually composed and quiet father was reduced to a loud, cussing, frustrated testosterone riddled male if he knocked over a pop bottle. Mom thought it was very amusing. I just thought it was stupid, especially by the time I was a teenager when I thought most things adults did were incredibly *stupid.*

The table sat right in the middle against the wall. Originally, there was a built in bar type table attached to that wall. It had a rounded end with shelves. Grandma put decorations on those shelves when she lived there. The top of the bar table matched the tops of the counters, a yellow and different tones of brown speckled type of counter material. Mom and Dad had the bar removed. They liked the flexibility of the table. The bar had also been higher and had stool style chairs with backs on them. If

I had been consulted, I would have chosen to keep the bar. It reminded me of Grandma and watching her make those apple dumplings and cut her homemade noodles after rolling the dough out on that bar.

If the walls of the kitchen could talk, they would tell of good smells from Grandma or Mom cooking, conversations past, laughter so hard that you would sometimes wet your pants, Christmas cookies rolled out and cut and baked by the all the women who had lived there, and there would have been tears. Mom stood at the counter after Grandma died, preparing our dinner and crying all the while.

Upstairs, the bathroom was the first door to the left. The antique bathtub with claw legs was by now encased with wood to make it "modern" looking, and the walk in linen closet had hooks to hang your nighties and bathrobes. Dede's bedroom was across from the bathroom. She only had one window over the roof of the side porch. Mom and Dad's bedroom were further down the hall next to Dede's room. My bedroom was across the hall from theirs and it had two windows, since it was in the corner. I could see the busy avenue out my front window and my friend Cindy's brown two-story house across the street.

I was in bed by 9:00 on school nights, except for Tuesday when I could stay up till 10:00 to watch "Cheyenne," a TV western I loved. I had a crush on the star, Clint Walker. I would lie in bed and watch the shadows on my wall move as the cars lights passed the house. I was lulled to sleep by their comforting quiet whoosh. I wondered why anybody would be out so late. I snuggled down into the covers feeling so safe there. The sheets smelled so fresh and clean like only things hung outside to dry can smell.

Mom always hung the sheets out to dry in summer. In winter, many years before she got a modern dryer, she hung clothes in the basement, on rope lines strung hither and yon, in a zigzag pattern. She put a fresh smelling fabric softener in the rinse then. The sheets and the clothes always smelled like all "good things" should smell, outdoor fresh and as white and pure as Ivory soap.

48

Chapter 8

"I Like Ike"

Society was changing by the mid fifties from the post war years. Gone was the mentality of Rosie the Riveter. Women were now expected to stay home and tend to their children rather than work in factories, as they had to support the troops during the war. General Dwight David Eisenhower ran for President of the United States in 1952 and again in 1956 and won a landslide victory both times. My parents and many others sported the "I LIKE IKE" buttons, which proved to be an irresistible slogan. Negotiating from military strength, he tried to reduce the strains of the Cold War with the Soviet Union.

The death of Stalin in 1955 caused shifts in the United States relations with Russia. Both the US and Russia had previously developed hydrogen bombs. With the threat of such destruction hanging over the world, Eisenhower, with the leaders of the British, French, and Russian governments, met at Geneva in July 1955.

The President proposed that the United States and Russia exchange blueprints of each other's military establishments and "provide within our countries facilities for aerial photography to the other country." The Russians were cordial throughout the meetings. Some people, however, began to get a little nervous about "those Russians."

I observed how the grown ups seemed to smile when they talked about Ike. I liked Ike because he made everyone happy. President Eisenhower is the first president I remember learning about or hearing about, other than my Mom and Aunt Rene or Grandpa saying things like "Roosevelt was a big CROOK!" Truman purportedly was like that too, but he was considered more innocuous. Grandma was not a political person or at least she didn't say anything to me about her beliefs. Along with everyone else I knew, I wore an "I LIKE IKE!" button. It made me feel like I was a part of things, on the cutting edge of political life. I was too young to remember anything about Eisenhower's initial election, but I was a *politically active* third grader.

In my school, a public school, the teacher started the day with a Bible reading and prayer. Then we said the Pledge of Allegiance. I remember the pride I felt for my country. By high school I was entering essay contests such as "What my country means to me…" There was never any doubt that the USA was indeed the greatest country on earth and the best place to live. How could anyone think otherwise?

Hula-hoops became popular in 1958. I had a green one. I hated green. Dede had a light blue one. I couldn't master the hoop thing very well, but Dede did. Mom entered us in a hula-hoop contest at the shopping center. It was a bright day for the event. They grouped the contestants by age groups in the roped off the parking lot. I lasted about 30 seconds. My hoop became erratic and went sideways, then dropped to loop my knees as I frantically tried to get it to *travel up.* It landed on the black tar parking lot. Some adults who noticed gave me an encouraging smile. Dede lasted 45 minutes. She only quit after 45 minutes because she had to go to the bathroom, (to make a *noise*). The winner of the contest that day lasted around 8 hours. They brought her a hot dog to eat, and she kept hooping while she ate. I have no idea how they handled the bathroom tasks. Perhaps they gave them a few minutes break to go after so long doing the hoop. Amazing. She won a trophy. I think it was a trophy with a child doing the hula-hoop on top and it had her name engraved on it.

Dede not only hula hooped, she also liked poems and made up her own, which she called "polums." She was also able to do the schoolwork I taught her when we played school, the same as I was learning in school at the time. This was quite a feat due to the fact that she was only four years old.

One of my favorite things was go out to eat for Sunday dinner. Later, when I was in fifth grade and we were then attending church, we went after that. We went to King Burger, a local restaurant, or Big Boy. The former had a jukebox and you could select what song you wanted right from the booth.

You put the coin in (either a nickel, a dime or a quarter, depending on how many selections you wanted), punched your songs on the push buttons and waited and hoped yours played before you were finished eating and had to leave. It was a busy place and first punched, first served. Big Boy didn't have a jukebox, but the Big Boy double hamburgers were good. Dad always got the same thing, a Brawny Lad sandwich. I think it had ham in it. It took me a few years to realize that there were "better *restaurants.*" I longed to go to them. Mom later told me that I had "champagne taste and beer money." That "attitude" has followed me to adulthood.

I thought that *champagne life* had arrived when Dad and Mom took us to Detroit to stay in a hotel one weekend. I could barely sleep I was so excited. I remember looking out the window of our hotel that night at the street far below. I was impressed. We were actually in a *real* hotel. They took us to a movie while we were in Detroit that they thought Dede and I would enjoy. It was *Rock-A-Bye Baby*, starring Jerry Lewis. I know the movie was for Dede and I because Mom didn't care for Jerry Lewis. She thought he was just silly, and not terribly funny.

Speaking of movies, the grade B horror films that came out from the mid to late fifties were splendid examples of no talent and no money productions. However, when you are from seven to ten years old, this never enters your mind.

My first and only venture was a double feature. The first feature was called "The Woman Eater." It had to do with a woman-eating plant but the only women this plant had an appetite for apparently had to be shapely and voluptuous. I didn't last long watching this because when the first woman I witnessed being trapped by this plant while she screamed, sent me running to the women's restroom. I thought I would be sick. I sat in the stall on the toilet after the wave of nausea passed looking at the deep pink walls and made the decision not to return to my seat since I did not want to repeat my performance. Between the features, Mom came looking for me. She told me to come back to my seat now since I was doing better. I also didn't like feeling as though I could not conquer this. Intellectually, I knew the movie was not real, as Mom had explained. I just wished my stomach understood this also.

"The *H* Man" was a color movie set in Japan. It was an anti nuclear movie, but at age ten, I didn't pick up on those subtleties. Mom explained it however. I watched in horror as the green liquid ooze emerged, (from an H bomb exposure), seeking victims and running up their legs and dissolving them into itself in order to survive. It made it's way through a sewer at one point. The only thing that would destroy it was fire. I was terrified. I didn't feel sick again while we were at the theatre, but after arriving home, the nausea returned. Nightmares and sleeplessness ensued. I resolved to never again go to those types of movies. I was emotionally convinced that there was green ooze slowly making its way up the stairs to my room. Shutting my door wouldn't keep it out, as it would go under the door. It could go up the outside of the house and get in that way. The possibilities for being dissolved into nothingness were endless.

Meals in our house were simple fare and were usually a time for family unity. For breakfast, I always had two pieces of toast (white bread) with butter and jelly or with butter, powdered sugar and cinnamon and a glass of milk. Rarely did I eat cereal, but if I did it would have been on a weekend. Mom always had the radio on in the mornings. She liked the talk shows. I sat there eating toast and wondered how anyone could be so cheerful so early in the morning. Obviously, they didn't have to go to school.

If we had lunch at home, which would have been elementary school since we came home for lunch then walked back to school four blocks away, it was usually a bologna sandwich with mustard on white (Wonder) bread and perhaps some Campbell's soup and a glass of milk. We ate it on a snack tray in front of the black and white TV and watched "Our Miss Brooks" or "I Love Lucy." Sometimes, Mom had a fifteen-minute soap opera on. I hated having to leave to go back to school because I wanted to watch *As The World Turns* with Mom. That was on after *Search For Tomorrow*. Those lunches were a bonding time with my Mom and I loved the soaps as much as she did. The soap families always had things going on. How could any one family have so much intrigue?

When we arrived home from school, supper (didn't call it dinner then), was ready soon after. On Sunday we ate in the dining room after church. Mom went all out. We had beef roast, or pork roast or fried chicken, mashed potatoes and gravy, vegetables, dinner rolls and dessert. We also used Moms fancy dishes on Sundays. Mom did her best to make everything so homey. She could also be "scary."

Mom's "Witch Routine" & "classical" tunes

Dede and I loved it when Mom would play "witch" with us. She had the best witch's cackle I have ever heard. We begged her to play it. She would usually chase us and I remember feeling real fear. We usually ran for the stairs with her close behind chasing us. We would take refuge in a bedroom or bathroom and lean on the door so she couldn't open it.

Mom ended the game permanently when she overheard Dede and I talking in the bathroom. I told Dede, "What if Mom really has gone nuts? People can. What if she really would kill us? We could jump out the bathroom window. We might break a leg but we wouldn't die." We really were seriously considering our next move. As I said, Mom overheard it. She called us out but I was afraid to go in case it was just a trick to get us to come out. We stood our ground. I cannot remember how she finally convinced us to come out, but since I did not want to spend my childhood in the bathroom, it worked. She would never play it after that, much to our disappointment.

Mom also taught us such timeless songs as Barbertown.

"As I went down to Barbertown a week ago today; I saw the funniest billy goat was ever fed on hay. The horns upon this billy goat were very far apart, and every time he took a step he left a little okeedokie fiddly-okie, take it as you like; if you go down to Barbertown, you'll see the same old site."

There was another one where a billy goat ate three shirts, coughed them up and flagged the train. Sometimes I still wonder at the apparent *billy goat* fixation.

Chapter 9

Summertime & School

The Langs lived across the street from us on Hope St. Hope Street was the side street to our corner house. The front of the house faced St. Johns. Hope St. had little traffic, unlike St. Johns Avenue, the main street out front.

The Lang's had several children. The two oldest girls were about my age. One was a year or two older and the second was a year younger. Nether of our mothers allowed us to cross the street to play very often. This just served to make the other child's yard even more inviting.

We were generally obedient but we whined about it a lot, or at least I did. "Pulleeese may I go over to Cat's to play?"

The answer was rarely, "OK."

Cat and I learned to ride our two wheeled bicycles together, she on her sidewalk and I on mine. We talked about bike sizes, 18 inch or 24 inch and 26 inch was for BIG kids. If we ever got a 26-inch bike, we knew we would have arrived. I got a new 26-inch green bike, probably for my birthday. Cat rode an old brown 24-inch second hand bike. We rode together on the sidewalk each on our own side of Hope Street, to the end of our respective blocks and back again. We sat on the grass that bordered the sidewalk below the lawns.

We talked and played games for hours. We also fought.

"My dad is stronger than your dad," Cat would say. I answered with something equally inane, "My dad is smarter than your dad and he could kill your dad if he wanted to."

"No sir! She answered. "My dad has a knife this long!" she motioned with her skinny little arms outstretched. "Well, my dad has a gun and he could shoot your dad," I replied in one-upmanship. Some unaware adults might think that only boys talked this way.

One time Cat changed the venue on me and said, "My mom says you are rich."

I was at a loss for words, and this didn't happen too often. I didn't think we were rich, but I decided to check this out. I admit I liked the idea if we were.

"Mom, are we rich? Cat says her mom says we're rich, cause we have lots of stuff."

"No," Mom answered. "We are not rich. Cat's dad has a good job but they have a lot of children so it takes more money. We only have two children."

It made sense to me. I am sure I repeated this to Cat. I wonder if she ever told her mother.

I recall that her mother and my mother did not get along. They never had any huge fights, but they did have a couple verbal exchanges that I gathered were not pleasant. Mostly Mrs. Lang just refused to speak to my mom, but she gossiped to neighbors.

This was a mistake. She told the wrong person that my grandfather was a attempting to lure children into the house. I have no idea how this got back to us, but Grandpa was understandably upset and Mom was very angry. It was the only time that I know of that my parents contacted a lawyer. The lawyer sent Mrs. Lang a letter detailing how she would be sued for slander if she kept this up. The letter did the trick.

I realized then that sometimes adults could be as childish as children. Since I really didn't like people my age, preferring adult company, this was a sobering realization.

A year or so later, Mrs. Lang came to our back door. I couldn't hear what was said. Mom told me that Mrs. Lang came over to apologize for what she said about Grandpa and for gossiping about Mom. She told Mom that she had become a Christian and was sincerely trying to live a better life as a Christian. Mom accepted her apology. Though they were never friends, Mom and Mrs. Lang had apparently come to some sort of peaceful coexistence.

Clarence was Dad's brother. He drove the bread truck, a box-like green truck with open side doors that folded open and closed to allow quick exits. In warm months they were always left open. Behind the driver were sliding glass partitions with trays of baked goods on shelves. From the back of the truck you could see through the small square windows on the back doors to the filled trays inside. The donuts looked so good.

Clarence was always smiling and he would hop out with a couple loaves of bread my mom purchased regularly. She rarely bought anything but bread. I imagine she thought why buy it when she could make it or buy it at the bakery more cheaply.

If we begged, she would sometimes purchase a couple crème filled chocolate covered Long Johns. Although this was a treat, there was an even better treat, ice cream.

The ice cream boy would come by every evening in summer. He bicycled behind the attached two-wheeled refrigerator cart filled with popsicles, drumsticks, ice cream bars and fudge bars. He had bells attached to the cart's horizontal handlebar, which he would manually jingle to announce his arrival to all the children. We heard him coming from two blocks away. We knew we needed to start begging then. If I was playing with other children when we heard his bells, we scattered home to ask for at least a nickel to purchase a popsicle. An ice cream or fudge bar was a dime and the coveted drumstick was a quarter. We didn't get the drumstick too often, as it was too expensive.

Occasionally a boy would buy a piece of dry ice. We watched as it sat there on the sidewalk smoldering and steaming. It seemed to have almost magical properties to it since the boys told us if you touch it, it would burn your skin off. It seemed magical because having ice that would *burn* seemed completely illogical.

Boys always liked danger. I never understood that quality.

Speaking of boys, they are entities that my mom did not allow as part of my and my sisters childhood. The neighbors across St. Johns Avenue had three girls and a boy. I played with the oldest girl. Her younger brother, John, would occasionally attempt to join us. Mom bluntly told him, "I don't have any boys here to play with. You can go home." I am certain Mom was doing what she could to protect us from some of the things she suffered from boys, such as cruel teasing. Conversely, it also prevented us from learning to relate to them more efficiently, a life skill that is necessary.

The time mom overheard me talking to one of my large baby dolls as if this was my son, she said, "Why are you doing that, making the doll be a boy?" I answered, "Well, I would someday like to have a son or sons." She replied, "For pete's sake, why?" I knew how she felt about boys and men in general, but I also knew I really did want to have a son. There would be no debating it with her. I just said, "Because." There was no logic to her feelings other than resentment due to her experience, and though I had my own issues with boys who could and had been very cruel, it didn't change my desire to have a male child. I also knew girls could be very cruel; they simply used a more subtle strategy most of the time. I guess she forgot about the homemade cloth doll that she pinned material to in order to make it an anatomically correct boy, as a very small child.

One of our favorite things to do was under the cloak of night protection. Mom, Dede and I would sometimes take a dip in our 8 ft. square wading pool, with metal seats on each corner, to cool off if it was particularly warm during summer. Mom certainly wouldn't join us in the daytime when she might be seen. We would lie on our stomachs and talk and watch the neighbors if they were out. People who were taking a walk would never know we were there in the yard and were able to see them, because we were very quiet as they passed. I am not sure what we may have discussed. All I know is that we seemed to laugh a lot.

One hot summer afternoon, things weren't so amusing, Mom had just done a large washing, and had been going up and down the stairs from the basement where the wringer washer and rinse tubs were, while carrying the full clothesbasket to hang the clothes outside, tote them in again and put everything away or pile them to iron first. After all that work, she was in much pain, and stood leaning against a chair in the living room. Grandma, who lived right behind us, came over. Mom was crying and was red-faced from the heat and her hard work. I worried, but observed from a distance. After a time, Mom was OK again. She said she had miscarried. She did not go to a doctor to be checked. This was the end of the matter. We learned later that since her blood was RH negative that this produces antibodies in the blood with each pregnancy and if the baby's blood is RH positive the antibodies attack the baby's blood through the placenta. This is why she miscarried. This was before the medical community developed Rho-GAM, the serum that prevents the antibodies from attacking the baby so RH- Moms can carry babies much more safely.

I had not known she was pregnant. I used to think about my lost sibling and wondered if I would have had a baby brother or a baby sister. I wanted a brother. My preference was always to have an older brother, who could have protected me from the bullies on the playground at school. I shared that desire with Mom and she asked, "Why?" with a baffled and ticked off look on her face. I had no way of knowing that I did have an older (half) brother and he had red hair, but Mom knew. The only red-haired boy I knew was Denny Smith, who was in my class at school, and he was one of the bullies. He had a butch haircut and many freckles. He taunted me and anyone else he felt had an "inferior appearance." He was truly a bad person if ever there was one, very cruel. I also thought his orange hair and voluminous freckles were possibly the ugliest things to have, so I wondered why he felt so entitled to be condescending. I never retaliated though. I was afraid of him and I was taught that you did not say things that would hurt someone else's feelings. Like most children, since I had previous assessments on my appearance by other not necessarily well-meaning classmates, I somewhat agreed that I was "inferior."

A popular hair dye TV commercial during this time featured a pretty blonde woman and a jingle, "Is it true blondes have more fun? Only your hairdresser will know for sure." This commercial, along with Marilyn Monroe and others indicated to me that blonde was better. I had brown hair. Dede had pale blonde hair. I thought maybe this was one of the reasons Dad didn't like me. Yellow was his favorite color. He said so.

One of the first times I became aware of my "general inferiority" was in first grade when we still lived on Ewing. I attended Irving Elementary School. I hated it and I hated my teacher, Miss Clark. I had tolerated Miss Ross, my Kindergarten teacher. Miss Clark had pin curled, short gray hair and thick little glasses that emphasized her beady little eyes. She only wore tailored suits with nondescript white blouses showing at the top of the jacket to school. I am still convinced that she hated me.

Miss Clark had three reading groups. The better readers were in group one, the okay readers were in group two and those who didn't read as well were in group three. I knew I belonged in the first group but I was placed in the third, I assumed, to humiliate me. The third group of children took a long time between words as they read aloud. The first group was able to read at a normal speaking speed. My only recourse was to read, when it was my turn, at not only a normal speaking speed over difficult words, but to read with expression. It was my way of letting her and the others know that not only was I an excellent reader, but that I knew I was an excellent reader, in spite of the reading group in which I had been placed.

I assumed Miss Clark hated me because I was ugly. A boy in my class had told me that I had hairy legs and that they were ugly.

"Look at Marilyn's legs. She has no hair on her legs. Why don't you look like Marilyn?" he said.

Marilyn was a girl in my class that had smooth legs. He was sincere and matter of fact, not really trying to be mean. At age six, he had somehow learned that males might *rightfully* comment on a female's presumed defects, as though his opinion as a male was the criteria used in judging beauty. Considering

Hollywood's standards of beauty over the years, and that Hollywood was and is run by men, not to mention the way products are marketed again using Hollywood standards of beauty for women, it would not take long for a boy or girl to get the message on who ran things. He simply assumed his perceived position as *purveyor of necessary-to-fix-yourself information* if you want to be viewed as beautiful by male folk. I accepted his assessment with little to no question.

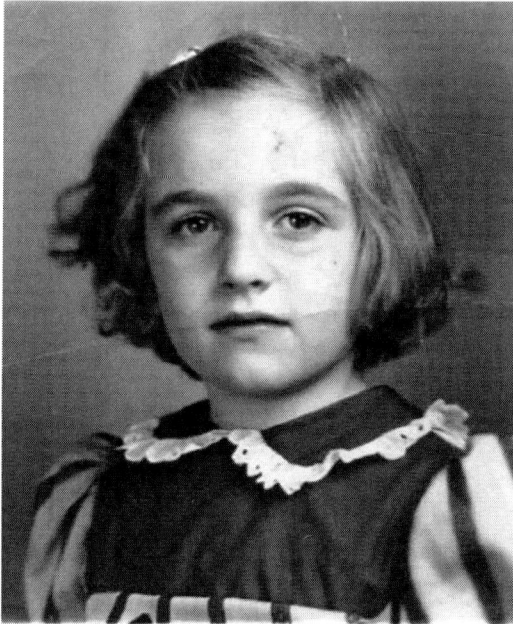

My First Grade school picture

Mom always told me that she used to look at this picture and cry. Earlier that same day, she had reprimanded me for something before I left for school. I don't remember this. However, she knew I was not happy at school. So, combined with the reprimand at home and then having to go to the place I hated, in the class of the teacher who I knew hated me, and only ever just wanting to go home, Mom thought I looked very sad in this picture. I do remember when it was taken. I knew I was supposed to smile. I thought I had. As I look at the picture, me at age six, and as a Mom myself knowing what I went through with Miss Clark, I can understand why it made Mom cry.

The following year, at a new school and in Miss Crist's class, I was quickly put into the highest-level reading group. Justice finally prevailed.

I joined Brownies in third grade, and then continued into Girl Scouts in fourth, fifth and sixth grades. Not only did Grandma, Aunt Bonnie and Aunt Rene buy Girl Scout cookies, Mom bought 60 boxes of cookies and put them in the upright freezer in the basement. The cookies were 35 cents to 50 cents a box. *Thin mints* were all right, but I liked *Savannahs* the best. Savannahs were peanut butter sandwich cookies that Girl Scouts still sell, but under a different name and they are now much smaller. Mom liked Savannahs best too. She bought 40 boxes of that kind alone. Mom was always my best customer.

My primary school years passed fairly uneventfully as I settled into the academic atmosphere at Jefferson. On the playground we played "Movie Star Tag." The playground was loose stone so it lent itself well to this game. You drew a box with a stick in the stones and put the initials of a movie star inside. The other child would guess who the initials belonged to, (i.e. M.M.=Marilyn Monroe, E.P.=Elvis Presley). If they guessed, they won that round immediately. If they didn't guess correctly, you had to chase them as they ran around some trees and back to base, where the initials were, before you tagged them. If they made it to base, you could not tag them. If you tagged them, then it was your turn to guess the names. I liked this game. I have no idea how you won, other than whoever got the most correct guesses.

I also liked the game *Rhythm*. The girls were the only ones who played *Rhythm*. Most of the boys awkwardly made fun of it. Some tried it but were not any good. Naturally, I assumed they didn't play it because they weren't as coordinated as the girls, so they made fun of it to cover up that fact.

A row of girls lined up and the leader stood in front of them. In perfect synchronization, our hands slapped down, one on either leg, then we clapped our hands together, then the right hand went thumb out, then the left went thumb out. The leader started the correct rhythm and spoke in the rhythm she wanted the others to follow. Sometimes she went very fast and sometimes very slow and all in-between. Each girl was a specific number. The leader was "*one.*" She said her number as the right thumb headed out, and spoke someone else' number as the left thumb headed out. Hands on legs, clap hands center, the girl whose number had been called said her own number, right thumb out and some other girls number, left thumb out. This continued till one of us made a mistake, like calling out a number greater than the number of girls sitting there, or getting out of rhythm, or going blank. If you missed, you went to the end of the line as the last number. The rest moved up. No mistakes, then you finally got to be leader. When the leader missed, she went to the end of the line. However, just as you were starting to have some fun, the teacher blew her whistle to round you up to go back in.

Sixth grade was my final year at Jefferson Elementary. I loved sixth grade. I loved Mrs. Nelson, my teacher. She was blonde, pretty, had a couple teen-aged sons and a husband who was in the Navy Reserves. Mrs. Nelson took us to the Naval Reserve Training Center on a field trip. Her husband hosted the event and showed us around. I remember one of the things we were shown was how to give a dummy artificial resuscitation. It was probably my first contact with the military. I was duly impressed, especially by the uniforms.

The next year I entered South Junior High School in seventh grade. My mother had attended South when it was a high school. New things were in store.

Chapter 10

Cincinnati to Lima

Aunt Rene had long since given up Miller, her married boyfriend who came to meals sometimes when we lived on Ewing Avenue. Rene had met and married John, a railroad engineer who lived in Cincinnati. He was originally from Tennessee and spoke with a southern accent. He started talking to Rene when she was waiting at the factory gate for the bus to come after work. His train was parked a block away at the depot and he had time before he had to take the train out again. She allowed him to walk her home to her little house on Ashton Avenue, a few miles away. She had moved out of Grandma's house at age 35 to buy the house on Ashton.

She and John talked about her beautiful flowers and how much he liked flowers too. He explained that he was going through a divorce. He had one son and his soon-to-be-ex wife was a drunk who had also cheated on him. After a reasonable time, when the divorce finalized and Rene finally dumped Miller, they got married by a justice of the peace. They lived in a duplex for a while, in Cincinnati. I went to visit them. I got to ride the B&O train there. John worked as engineer for that railroad. They lived on a hill. I loved visiting them. I thought hilly Cincinnati was beautiful.

Once, Rene and John took me to the Cincinnati Zoo and I rode a fast roller coaster type ride by myself. I forgot to strap myself in and almost flew out. The guy running it never checked to see if I was belted in. He glared at me while the ride was going and gestured wildly. I knew he was mad but I didn't realize he was motioning toward the strap. I didn't know there was a strap. He never checked like the seemingly more conscientious people running rides today. When the ride was over he was still mad. I thought he was just mad and overreacted because he thought I was ugly.

Now, when I think back to that, with the stringent rules now, he would have been fired. Perhaps he would have then. He likely didn't stop the ride because he didn't want to call attention to the fact, any more than he already was, that I was not strapped in and he hadn't done his job.

I left my new straw purse on the seat of the ride. My dad's boss had given me the purse as a gift. It was from Florida and it had pretty colored shells on the top. It was expensive, Mom said, even though it was a little girl's purse. The purse had $2.00 in it. I was so distraught that John called the zoo later to see if it had been turned in. It hadn't. I mourned the purse and hoped whoever took it was miserable. It was probably that mean ride operator.

I also burnt my thumb on Rene's percolator one morning that same week. While I was outside in backyard later, I decided to cool my throbbing thumb by sticking it in her birdbath. It might have worked, but it had rained and my feet slipped on the wet grass. I fell forward, hitting my two front teeth on the edge of the cement birdbath. Rene rushed out as I screamed and there was blood all over me. She washed me up and I could tell she was scared at what my parents would say about my teeth. I was more concerned with my bloody knee. Mom took me to a dentist when I got home. He said that since I was still growing, my teeth would have to wait till I was in my mid teens to be capped. I was relieved it was a long way off. Although I didn't like the upside down "V" of my front teeth, since the other children didn't make fun of it, it was a tolerable defect.

Rene and John eventually moved to Lima. It was nice to go visit them in Lima as well. John was a handy man and decided that they could build their own house in the country. They built the cement block garage first and lived in that as they built the house. He obtained the necessary tools, including a cement mixer, for the foundation. I watched them working on the foundation and had fun seeing their progress. They could honestly say they built it from the ground up. Rene helped with everything. She was on the roof hammering nails right along with John. They were in their 40's. She enjoyed telling of the big rain they had one day while on the roof. The cars were passing by out front as it was a major route from Delphos to Lima. It poured and there they sat. They laughed as cars honked at them. Rene talked as if this was the best time of her life. Every year we went out to their house for Thanksgiving and they came to our house at Christmas. I spent an enjoyable week there every summer.

The house had two-bedrooms with a full basement. I stayed in the second bedroom when I visited in summer. There were lots of cars passing by where they lived and the railroad tracks just beyond the busy highway added to the noise. It was fun to watch the trains pass by. Sometimes the engineers waved at me. I could hear all those comforting sounds when I went to bed at night. I learned to sleep through it.

Their house was very homey and comfortable with Early American style furniture. It smelled of John's cigars, and due to the association of that smell with him, I learned to like the smell.

This is a picture of their house....

John was a beekeeper as a hobby and he had 40 hives in various fields nearby. Farmers liked this as the pollination from the bees also pollinated the crops. I enjoyed watching him rob the hives. I helped him strain some of the honey and cut the comb for some of it to go into boxes labeled with J. W. Stephenson on the front, R.R. 2, Delphos, Ohio, their address. The boxes were green and yellow with a honeycomb pictured on the front and a clear plastic window so you could see part of the comb honey inside. The strained honey went into jars and a label with the same information was stuck on the jar. In some jars there was strained honey as well as comb. John and I delivered the honey to various customers, small stores as well as Pangles, the large local grocery store in Lima. They all wanted John's honey. It sold as fast as he could supply them.

John was a man who never met a stranger. He was loud, and happy most of the time and as I said, he smoked big smelly cigars. He took me to ride go-karts. I was nervous as I attempted to guide the cart around the curves, but he raced past me making two or three rounds to my one. He yelled, waved, and laughed as he passed.

Mom told a different story of the "happy" time at Rene and Johns home. Rene called her on a regular basis when she and John had fights. I never heard about those calls until I was much older. I felt loved. John was the laughing, outgoing, "approving" father figure that I didn't seem to have with Harry.

"Well, I'm going to SAY something! It isn't right!"

"No, John, you can't. You can't. Mable and Harry would hate us. It isn't our place."

"I don't care. This isn't right! If they don't tell her then I will."

"John, maybe so, honey, but we can't say anything to Cherié."

Rene told me she and John had this conversation several times till he finally let the topic go. Rene had told him everything about the adoption, and about Hubert, as she told me many years later.

These are two pictures of my Uncle John, the beekeeper. Yes, those little flying dots are bees swarming about him.

I descended the stairs one summer morning and Mom greeted me with "I have some good news!" She was grinning.

I blurted, "Rene is pregnant."

Mom's mouth fell open. "HOW did you know??"

I didn't know *how* I knew. I just did. I was happy for her.

Five months into her pregnancy, as the doctor held the stethoscope to Rene's belly, he was unable to get a heartbeat.

John had bought baby clothes.

Rene warned him, "Now dad, we shouldn't do that yet," but John was so excited about becoming a daddy again. Since his divorce, he had lost touch with his son.

Rene always had heavy menstrual periods, but the last few years they had gotten increasingly worse. Rene had a very large abdominal tumor, which turned out to be benign and it had likely been there for years. She had to have a hysterectomy. The medical community allowed the dead baby and the tumor to share Rene's abdomen for several months before they were removed.

Rene had been hemorrhaging monthly. And then it was over.

No more hemorrhage. No more tumor. No more baby. Her baby was a boy.

It was sad, yes. I had a hard time with sadness. I didn't like the way it felt. So, I tried not to think about it. Some people get to have kids. Some don't. It is difficult to be philosophical when it hurts so much, even if it is for somebody else and not you, but I sure tried.

Chapter 11

"Growth"

When I was seven, I wrote up a questionnaire for my parents..

Mom and Dad always circled the *right* answer on my questionnaire.

"Do you love me? (Circle yes or no) Yes   No

Thank you for your assistance.

Sincerely,

Chérie A. ..."

When I reached my teens, Mom asked me if I felt insecure at that time. I told her no. I was fascinated with my new discovery of forms and I had seen surveys where they asked questions and you were to circle your answer. I also liked office materials and organization and words. I had just learned how to close a letter using the word "sincerely." If I wanted to do a questionnaire, there were not many options other than Mom and Dad. I had no idea this would foster my mother's worry about me being insecure.

I was given a children's Bible about this same time. It had a blue and gold cover with a tall angel on the front. The print was large and there was a line drawing every few pages. Though we didn't go to church until I was in fifth grade, Grandma sometimes told me Bible stories and would sing hymns while we sat on her carport glider swing. I loved that. She had such a sweet old lady voice. It was so peaceful sitting there with her. Mom told me stories too and she told me God loved me.

Perhaps due to Grandma being sick much of the time, or perhaps it was something on TV, which prompted Mom to tell me that *all* people die and that I also, would some day die. I cried myself to sleep a few nights after that. I didn't want to die. This was something big. I couldn't find a way around it like I could when I did something I shouldn't and was able to talk Mom out of any punishment. When she told me, I was scared, angry, and baffled.

My reaction to the unwelcome news was a heartfelt "Then what's the point?" Mom seemed surprised and then answered, " Well, you enjoy being alive don't you?" "Yes," I said.

However, I thought this reasoning was very lame. I am not sure if I voiced it aloud or just thought it, "If enjoying being alive is the reason we are alive, then how do you enjoy it when you know you are going to die?" It made absolutely no sense to me whatsoever. I knew I could argue with Mom but I also knew it wouldn't do any good.

"And anyway, you have your whole life ahead of you. You don't have to worry about that now," she concluded.

"Well, gee," I thought, "How am I supposed to enjoy *any* of my life when I know what is coming?"

She ended the conversation as though she had fully answered my questions. I didn't feel that she answered my questions in any way. It was awful. If the whole point was that I enjoy being alive, then why do we have to die? It didn't make any sense. She was supposed to know everything. She was Mom. I went to her for this and other important questions. Sometimes she said, "I don't know." If she "didn't know," then who would? It was so frustrating!

I couldn't sleep that night. I stared at my bedroom wall, as I laid there awake in the dark. I realized there was no way I could get out of this or get around it. I could get around Mom or Dad sometimes with my verbal abilities, but God was another matter. I knew He knew all and that no amount of cajoling would work with Him. I felt scared and trapped. There was little comfort from Mom or any other adult who said to me, "Don't worry about it. You are young. You have your whole life ahead of you." I thought that they had lost their minds. It defied all logic. Was this what grownups did with everything? They talked themselves into an inane calmness by telling themselves it was a long way off?

I talked to God about it. "Why God?" I asked. "Why did you do things this way? You could do something about it if you wanted." I was expressing my own fear, and honestly seeking understanding.

Knowing how disturbed I was, Mom had added further comment, "If people didn't die, there wouldn't be room enough in the whole world for everyone."

Logically, I knew *this* rang true, more so than her earlier illogical "enjoyment of life" answer. Though this made sense, somehow it still didn't add up. If God was loving, as I had been told and I knew He was, then why would he want his children to suffer by dying? I knew with this newly acquired information that nothing would ever be the same again.

One day when I was nine years old, I didn't have anything else to do so I went to my bedroom with my big blue and gold bible. I sat on my bed and I read the story about the crucifixion. There was a line drawing of soldiers with a hammer while Jesus was pictured lying down. I knew about the crucifixion from when Grandma or Mom told me stories. This time was different though.

As I read where the soldiers hammered nails in Jesus hands to put him on the cross, it dawned on me for the first time what that actually meant. I stared at the palm of my own hand. I visualized what it would feel like as I watched someone hammering a nail into my own palm.

I thought, "Boy, that would *really* hurt."

I kept on reading. Jesus had done nothing wrong. I knew that I was not always good, and I knew that He was good and didn't deserve this. I knew He died for me.

The thought snowballed.

He suffered *all this pain* for me.

The enormity of that weighed on me.

I was so sorry.

I began sobbing out of deep compassion for the pain He suffered. As I sat there, the most wonderful feeling of love and peace enveloped me. I didn't know what it was. I just knew it felt really good. After awhile, I went back downstairs and didn't say anything about it to anyone.

I repeated my reading on a couple other occasions. Each time, the same love and peace enveloped me.

Years later I would understand my experience better. All alone in my room, at the age of nine, unchurched and not informed, God touched my heart in a beautiful way. I had what some call a salvation experience. No, I didn't become the perfect child, but nothing in my life was quite the same.

There was a girl who lived a block away. She was a year older than me. She never wore shorts or slacks, just homemade dresses. She had long hair because her family didn't believe in cutting girl's hair. One time she invited me to go to a night service at her church.

Her church was the white one in the middle of the next block also facing St. Johns. Since it was close, Mom said I could go. We sat together in the crowded service, standing room only. I had been to church before but the churches I had been to were nothing like this one.

The guest minister was preaching up front as all sat in rapt attention. He was very loud and gestured a lot, as he paced back and forth. I sat near the alternate side door, which was open to allow a breeze into the non-air conditioned building. Many of the women held wooden handled hand cardboard fans with a color picture of Jesus on it and they fanned continually.

In here were lots of people; the women all dressed the same way the girl dressed, though some had their hair in greasy looking buns. The men looked almost normal, but some looked, (and smelled), as though they needed a bath.

I could see the sidewalk out front and the cars going past. The street, the cars whooshing by all looked so familiar and comforting. I wanted to be out there in that comfort. Wouldn't you know it that one of my male schoolmates, Lonnie, would pass by outside with two of his friends. They could see in, of course. They were being loud but I couldn't hear what they were saying although it was clear they were making fun of the service. I did hear clearly when Lonnie spotted me however. "Hey!" he said to his friends in a shocked voice, "Look! Chéri's in there!" (except he used my last name, not Chéri, again something that seems to be what boys do most often). Since I had a very low opinion in general of Lonnie, this didn't bother me too much. The boys moved on quickly, however. They were probably going down to the ice cream stand on the corner of Fourth Street and St. Johns. I envied them. A nickel cone was pretty small, but a 10-cent cone was good sized and satisfying.

The minister continued to shout. He talked about God and being saved and coming forward. I already knew about being saved, and though I knew the strange girl who invited me would have liked me to go forward, that would have meant I would have had a closer encounter with the loud preacher and all the sweaty people who went forward. I couldn't take any chances. Anyway, I knew you didn't have to be loud to be saved. I knew Jesus loved me and I knew I loved Jesus. I just wanted Him to get me out of there. I learned from this experience that churches are different and this was a "Pilgrim Holiness" church. I had no idea what that meant. I just didn't want to go to any of those again.

I told Mom about the experience. She was nonchalant about it. She said that people are different and that some people need more emotion in their church services. She had OK'd it for me to go. I am certain she knew what the church was about since it was a half block away and you could hear the singing in summer since they left the doors open to be cooler. And Mom also knew that this would be a new experience for me.

I always thought of her as overprotective. She was in many ways, but sometimes, she came through. She allowed me to have the room, to question and to grow, even when she didn't have any answers.

She was equally nonchalant when I asked her about Oral Roberts who had his own show on TV then and it was filmed in a tent where lots of people went to get healed. On the show, they were always healed. I watched it several times with much interest. Finally I went to Mom for those same answers.

"Is what Oral Roberts doing for real? Arc those people healed?"

She replied honestly, "I don't know."

"OK."

I finally learned something, acceptance of not knowing.

I also attended church with my best grade school friend, Juanita, and her family once. We went to Mass and it was in Latin. I loved the looks of this large old church with the high ceiling, wall frescoes and along with the somber Latin intonations it appealed to my sense of art and aesthetics.

It was shortly after this time that Pope John XXIII became pope. I remember the teacher had a newspaper clipping on the bulletin board, along with information on the Second Vatican Council. Catholics would not have to eat only fish on Fridays and the Mass would now be in English in the US. Although I liked the sounds of Latin, it made much more sense to me to have it in a language that people could understand. It would seem they would get more out of it.

Dad took a lot of business trips. In winter, he went to Ft. Lauderdale, Florida with his boss and his family. He chauffeured them, did errands for them, and was a charming right hand man for Mr. Galvin. In summer, when the Galvin's traveled to a resort in Petoskey, Michigan, Dad went as well. I always envied his travels.

Mom told me when I was a teenager that we could have gone with him all those times, but I didn't know that at the time. Mr. Galvin had offered to pay all our expenses. She made the decision that staying put would be better for her children. They had school. Actually, Mom was always a *homebody, as well as shy,* and did what *she* preferred. Judging by all the niceties we received over the years by Mr. Galvin, I am certain he may have provided a tutor if Dad had requested it for us.

Mom and I were different. She had loved school. I hated school, for the most part. I can only imagine what true *education* we may have received if we had been able to accompany Dad. We would also have had the time to bond with him, something that was sorely needed, and he would not have had to spend his off time by himself in a hotel room. He did enjoy the greyhound dog races as well as sulky races, but he admitted he became homesick and said how much he missed us.

Had I known all this and been older, and had I known Mom as a young woman, I would have been baffled at the way she had changed, at least on the surface. And I would have been inaccurate. She was still the same person who grabbed for the brass ring, whatever it took. She grabbed the ring and was living the American dream of women everywhere at the time. Why would she want to change that? She also wanted a stable home life and routine for her children and herself. Perhaps her earlier life had been so different that the calm by contrast was very welcome. I do know that she missed Dad as much as he missed her. She often cried when he called because she missed him so much.

One time, when he made one of his bi-weekly calls home, he mentioned another of Mr. Galvin's employees who had come on this particular trip. The woman worked at Galvin's house. Mom flipped. "What is SHE there for?" She was in tears. I saw her crying while on the phone. After she got off, she told me what dad had said. I was angry. But I told her, "Oh Mom, you know Dad would never cheat on you." I had not stopped to consider her history with Putter, but even if I had, I would have seen Dad as such a totally different person than Grandpa. I was a naïve young teen. Though this was true that Dad was not Grandpa, people make mistakes in life. Dad likely told her about it because he may have been tempted and wanted her to react, or he may have thought she would find out and think the worst so he told her so she wouldn't think he was hiding something. Perhaps he even felt she might consider all of us accompanying him from now on.

Dad called later to tell her how much he loved her and that she was the only woman there would ever be for him. Dad also spoke to Mr. Galvin. Mr. Galvin said, "What did you tell her for?" When Dad told Mom what Mr. Galvin said, she was even angrier. Mr. Galvin sent the woman home. No more was said on the matter.

Mom was amused years later when I met this friendly woman at some social function. I barely spoke to her and though I smiled at her compliments about my wonderful father, I was thinking, "Yes, I bet you do think he is wonderful and you better stay away from him." I am sure disgust was written all over my face.

Chapter 12

"Grandma's Apron"

&

Chamber pots

My grandmother and mother were very close. Long after Grandma died, I would find Mom crying. I would ask her what was wrong and she would say, "I just miss Mom is all." To view my life and Mom's life, especially the latter, would be missing a vital aspect without a closer look at her own mother. It would be like looking at a human body that contained no heart. They were like two layers of a cake with only a small sliver of frosting to separate them. To understand Mom, Grandma must be there.

It's funny the little things you notice when you are a child. Although I didn't give it a lot of analysis at the time, I always noticed Grandmas, and she was never without it, apron any time I saw her. They were colorful ginghams mostly, with little flower patterns. Unlike Mom, whose aprons were tied around her waist, fell over the front part of her skirt and were only worn when she was cooking, Grandma wore full aprons all the time. The bottom covered her skirt, but at the waistline, where it was tied behind her, the top of the apron covered most of her chest and it had wide straps, sometimes with ruffles, which went over her shoulders, down her upper back, and were sown to her waistband. Across the back of and sewn to the straps was usually a middle strap of material connecting them, which made her apron much like a dress. She put it on over her head and then tied the waistband ties.

You could tell she took pride in her appearance. Her aprons were always clean, starched and ironed just as she did her dresses. She must have had several aprons because I never saw a soiled one. She probably changed it as soon as it became soiled. I can still see her elderly figure as she walked slowly down the sidewalk to our house next door.

Her salt and pepper brownish thin hair was neatly pinned inside her matching hair net. Her dress and apron were colorfully coordinated. She always wore support hose, which were gartered just under or over her knee. She only wore one sturdy style of shoes, completely geared for comfort. They were black leather oxfords, with 1-2 inch chunk style heels. As I see her in my minds eye, the way she dressed perfectly epitomized the way I have seen pictures of the way most women dressed in the 1930's.

She had a deep love for her family and her sharing of her delicious cooking frequently showed this. Although I was able to appreciate most of the dishes she made, I recall a couple that even as an adult I would not eat.

When I walked into her kitchen one afternoon, she was frying brains (pigs) for Grandpa's dinner. It smelled terrible. I held my nose and asked her what the grayish-white mass was in the skillet. I was horrified when she told me. I ran home to report to Mom what *Gramma* was making, as though Mom didn't know what things her mother cooked.

Another of her dishes that I would not choose to eat was squirrel soup. Grandpa liked to hunt squirrels and I enjoyed, possibly with maudlin curiosity, watching him clean and dress the carcasses.

One day when I was in our backyard close to Grandma's carport, she came out her kitchen door carrying a bowl of soup with the spoon and said, "Here, taste it." Though it smelled good and the rich broth looked good, along with the vegetables was meat. I replied, "What is it?" One couldn't be too careful.
"Just taste it!" she said.
"What is it first?"
She looked exasperated. "Squirrel soup."
"No, I don't want it." I made a face.
"Don't be that way! Try it once" She held out a spoonful.
Grandma had a determined look on her face. I also didn't want to hurt her feelings, but would have chanced it if she hadn't been so close with the spoon outstretched.
She put it in my mouth and waited as I chewed. It was surprisingly tasty, but I still couldn't get past the fact that I was eating squirrel meat, the very meat of the squirrels I had watched Grandpa skin and clean, with the piles of innards lying on the newspaper he had laid out for this messy job.

She waited till I swallowed for my response. If I told her the truth, that it surprisingly tasted fairly good, she would have expected me to eat it again at some other opportunity. I wasn't totally stupid. I couldn't chance it. I made a face. She walked away shaking her head and mumbling in disgust. You can coerce a ten-year-old to do some things, but you cannot make them like it.

In spite of these less than favorable incursions with undesirable "food," most of Grams culinary ventures were exquisite. She made wonderful homemade noodles. I loved watching her roll out the stiff dough on the floured table, fold the dough several times and then cut through the layers in strips. Voila! Noodles!

She also made heavenly apple dumplings, pies, homemade potpie and "Rivel Soup." The latter contained clumps of dough (i.e. "rivels") with a thick creamy sauce served on a plate over which you sprinkled sugar. It was hearty and very satisfying.

My favorite times with Gramma, however, were in summer when we spent time on her glider swing in the carport. She got out her hymnal and sang many hymns. If I knew them, I sang along. She liked "The Old Rugged Cross" and "In the Garden" best, but her all time favorite was "Just A Closer Walk With Thee." I liked "In the Garden" too but I liked "What a Friend We Have in Jesus" best. And I meant those words as we sang them.

> "What a friend we have in Jesus, all our sins and grief's to bear;
> What a privilege to carry, everything to God in prayer."

"In the Garden" was special because I could just see Jesus as we sang the words.

> "I come to the garden alone; while the dew is still on the roses, and the voice I hear falling on my ear, the Son of God discloses.
> And he walks with me and he talks with me, and he tells me I am His own. And the joy we share as we tarry there, none other has ever known."

Gramma may have had a somewhat tenuous singing voice, likely due to her age, but she sang enthusiastically anyway. I loved hearing her sing "Just A Closer Walk With Thee." She smiled as she sang with her eyes closed. I knew she felt sincerely every word she was singing.

> "I am weak but Thou art strong
> Jesus keep me from all wrong
> I'll be satisfied as long
> As I walk, let me walk close to Thee
>
> CHORUS:
> Just a closer walk with Thee
> Grant it, Jesus, is my plea
> Daily walking close to Thee
> Let it be, dear Lord, let it be."

I loved listening to her and being with her at these times. She seemed so happy. I believe it was her way of sharing her faith and love for God with her granddaughter. What a legacy! It could not have been dearer.

We visited Aunt Cleo infrequently. Actually she was my grandmother's sister, so she was my great aunt. Cleo and her husband Carl lived on a farm. They had one son, Earl Lee. Mom told of how she used to stay the night there sometimes when she was a child.

I remember walking around outside and wishing there were some animals. How can a farm be a farm with no horses or cows? Cleo's house smelled like eggs. They did have chickens. I didn't particularly care for the smell. Cleo's stove was the kind now in museums. They probably were at that time as well. I was told she would have to light it and stoke it to make it work.

Cleo and Carl had an old TV set with a tiny picture tube. Their carpet was a floral pattern of bygone ages. Upstairs under the bed when we were playing, I found what I thought was a *very large coffee cup*. It had some unpleasant stains and smell inside. I asked about it. I was told it was a *chamber pot*. Since they had only an outside potty, this was for convenience. I was disgusted.

Cleo and Carl were living more like the 1800's. Can you just imagine for a moment, the worth of these antiques now?

Chapter 13

Punky

"Mah-om," I yelled, "Dede's throwing a fit again!" My parents referred to Dede's frequent temper tantrums as "throwing a fit." Her *fits* would last anywhere from 45 minutes to 3 hours depending on when she began to get whatever it was she needed to satisfy her, which she pretty much always did, though she wasn't easily satisfied. If we had visitors, it did not matter; a fit would be thrown when it suited her. Most of the time, I tried to steer clear. I would go outside in summer and try to find someone to play with till it passed. If it was at night, there was little I could do to escape. Much of my childhood was spent trying to just stay out of the way while Mom and Dad dealt with Dede.

Dede's fits usually had to do with the misplacement of her favorite toy she had named *Punky*, a little stuffed elf doll. Dad hunted for the elf from upstairs to the basement, all nooks and crannies, until it was located. If Rene and John were visiting, he would excuse himself and hunt it down. I am sure he did this because he knew she would not stop till she had her way, and Dede always got her way or she would throw a fit. The tantrum always escalated. Corporal punishment was rare in our household. I also doubt Mom had heard of time-outs and the concept would probably not have worked, even if she had.

During these tantrums, Dede would hit either Mom or Dad and continue her loud squall. I watched in horror when she hit Mom. I kept thinking, "Why doesn't Mom DO something?" I knew if I was a mother that I would not permit my child to hit me. There was no reasoning with Dede when she was on the floor kicking and screaming.

Sometimes Dede tried to pick a fight with me as children do. I tried to avoid picking them with her, as I knew it could set off a tantrum and I didn't want to hear it. Sometimes I did fight back (usually a verbal thing), but one day I realized that was what she wanted me to do, plus I thought it was real stupid and *little kidish* anyway, *back and forth, back and forth, tit for tat, for what?* Then Mom would yell, "STOP FIGHTING!" The next time she came to me with her chin stuck out and made her usual taunting babyish remarks geared to get a fight going, I said, "I don't care what you do. Doesn't matter to me." The look on her face was utter shock. She certainly hadn't expected that. I walked away.

Later that day Mom told me, "Cherié, I heard what you said to Dede earlier. That was very mature of you." I decided from then on I would really try to be "mature" whenever something like that came up again. Unfortunately, this has proven to be a necessity in adulthood as well.

Dad got so exasperated at times with her that he picked up the phone and dialed the Children's Home. The Children's Home later closed, but we were told it was for children who were orphans or children whose parents no longer wanted them or was unable to keep them. The calls were scary.

One time, however, I was at the right angle and discovered that he kept the button on the phone depressed. He was faking!

Dad had his "conversation" and asked, "Could you stop by? We have a problem ..." Dede became quiet. I could see the fear in her eyes. It did stop the tantrum momentarily. There were times after he got off the phone that she begged him to call the home back and tell them not to come. He would, after a time, make the follow-up "call."

As much as I hated the tantrums, I didn't like the fear she was experiencing either. I secretly told her, "Dad doesn't really call the Children's Home. He pushes the button down." This provided her with some relief.

I am sure the call charade was made out of *sheer desperation* to find some answer to stop the tantrums altogether.

Mom said that Dede stopped throwing tantrums when she would pick her up and rock her, showing her love. Mom thought this was the key. A woman at church had given her this tip when she shared the problem with her. It may have been the right thing. It may also be that Dede would have outgrown it. Rene told me that John hated it when they were there and "Harry would drop everything to go look for Punky." John told Rene he thought Dede was "spoiled, catered to and it wasn't doing her any favors."

When I heard these types of comments, I was torn. I felt loyal to my family and I didn't want them to be criticized by anyone, or at least not to tell me about it. I also felt I shouldn't say anything to my aunt and uncle to "back off" either. That didn't seem proper and I didn't want to hurt their feelings. And down deep inside, as much as I didn't want it to be true, I figured there was a lot of truth in what they said. I tried very hard not to think about it one way or another.

When I was seven or eight and she was three or four, we were alone in the kitchen. There were dishes in the sink that were in the process of being washed. On impulse, I grabbed a knife and said to her menacingly, (and inaccurately,

just like I had seen those in TV shows or in movies do), "I could kill you and Mom would never know." The only sound missing was the "bwaahahaha!" She looked like she actually momentarily believed me, with the same look on her face as when Dad pretended to call the Children's Home, and was silent, a *rare* occurrence. She had no comeback for a change. I dropped the knife back in the sink and admitted, "I was just kidding," which was the truth. It wasn't one of my better childhood impulses. It brought the same *not good* feeling inside that I had when I squashed a fish worm with my little shovel when I was two.

Regardless, the tantrum phase *seemed* to have stopped after a couple years of regular misery for all in earshot. Perhaps tantrums that are not dealt with in a productive manner at the time could manifest later in life in another form. Adults can have "tantrums" but they are usually more subtle, as well as potentially more destructive. Perhaps to someone who isn't aware of the history or the tendencies, it could inaccurately appear that the person is intelligent, normal, and justified.

Sometimes Dede and I would play "school." I taught her whatever it was that I was then learning in school. She picked up learning very well and seemed to enjoy the *academic structure* I created.

Mom told others later that she realized Dede was *gifted* when she would give her numbers to add up and she did it correctly in her head. They were double numbers. She was four.

When Dede started school, she was a very good student. She was involved in school activities and had several friends. One day in elementary school my class was discussing siblings and relationships. A boy talked about his older sister and how smart she was and that he could never measure up to her standard. Others shared similar stories about older siblings.

I was a *failed* older sibling!

Dede was the smart one. I did well in subjects I enjoyed, but Dede excelled in *every* subject whether she liked it not. Based on the evidence, I concluded that I was probably quite dumb.

If Dede brought home a grade card with one B and the rest A's, Mom would ask her about the B, Dede told me. I never heard those conversations. Mom apparently discussed each of our school issues in private. It is possible, as Dede has stated, that she strived to be such a good student, even though it came fairly easy for her, because she felt she "might be given away," due to residual fear left from when dad pretended to call the children's home, and she was aiming toward perfection so he would keep her. And maybe that is a bit of a *stretch*.

My grades were *considerably* lower and Mom questioned me about them. Math was always my worst subject. Story problems were the worst. If the problem stated that a family went on a trip and went X miles in one day, then based on that information, how long would it take them to arrive at their destination, I would answer, "Well, it would depend on how many times they have to stop to go to the bathroom and to eat lunch.

How can you *know* how long it would take?" I thought I made all kinds of sense. I still do. I think Mom finally gave up her notion that I would ever be able to do well or to *succeed* in the work world.

She said, "Well, you don't have to know what 2 and 2 are to change a diaper."

Dede was always the one who was expected to "succeed," because, as Mom pointed out to me on many occasions,

"You are just *not* college material. ... Dede is."

I wonder now if Mom's views had something to do with our two father's different professions. Harry was a skilled chemist. Hubert was a truck driver, and had a southern background, although his ethnicity was Italian and German. Mom had a distinct prejudice about people from the south. To her, they were all "hillbillies."

Mom's comment, "You are not college material," came up again as I was about to graduate from high school. My grades improved in high school, but math was a continual *low* grade. I was, however, very proud of making it far enough to be graduating. I had a white cap and gown and my red and gray tassel. When trying on my robe, I stared with pride at the glowing image in the living room mirror.

I smiled. "Won't you be proud of me when I walk down that aisle to get my diploma, Mom?" I asked.

She answered "Yes, but I'll be even prouder when you walk down another aisle."

My stomach sank. I was stunned.

I asked her about her comment when I was in my early 30's.

She said, "Well, it's just that I knew that is what *you* wanted."

She was right. I did want that. I also wanted her to be proud of me for this accomplishment, my high school graduation, with no qualifiers. It still stung. She apologized.

I went back to college after my five children entered school full time. Mom proudly attended both the ceremonies for my Bachelors Degree in 1986 and my Masters Degree in 1987. I was on the Deans' List, in two honor societies, and a member of the Honors Student Association.

During the first year of college, I kept thinking the professors would discover their error in giving me A's. It was just a matter of time till they realized that I was *not smart*.

They continued to issue the A's. I finally concluded, "Maybe I am not so dumb. Maybe I am smart after all."

Chapter 14

Camp and Carnivals

The summer before I entered seventh grade, I went to Local 12 Summer Camp. It was supposed to be for a week. I was 12 years old. My neighbor, Cindy, was going also. Both of our dads worked in the same place and this was a work related camp. She had been there two other years and loved it. I took her word for it. We had to get immunizations before we left.

We were bussed to someplace in Michigan to a lake called Sand Lake. The lake was pretty. The wooden cabins had several metal bunk style cots to accommodate 12 girls and our 16-year-old camp counselor. Our counselor was nice. Her name was Lana.

Lana made the mistake of stating that the first night is the hardest and that is when girls get homesick.

"NOOOOOO!" the girls responded in unison.

I wasn't so sure.

For one, it was my first time away from home for this long. The more I thought about it, the longer one week seemed. I pictured my yard at home and Mom out sprinkling her flowers.

We went to dinner at the large noisy cafeteria. The food was OK, at best.

Cindy, though she was in my cabin, already knew some of the other girls and played with them.

I was on an upper bunk. There was a very large, fat black girl below me. She enjoyed pushing on my bunk with her feet and bouncing me, starting the first night there. Her name was "Midge." I had not had contact with "African-Americans" before this and I wasn't enjoying the contact I was having now. I was reserved. They all, at my camp, were loud. I believed in the Golden Rule. If they did, then they were not showing it. I was scared of Midge. She was knowledgeable beyond her years and said some vulgar things I didn't completely understand. However,

I did recognize the tone and intent and I knew what some of her terms referred to by her tone.

All I could think was that I wanted to go home. I decided I could not stand a whole week of this. I was obsessed with thoughts of home. By late the second day at camp, I did nothing but cry. There was neither rhyme nor reason. I was not thinking clearly. I just knew I was in totally foreign territory and most of the inhabitants there seemed like enemies.

Lana told me to go to the campground director, who sat at the side of the lake in a chair, smoking and watching the kids swim. She pointed him out. I went to him several times but he seemed to ignore me.

When we had an activity, I went along, but stood at the sidelines by a tree and quietly cried. Cindy told me I was a crybaby and why didn't I just try to enjoy myself. I told her I just wanted to go home.

I would lay in my bunk and daydream. Mom was in the front yard watering the flowerbeds in my daydream. She loved to do that. I could virtually smell the metallic water from the garden hose, so real was this daydream. I counted the cracks in our cement walkway up to the steps in my dream. Mom would turn and smile at me. This would inevitably set off a new rush of tears. I realized at camp just how much I loved her and loved my home.

On Tuesday, Lana took me to the camp nurse. The nurse gave me a pill to take and kindly informed me that my parents had been called and were on their way to pick me up. I was relieved. My continual tears stopped and the world looked great. I told the other girls that whatever was in that pill really worked. I couldn't cry if I wanted to and I tried just to prove it.

I realize now that the nurse gave me the drug so I would not be so upset when my parents arrived. They didn't want a lawsuit. If they had given me the pill to start with, I may have been able to last the week out. It is likely that whatever she gave me, she would not be allowed to give to a child now.

When my parents drove in I was all smiles as I greeted them. We gathered my things and I said good-by to the other kids.

They looked at me like I was a different person. I was. I had taken the *magic happy pill*. Better yet, I was going home.

My parents never said anything negative about my need to return home early. I don't remember much of anything being said one way or another. It was simply accepted.

Mom had become the quintessential housewife and mother of the 1950's and into the 1960's, and had given up the buck-the-system actions of her past. She absorbed into the mainstream, touted its virtues and donned a clean housedress. She joined the PTA once Dede was in school, and cooked creamed chicken in the school kitchen to make sandwiches for the annual fund-raising carnival.

One time I came into the school kitchen where she was cooking with several other women. I think I was in 7th grade, but had come back to my grade school for the carnival because Dede still attended there. There was a tall, silver-haired distinguished looking gentleman visiting the kitchen ladies. He was smiling and sounded intellectual, but friendly. I thought he looked handsome. I listened to the adults chat as they worked and he stood there. I looked at him and politely said,

"You are very nice looking."

The room stood still. The women quit talking. He looked at me surprised. He did not say "thank you" as I had been taught to say when someone was nice enough to give you a compliment.

Mom always said, "If you like something about someone tell them. People like to get compliments."

So, I did.

He looked at Mom and said, "Oh Mable, you better watch out for this one!" I looked at Mom's disheveled, sweaty face, but she wasn't smiling.

She looked mortified.

She said, "Cherie!"

Had I committed the crime of the year!

All I did was compliment someone.

"What?" I responded.

She dropped the matter. She knew I was innocent.

Mom was usually very perceptive when it came to knowing me. I think she was embarrassed and felt she had to react the way she did for the benefit of others there who would have expected the correction. But she also knew admonishing me further in the kitchen would have meant embarrassing me so she could *save face*. She backed off. Mom was not the sort of person to throw her own child under the bus.

Chapter 15

"Where have all the flowers gone ..."

"Those Russians" were proving to be as obnoxious as people earlier thought they potentially were.

We studied current events in school and I was becoming more aware of the world at large. Stalin's successor, Nikita Khrushchev, got my attention in 1960 when he repeatedly disrupted the proceedings at the United Nations by pounding his fists on the table and shouting in Russian. It was reported that he took off his shoe and banged it on the desk when he was angered by comments made by the Filipino delegate that charged the Soviets with employing a double standard. Khrushchev twice interrupted a speech by British Prime Minister, Harold Macmillan, with his shoe banging. The unflappable Macmillan famously commented over his shoulder to the Assembly President, that if Mr Khrushchev wished to continue, he would "like a translation."

I discovered that I enjoyed witty commentary. The aplomb of Macmillan and his refusal to allow boorish behavior to intimidate him amused me. It was the stupid behavior by Khrushchev that began to grow the political seed in me.

That seed was developed further a couple years later with the onset of the Cuban Missile Crises. I was in junior high school during this episode. Everybody seemed to love President John F. Kennedy, the youngest president our nation had ever had. He seemed to have handled the crises well.

"It shall be the policy of this nation to regard any nuclear missile launched from Cuba against any nation in the Western Hemisphere as an attack on the United States, requiring a full retaliatory response upon the Soviet Union. To halt this offensive buildup, a strict quarantine on all offensive military equipment under shipment to Cuba is being initiated. All ships of any kind bound for Cuba from whatever nation and port will, if found to contain cargoes of offensive weapons, be turned back. This quarantine will be extended, if needed, to other types of cargo and carriers. We are not at this time, however, denying the necessities of life as the Soviets attempted to do in their Berlin blockade of 1948."

President John F. Kennedy, October 22, 1962

Terror, sheer terror is the only words to describe my feelings at this precarious time, the Cuban Missile Crises. I felt we were going to be blown to bits at any moment or incinerated with atomic fall out. Many people built fall out shelters. I wanted one too, but the only thing Mom did was to have extra cans of food and gallon bottles of water stored in our basement. I am sure she must have realized that if the worst occurred, the basement would not do a thing. She probably stored things there to appease her children.

"Mom, storing food down in the basement won't work. There are windows. We would not be protected. This isn't enough," I told her.

"Well, it will have to be," she said.

I had seen a show on TV where a family had a fall out shelter and they went in it after a blast occurred. They had to bar the door from neighbors who sought refuge there, because they were only prepared for their own family.

I knew if anything happened and we survived, that we would be the doomed neighbors locked outside the door.

The only thing that kept me from going into total panic was my parents, especially Mom. Both were calm. I knew Mom was concerned, but she didn't seem scared. Maybe it would be all right after all. The crises passed. The world calmed. The sun came out again.

At school, they taught us to hide under our desks if something happened. We had drills on this the same as we had fire drills or tornado drills.

I had learned by this time, that Mom and Dad couldn't fix everything. They were adults, but they were in many ways as vulnerable as I. That realization terrorized me more than Khrushchev.

Grandma was gone now. She died about the same time as the Cuban Missile Crises, but was too weak to pay any attention. Grandma was only 69 years old when she died. She seemed older than her years. She died of a form of blood cancer, but not leukemia.

A few years before her death, Grandma decided she was going to leave Putter. Mom told me about this, years later.

Mom said, "I talked her out of it."

"Why?" I asked. "After all he put her through, why not?"

"I told her that after all these years what would be the point? At least she had someone in the house with her. She had stuck with him this long."

Perhaps Mom was right. OR, perhaps Grandma should have left him. It seemed to be long overdue.

Grandma's death took place in the hospital while Rene was visiting her. She couldn't breathe and begged for help as her lungs filled with fluid.

Rene screamed for help.

The nurse hurried in and attempted to calm Grandma, "Now, calm down Mrs. Putman, calm down."

Where was the "help?" She was begging for help.

Rene was frantic.

She watched as her mother struggled and the nurses shoved Rene out into the hall.

I had nightmares about this for a long time. Though I knew people died, this was the closest person I had lost. I was 12.

Mom took Dede and I for the two evenings of visitation at the funeral home. My cousin, Barry, Aunt Bonnie's youngest son who was older than me, was there also. The three of us spent most of the time in the coffee room teasing each other and laughing. We talked about school. We took things to do, quiet games to play. I asked my cousin, "Doesn't this bother you, Grandma dying?" "Well, yeah!" he answered. When children don't really know how to handle a situation, sometimes they make up stuff to convince themselves that they are handling it. Perception is everything. Maybe we were handling it. While we coped in the coffee room, the adults did the same in the other room.

Grandpa had come to the visitations as well. He arrived early for the funeral. He sat by himself on one of the folding chairs. He wept. By this time I knew what type of husband he had been. Mom and Rene both commented that maybe he was feeling badly for the way he had treated Grandma all this time.

The day of Grandma's funeral was somber, as funerals are. When it was time to go up to the casket to view the body once more before leaving for the cemetery, I was in line just ahead of Mom. I looked at the body. They had dressed Grandma's body in a pale blue chiffon robe with little rhinestone balls that trimmed the tie at the neckline. Mom purchased it since Grandma had told her what she wanted to be buried in and the color. It wasn't exactly the same as she described but it was as close as Mom could get it.

I was about to move out the nearby door when Mom started to cry violently. I watched horrified when she leaned over her mother's chest, put her hands on Grandma's body's shoulders, sobbing and crying, "Mom, Mom." It was heartbreaking. It was the first time I saw my mother so completely overcome with emotion. Funeral officials apparently thought she was going to try to lift the body. They came quickly to ease her away and and I kept gently saying, "Come on Mom, it's OK."

My mother never got over Grandma's death, not that one ever gets over some things. They had been through a lot together. She admitted that the only thing that pulled her out was the fact that she had two girls to raise.

Chapter 16

Tween & Teen

"I will not go to the dentist; I will not go," I said.

I hated dentists. I had nothing but pain every time I went. This was before the days of fluoride treatments for children, or if they had them, to my knowledge, I wasn't a recipient. I had many cavities over the years.

The first dentist I remember going to was Dr. Crawford, who specialized in children's dentistry. The Galvin children (Dad's boss' grandchildren) went there, so he must be good. This was always Dad's reasoning. It used to irk Mom. She felt he liked and was sometimes more interested in their family than his own. He spent much time of his time with them. I am sure he would have spent more time with us had Mom allowed us to go on the business trips with him as Mr. Galvin suggested. How could a person have it both ways? Some things just never made any sense to me.

Dr. Crawford had earphones that played music if you turned the green button on the control box he sat in your lap. The red button was to be turned if you had pain and a loud gush which sounded like air assaulted your ears. He didn't use Novocain.

No amount of pushing a red button *ever* helped me when he was filling my tooth. It hurt.

It hurt badly and I had had enough.

I knew that I was physically large enough to cause a problem if I was to absolutely refuse to go to the dentist. When it came time for the appointment to be made, I simply told Mom I was not going.

"What?" she said. "You are too."

"No, I'm not," I answered firmly. "You can make me go, but if you do you will have to drag me and I will kick and scream the whole way. If this is what you want, then OK."

I meant every word. She knew it.

I won the first battle. She let up and called the dentist and explained her predicament. I got a letter in pencil from him scrawled on one of his dental pads.

"Dear Cherié,

I am really sorry if I have done something to hurt you. I hope you will give us another chance.

You know, Cherié, some day you will want some young man down in his knee to you. Well cared for, pretty teeth will help ensure this happens.

Please reconsider and give us another chance. Tell me when something hurts you and I will try to take care of it.

Sincerely,

Dr. Crawford, DDS"

I decided to give Dr. Crawford a chance. I went. He gave me a shot of Novocain and *immediately* started to fill my tooth. It hurt the same as it always had. By the time I left the office, my entire gum, tooth and cheek were numb. I wiped the drool with a tissue. *If* he had waited for the Novocain to take effect, this might have been OK. I told Mom I would not go back.

We changed dentists. Maybe the Galvins didn't know everything just because they were rich.

Mom explained to our new dentist that we had some painful experiences with another dentist and that Novocain should be used. He used Novocain, but he didn't wait long before drilling either. Still, he waited longer than Dr. Crawford.

This dentist was the one who did a root canal and capped my two front teeth that I had broken at Rene's duplex in Cincinnati when I was nine. Yes, he used Novocain then. It hurt anyway. Everything hurt. It hurt worse than anything I had ever felt. I don't think he even cared. His name was Thornhill. I always pictured roses and thorns when I thought of him and how thorns would prick and could if pressed correctly really hurt. How apropos.

I didn't think he did this because I was ugly as I usually assumed when people seemed to be mean. I think he did it because he enjoyed giving pain, the same as Dr. Crawford. I resolved that dentists must be evil people to go into that profession to administer pain. I was 22 years old and married before I would change that opinion, when my dentist was Dr. Deck.

I challenged Dr. Deck. I told him of my experiences. I told him what I thought of dentists and their choice of professions. He looked genuinely hurt. He said, "I became a dentist so that I could help alleviate tooth pain."

I gave him a chance.

He used Novocain and he waited till it was numb. If I felt pain he would use more Novocain. He sang while he worked. I cannot remember ever feeling pain with Dr. Deck.

When Mom was in her 40's, she fixed her own tooth pain, what was left of her teeth anyway. She had them all pulled. Then it meant a hospital stay. I still remember what her gums looked like all stitched up. I also remember her talking about a terrible toothache she had when I was a child. She told me she stuck a straight pin into her gum. I was horrified.

"Didn't it hurt?"

"It was a 'feel good' kind of hurt."

She made the mistake of telling her dentist. He screamed at her that she could have "died from those sort of shenanigans." He was right, of course. I always knew that deep down, Mom understood my angst about dentists.

Becoming a woman…

It was exactly one week after my 13th birthday. I got up and went to the bathroom and sat down.

"MOM!" I screamed, sobbing, an onrush of emotion.

Mom ran. She thought I was dying.

"What happened?" she asked breathlessly.

I continued to wail, "I started my period."

Getting my menstrual period was a long awaited and desired event. When it finally happened, I was overcome. Maybe it was hormones.

"Why are you crying? You are a young lady now."

That was the name of the booklet Mom had given me two years earlier to prepare me for the female things that lay ahead. My body was doing natural things.

I was *finally* a woman, at long last.

The previous year I had begun to grow armpit hair. I just wanted to get my period like some of my friends had already done. I was standing in the hall upstairs. "At least I have perspiration," I thought to myself. Perspiration, which smelled, was a sign of impending adulthood.

It is weird. I also felt that on some level, I was finally equal to Mom. It was a first. I could now produce a child. Although Mom didn't say too much one way or another, I sensed that she was happy about it. If this had been a musical, "I Enjoy Being A Girl" would play here.

Rainbow Girls

Dad was a lower order Mason. If he had been in a high order, I am sure he would have to have attended regularly. The only Mason function he ever attended was the annual Father/Daughter Banquet. Since I was the oldest, I went. Dede's was too little to go and be trusted not to get upset about something, anything, and throw a fit. It was a dress up affair and I was on my best manners. We sat across from other dads and daughters. It was in a room in the Masonic Lodge like the fancy ones you see in the movies. The table was covered with a white linen tablecloth and we had linen napkins. I always enjoyed this outing. It appealed to my *champagne taste*. I am sure my champagne taste was developed partially from going to movies on a weekly basis and seeing the glamour exemplified there. I also heard the stories Dad told about the aforementioned rich Galvin lifestyle.

The International Order of the Rainbow for Girls is the "only youth club that teaches things that matter most, leadership, confidence, and citizenship." At least that is what their literature states. The Masons are the parent organization to Rainbow. Mom suggested I join Rainbow. Since I knew a few girls at school who were in Rainbow, I decided that I would join and it seemed to please Dad, so this was an added benefit.

I am sure Mom was encouraging this because she thought it might help Dad and me bond, the same as she encouraged attending the banquet.

The initiation ceremony was also held in the Masonic Lodge. This was a dress up affair that could only have been in my dreams. We had to wear full-length formals! Mine was pale blue with cap sleeves, a sweetheart neckline and a bodice with sparkles in it. Vivid colors looked better on me though. I would rather have had a red one, but Mom liked pastels and would never have agreed to allow me to look like a "gypsy." That was her opinion of vivid color.

The ceremony was held with great solemnity. The *initiates* were grouped in threes. There were stations to represent all the colors in the rainbow. Each color represented some virtue. As we traveled from station to station, the person posted there would hand us each some token and deliver her memorized speech. We were to answer appropriately when questioned with a "yes."

Call it nervousness due to the evident gravity of the situation, but hard as I tried not to, I found all this quite amusing. It wasn't that I didn't believe in those virtues. I did. It was the pomp, the pretentiousness that I perceived as so over the top that struck me funny. Here were a bunch of 13 year old girls, dressed in formals, walking like we were on a death march from station to station in unison, while a group of the "elect," other teen aged girls who were already members watched from the gallery section as we joined their ranks.

The process began when potential members put in their request to become a member. Those who were already members voted whether the candidate would be accepted as an initiate. The vote was conducted with white and black marbles. Each girl put either a white or a black marble into the box. If any girl put in a black marble, the candidate was rejected. I am sure the adults running the organization cautioned the members not to blackball for a petty reason.

I was accepted, no black ball.

All this was going through my mind as I walked *so slowly* through this long ceremony.

That is when I began to giggle.

I was horrified.

I giggled some more.

The fact that I could not seem to be able to stop giggling made it even funnier. I began to notice how silly we all looked doing this. The solemn faces of those in the gallery looked even funnier. Everything became funny.

Giggle.

Stop it!

Giggle.

I wanted to escape. All eyes had to be upon me.

The girl next to me turned and glared.

I was waiting for the boom to fall where they would publicly call me out and tell me to leave.

Nobody asked me to leave.

Somehow, I made it through the ceremony.

I was relieved.

I went home and told Mom about it. She was sympathetic.

I went to a handful of meetings after that. The girls were snobs. It was boring. We sold candles at Christmas time as a fundraiser. Mom bought some. I sold a few more to relatives.

The candles were pretty. But the Girl Scout cookies tasted better …

On looking back at this ceremony, it reminds me of a segment of the popular *Mary Tyler Moore Show*. Mary attended a funeral for a clown. As the eulogy was given, she found it increasingly difficult to keep a straight face. A major portion of the show is Mary stifling laughter till she can no longer stand it and leaves.

I told Mom about the whole thing, of course. She grinned about it and tried to encourage me that it was all OK. Nothing terrible had really happened. I thought she just might be lying but I liked the lie and was comforted. Sometimes it is best not to look the gift horse in the mouth.

Friends

Edith was my best friend at school, beginning in seventh grade. She had an older sister and an older brother. I went to slumber parties at her house and I had slumber parties at my house. Slumber parties were my favorite thing. We always had pizza and played games, watched TV, and made phone calls to strangers to ask them things like

"Is your refrigerator running?"

Usually they answered "yes" and we replied,

"Then you better go catch it."

We hung up and laughed till we couldn't breathe.

Edith was 5'2" tall and weighed from 98 pounds to 102 pounds the whole time I knew her. I felt like a blimp beside her tiny little frame. Life was just not fair.

Edith never ate her apple crisp at lunch. Sometimes she gave it to me. It was my favorite food in the cafeteria.

Sometimes we had food fights. That was my favorite thing, particularly when lots of kids got involved. The cafeteria workers and the teachers who monitored soon put a stop to it but it was fun while it lasted.

I also had an imaginary boyfriend. I did this to entertain my friends at lunch and although they didn't have any boyfriends, it was obvious other girls did.

I made up a name and *he* wrote lengthy romantic letters to me from his home in Anaheim, California where I had *visited* the previous summer. Of course I hadn't really visited, but if you are going to lie anyway, why not make it really impressive! Disneyland is in that area and if desire had anything to do with it, then I *had* visited, in spirit anyway.

If we weren't talking about the boyfriend, then the topic might be a new medical TV program which featured a young intern, *Dr. Kildare*, played by the actor, Richard Chamberlain. I had a crush on him and wouldn't have missed the show for anything. My girlfriends weren't as smitten as I, although they thought he was cute.

Rona was Edith's other friend. We competed for Edith's attention. Rona argued with me about things in the Bible. The cafeteria was our forum. We just didn't see it the same way. She thought the streets of heaven were made of gold like the Bible says. I thought that was probably a metaphor for something wonderful, beautiful since rock hard gold would not make me happy. I liked fields of wild flowers better. To me, that would be "gold."

Because of this, Rona felt I was going to go to hell and told me so. I just thought she was an idiot and couldn't understand why Edith liked her, but I kept my mouth shut.

Rona announced she was going to have a slumber party and she invited me, likely because she felt obligated, I thought to myself. She also knew Edith wouldn't like it if Rona left me out.

I arrived at the party and Rona's mom seemed nice. She had lots of refreshments for the party. We watched TV for a while and then the other girls wanted to go upstairs so I couldn't finish watching the program.

We chatted for while but I mostly listened. Rona brought it up. She started on the streets of gold again. She told the others, "Listen to what she thinks." I told them. I didn't know any of these other girls. They didn't go to our school. I imagine they were some of her church friends.

After I gave my opinion they all pounced on me the way Rona always did. I remained nonplussed and didn't budge. After one of them began to pray for me out loud because I was doomed to hell, the others joined in and most were crying. I had not experienced anything like this since I attended the Pilgrim Holiness church service with that girl I used to know where the preacher shouted.

I didn't feel like crying. I was uncomfortable and wanted to go home. I felt sorry for these girls who were so upset about my eternal home. I knew where I was going. I was sad that they couldn't understand it.

Rona was a Baptist.

Edith was attentive, but had remained silent through the whole exchange. She was Methodist.

Though I have met Baptists since then that I felt the same way as I felt about Rona and her friends, I have also met Baptists that I have gotten along with quite well.

I told Mom about it. She became very quiet. I don't recall her saying much about it. I think she thought I handled it well. Knowing her, I think she was probably angry that I had been put in this position. If you are familiar with the terms legalistic and Pharisee, then you know how I felt when directly confronted with it. I suspect this "party" may have even been a set up.

Seventh grade was made more bearable by having an older friend in ninth grade. Her name was Sharon. Sharon had a crush on Frankie Avalon, a teen idol at the time. I thought he was cute too but I didn't feel the same way as Sharon. She formed the Frankie Avalon Fan Club. We met in her home with one other girl. Sharon even wrote to the national fan club in order that we could get even more Frankie information and items. She decided we needed a password. We put our heads together and came up with Eiknarf Nolava. That is Frankie Avalon spelled backwards. Who would ever know. We also made up our very own fan club song. I was most instrumental with this one, no pun intended. It brought out my creative side.

> *Frankie Avalon, he's real gone,*
>
> *He's our favorite singer too.*
>
> *We love him truly,*
>
> *You know surely,*
>
> *Frankie, we love you.*

We sang the song *every* meeting we had. After the second or third meeting the fan club dwindled out.

Mom didn't like Sharon, for some reason. I think she thought she was too old and streetwise for me. She was probably right.

My First Baby-sitting Job

I began a regular baby-sitting job, also the summer I was 13. The woman on the corner had two children. Patricia was six and Johnny was four. Their mom, Vilma, was from Sao Paulo, Brazil. Her native tongue was Portuguese. She had a thick accent. It sounded charming to me. I earned fifty cents an hour and sometimes only thirty-five cents an hour, after Vilma told me she couldn't otherwise afford me. Because her children loved me, Vilma loved me. She loved Mom as well, and confided in her.

Vilma's absentee husband (John) was an airline pilot. John was 40 years old, tall, tanned and handsome. I could not imagine any sane woman not finding him attractive. Unfortunately for Vilma, many women did find him attractive. She somehow managed to obtain sexually explicit "love" letters written by a flight attendant from Sweden. I was permitted to see some of these letters since Vilma gave them to my mom for safe keeping while she went to her lawyer to nail John to the wall in their upcoming divorce. All this was pretty ripe stuff for my small city traditional upbringing. Vilma eventually did manage to take John to the cleaners and he married the flight attendant, only we called them stewardesses then.

Mom showed me one of the tamer letters. The writing was small, neat and squiggly. My young, innocent eyes lingered over the line where she wrote about her fondness for her "hand warmer." Mom explained to me what she meant and to what this referred. It was a sort of epiphany for me, in fact.

Again, if this was a musical, "Trouble in River City" from the "Music Man" could not capture this moment more.

Vilma was also a very superstitious woman. Since she was from a rather exotic area of the world where voodoo is not uncommon, she came by her feelings honestly. If John's mother, who lived in Trinidad where John was from originally, sent her presents for her grandchildren, Vilma never opened them. She burned them. She thought they were cursed since her mother-in-law hated her and would literally hurt her and the children through the gifts. This didn't seem logical to me since I had only experienced a loving grandmother and I couldn't imagine a grandma trying to hurt her own grandchildren in spite of the way she may feel toward her daughter-in-law. I also questioned that it was even possible to do that, hurt someone through an object if you could get it into their possession, if that was her evil intent. Vilma was quite passionate about it though and it was obvious she believed it.

It should also be kept in mind that Vilma's father was a physician, had money, and she was not without a good education. John was likely attracted to Vilma's father's position and money, to hear her tell it.

Another piece of evidence to Vilma's foreign culture upbringing was she and her children's love of raw hamburger. She said this was a delicacy. Mom was horrified. I was simply disgusted, both at seeing them eat it and at what it must taste like raw. I couldn't think too much about it or I would surely have gagged.

It was most fun when Vilma, a social butterfly, would have some of her Brazilian and Hispanic friends over. They knew how to party. Lights would be strung. Food (including the raw hamburger) would be laid out. I tasted *some* of the food and it was very good. They spoke Portuguese and also Spanish, so it was almost as good as traveling to a different land.

I secretly hoped some of the exotic flavor would rub off on me. I wanted to someday be a mysterious woman who was totally intoxicating to men.

Mom liked Vilma as well. I think she was as intoxicated by the cultural diversity as much as I was, but she was not going to allow it to bowl her over. She was the adult and the confidante. I am sure it was a place she never imagined herself. She had become international in a real sense. The world became smaller.

A few years later Mom began to dislike Vilma when Vilma hired another girl to baby-sit from time to time. I imagine Vilma thought the competition would do us good. She bragged to me about how smart the other girl was. I thought she was being mean spirited but I didn't really care at that point. I had learned that if you *care,* things hurt more. I chose to be in a pain free survival mode.

Chapter 17

Becoming a "young lady"

In May, 1961, Alan Shepherd was the first American launched into space. On April 12, 1961 Soviet cosmonaut Yuri Gagarin had become the first man to reach space. The reason Russia beat us into space was due to delays caused by unplanned preparatory work, as well as the Russians willingness to cut safety precautions that the US was not willing to do. We originally intended to launch in October 1960.

A TV was set up in the large study hall at school, room 207, when Astronaut Shepherd was launched. If we had study hall anywhere else in the building, or our teacher permitted it, we were allowed to go to this room to watch the TV. Coverage lasted all day. It was impressive. Imagine having a man in outer space. I continued to be very proud of my country. I also liked getting out of class and made sure I asked if I could go watch the coverage whenever a teacher seemed approachable.

My least favorite thing in school by this time, even over math, was gym class. When we had our period, we didn't have to take gym that day. The teacher lined us up at the beginning of class to take attendance. We had a royal blue, one-piece, short jumpsuit we had to wear for gym. We had gym two days a week. If we had our period, when our name was called we answered, "reporting," instead of "here" and that way she knew you were on your period. Even if my period lasted only one gym class day, I was always "reporting" the second gym class day. What was the teacher going to do? Look?

Miss Baker was my seventh grade gym teacher. She was over six foot tall and wore size 15 shoes. I used to stare at her feet. I couldn't believe it. She never wore makeup had deep acne scars, and looked like a guy.

Miss Dotson was my eighth and ninth grade gym teacher. She was five foot tall and weighed well over 200 pounds and wore makeup. Though some gym teachers took part in the activities, Miss Dotson never did. Mom philosophized, "If a gym teacher is going to try to make the students do something, then she should be able to do the thing herself or she has no business asking someone else to do it." I agreed, but I was not inclined to tell Miss Dotson that. Some things are better left unsaid.

President Kennedy was a stickler for physical fitness, we were told. So, we had to take a physical fitness test. The test had several parts to it. One part of the test was the 600-yard walk-run. We were to do this as quickly as we could. I was always one of the laggers who could barely make it in. We were not allowed to have a drink of water till we finished. It was the closest I came to dying in junior high school.

The locker room was a total embarrassment. We were required to take a quick shower after gym. The teacher had a helper who checked to make sure we did take the shower. We all did our best to wrap ourselves in the postage stamp size towels till we got in the shower, an open room with shower-heads. Some of the girls splashed some water on their shoulders so it looked as though they showered. I tried this too. It worked some of the time. We had about five minutes to strip off our gym clothes, get in and out of the shower, get dressed in our street clothes, comb our hair, apply lipstick and head out. The bell usually rang before we got out there and we ended up sweating and tardy to our next class. Sometimes the teacher gave us more time.

We were also supposed to take our gym clothes home to be washed. Mom asked me to bring them. I kept forgetting, but they got home a few times. My gym clothes may have been able to walk on their own by the time the semester was over.

Most of us had been taught to be modest. How could any be modest in that atmosphere? I was just beginning to grow breasts, an AA cup size. Mine weren't the smallest, thank God. That distinguishing title fell on Connie. Poor Connie. Those with larger breasts teased her. She wore a little *no cup* style bra, and one matronly looking, overly endowed African-American girl said to her, "What are you wearing that for? You ain't got nothing to put in it."

I dressed hurriedly hoping she wouldn't look my way, although we were all larger than poor Connie.

By high school, we had all the breast growth we were going to get. *Some* things do improve over time.

Mom was nonchalant about my concerns over breast development. She noted that I wasn't as flat as she had thought. She hadn't seemed to notice that I was in need of a bra, although it looked to me as though I did. Her one comment when I put on an AA bra for the first time was "Oh my gosh! You DO have breasts!" Though I was pleased for the acknowledgement, I wondered how she could have missed something so obvious.

When I was 14, and in ninth grade, Blanche moved to our school. Blanche wore glasses and had wavy, neck length, chestnut brown hair. She was about 5'7" tall. She dressed like the rest of us. That day she wore a plaid shirt-waist dress. I couldn't understand it when we were in the lunch line chatting and the boys at a nearby table acted as though they went nuts. They ogled and she was obviously being discussed. She acted as though she didn't notice. Perhaps she was used to this type of attention. Blanche had an older boyfriend.

I tried to look at Blanche with the same perspective that the boys did. It was then I understood. Blanche had full-grown breasts in *ninth* grade! She must have started the growth process early. I bet nobody ever made fun of Blanche's breasts in the locker room. Regardless, I was convinced that boys were simply stupid.

Ninth grade was my favorite year at my junior high school. We were technically high school freshmen. This afforded greater status. The senior high school made up the other three high school grades.

I had a crush on three male teachers. Mr. Mitchell was a 6'5" English teacher. He was handsome. I did not have him for English. I did not have a crush on him. I never aimed that high. However, my 7th and 8th grade math teacher seemed to have a crush on him. Mrs. Stitely was one of those teachers who seemed to enjoy embarrassing students. She was just plain mean, and enjoyed calling on students who she knew didn't know the answer.

"Go put your answer on the board," she said, "Move to the side a little so we can all see."

What they saw when I accommodated her was a blank chalkboard. Sometimes, they saw that blank chalkboard for 44 minutes of the 45 minute period because Mrs. Stitely liked to see students squirm. The only advantage to standing with your back to the class is they cannot see your red face or that you are about to start crying.

Mrs. Stitely got positively giggly around Mr. Mitchell. It was obvious even to my untrained female eye that she was flirting with him. It was sickening watching her coyly touch her face and hair as she smiled up at him.

In class, Mrs. Stitely was never giggly or pleasant. As we worked quietly at our desks, she played with her bra strap. I wondered why she didn't shorten the strap so she could quit playing with it. Maybe she enjoyed it. Perhaps it was an adult form of sucking your thumb or needing a comfort toy.

The only interaction I ever had with Mr. Mitchell was when I was walking past his class to the restroom. The period bell had rung and he was about to go back into his classroom. I had just started my period and knew I had a large red stain on the back of my skirt. I said "Hi, Mr. Mitchell." He said "hi." I kept walking, knowing I couldn't hide or otherwise hide the back of my skirt. I never looked back. I knew he was still there and had seen my skirt. I was mortified. I wanted to run, but we weren't supposed to run in the halls.

I now realize that if Mr. Mitchell saw my skirt, he probably thought, "Aw, the poor kid." We *just die* so many times in junior high school.

I had a crush on Mr. Gingrich, my general science teacher, who was short, cute, 26 years old, and married. I volunteered for duties after school to assist him. I did special projects. I did anything to keep me in his proximity.

One day in class we were talking about water treatment. I raised my hand and told of water that had "crawlies" in it when viewed under a microscope.

He asked, "Was it tap water?"

"No," I replied, knowledgeably, "It was water out of the faucet."

He grinned. "That is the same thing."

I knew that! Really! I had a momentary lapse. My brain synapses had quit firing in his presence. That had to be it.

I was embarrassed, but he was so sweet about it that it was simply amusing moreso than embarrassing and endeared him in my eyes even more.

Mr. Gingrich introduced us to the book Silent Spring, by Rachel Carson. Was our environment really that bad?

I tried to do my part. I didn't litter.

I was also in love with my band director, Mr. Beck. Mr. Beck was in his 40's, wore horn-rimmed glasses and had a potbelly. I didn't care. He was so nice. I played clarinet.

One day he visited my classroom to see me. He bent down on one knee. The kids went wild. "He's going to ask her to marry him, he's going to ask her to marry him!" they shouted. I was embarrassed but gleeful. He said, "Cherié, would you do me the honor of taking part in a clarinet quartet for contest this year?" How could I refuse such charm?

What he didn't tell me was that Contest was 3 weeks away. The other 3 girls had been practicing for a long time. What made him think that I could do this in such short notice, if at all? I didn't want to embarrass myself and pull their rating down at Contest. He promised that he would have me ready.

We practiced with the group to start. I was lousy. Then he gave me private lessons. Never had I been put through paces like that. Our selection was played at a brisk pace much of the time requiring swift fingering. "Pa, pa pa PUM ta ta TUM, and 2 and 3 and 4 and…" he said, as he also slapped the time out on his knee. Our sessions lasted from 30-50 minutes of constant work. I felt like I imagine recruits feel in boot camp.

The next time we practiced as a group, the other girls exclaimed at how much I had improved. Mr. Beck taught me a couple musical tricks along the way. For one thing, you keep going and muddle through if you lose your place or make a mistake until you can pick it up again.

Contest day was at a neighboring high school. Students from all over the area were there. I was so nervous. Everyone was on edge. We performed our selection for the judges. We waited for our rating. Finally it was posted. We had an A! I was ecstatic. Sometimes, you are capable of a lot more than you think, if there is some type of coach there to persist and pull it out of you.

On emerging hormones …

It was night and I was in bed. I was 14. I had been crying. I was worried. I knew how much I was attracted to male people of all ages. Although I also had some knowledge that this was due to body changes, I doubted my ability to resist temptation if it was offered. I had every confidence in my "slutability" factor, a term (i.e. slut), I learned from my older girlfriend, Sharon.. It both horrified and terrified me. Moving into panic certainly didn't solve anything. I knew Mom wouldn't have any answers for this any more than she had answers for any other of my major questions in the past. I would also have been too embarrassed to ask her if I thought she did. So, I went to the only Person I knew who I felt could hold sway over anything, the One I always went to for major deals.

"God," I prayed from my heart, "I am getting older now. I am growing up and we both *know* me. We both know I will probably get into some trouble sometimes while I am growing up and when I am grown up. Well, when that happens, I want you to please pull me back to you. Even if I don't want you too then and ask you not to do that then, don't listen to me then, listen only to me now. Please, whatever it takes, just pull me back to you. Keep me safe. In Jesus name, Amen." I slept.

On a somewhat lighter note, at age 15 and a high school sophomore, my friend, Sharon, now a high school senior, invited me to go to an *instruction* in Catholicism with her. She told me that her current boyfriend was Catholic, so this was her motivation. Mine was to keep her company and also to assuage my own curiosity about Catholicism, which began when I had attended the Mass, still in Latin, with my friend Juanita, and her family while in elementary school.

When I saw the movie, "The Nun's Story," starring Audrey Hepburn when it came out in 1959, this also set off a whole new set of questions about the Roman church. Hollywood made its unique impact on my development in many ways. Of course, when I later saw "Lolita," the one starring James Mason, Shelly Winters, and Sue Lyon, it was less of an impact and generated more of a stirring of the emotions of "I don't think I want to grow up any more" type feelings. "YUCK!"

Chapter 18
"The World Changes"

January 15, 1962 - During a press conference, President Kennedy is asked if any Americans in Vietnam are engaged in the fighting. "No," the President responds without further comment.

September 2, 1963 - During a TV news interview with Walter Cronkite, President Kennedy comments on America's commitment to Vietnam "If we withdrew from Vietnam, the Communists would control Vietnam. Pretty soon, Thailand, Cambodia, Laos, Malaya, would go..."

November 22, 1963

I was a sophomore at Lima Senior High School. It was a large school. There were over 500 students in my class alone.
I was in Health class (all girls) toward the end of the day. Miss Shue, who was also a gym teacher, was busy getting our information on our latest self-improvement projects. My project was to quit biting my nails. I couldn't attempt to do what was even more obviously needed, which was to lose weight. I had to pick a project that I had some hope of being able to do with some measure of success if I wanted any kind of a grade.

The PA speaker clicked on about 15 minutes before the bell for the last class of the day.

"Students, teachers, may I please have your attention," Mr. Scheurman, our principal paused, and then continued.

"The news media reports that President John F. Kennedy was shot as he rode in the motorcade on his visit to Dallas. He was rushed to a hospital in Dallas. We will give you more information as it becomes available."

Miss Shue hesitantly resumed class. We were very quiet. Less than five long minutes passed.

We heard the PA click. Mr. Scheurman spoke softly, "They have just announced that although they did all they could to save the President's life, they were not able to.

President Kennedy is dead."
There was a synchronized gasp, then silence.

Numbness. Disbelief. It couldn't be true.

My 15 year-old mind could not grasp the words I heard.

We are the United States of America. That does not happen here.

Presidents had been shot in the past. Lincoln was an example. But that was a long time ago.

Nowadays, things like that only happen in third world countries.

Mr. Scheurman continued, "We will dismiss at the sound of the bell. The busses have been notified that you will be out early today. They are already lined outside."

The bell rang.

We went to our lockers.

The locker doors clanged opened and shut as usual along with the scuffling of student's feet in the halls and the dropping of books, but the usual cacophony of voices was conspicuously absent.

The real world had invaded our school.

November 22, 1963 - Lyndon B. Johnson is sworn in as the 36th U.S. President. He was part of a succession of Presidents who had been coping with Vietnam and oversaw massive escalation of the war while utilizing many of the same policy advisors who served Kennedy.

By year's end, there were 16,300 American military advisors in South Vietnam. South Viet Nam had received $500 million in U.S. aid during 1963.

March 6. 1964- Defense Secretary McNamara visits South Vietnam. Following his visit, McNamara advises President Johnson to increase military aid to shore up the sagging South Vietnamese army. McNamara and other Johnson policy makers now become focused on the need to prevent a Communist victory in South Vietnam, believing it would damage the credibility of the U.S. globally. The war in Vietnam thus becomes a test of U.S. resolve in fighting Communism with America's prestige and President Johnson's reputation on the line.

The cost to America of maintaining South Vietnam's army and managing the overall conflict in Vietnam now rises to two million dollars per day.

During this volatile time, it seemed as though the country was of one collective mindset. Nobody who is sane likes war. The only seeming variance of perspectives was how it should be carried out.

I wanted to be supportive of my government as much as I was able at this age. However, I couldn't shake the queasy feeling. As much as I was trying to be my perception of a "normal" teenager, it was becoming increasingly difficult. Mom and Dad assisted my efforts by not talking about it, whether they were aware of that or not. If they didn't discuss it, it made it less real. They were my barometers of *reality*. We all saw the same news reports on TV every night, the same footages from Viet Nam. I wonder if they ever discussed it with each other.

Chapter 19

"Travel"

New York World's Fair

Ironically, although either nobody perceived the irony or simply didn't comment on it, the theme of the 1964-65 New York World's Fair was "Peace Through Understanding," while the Viet Nam War raged. The focal point of the fair was the Unisphere, a 12 story high, spherical stainless steel representation of the world. It was commissioned to celebrate the beginning of the space age and to represent the theme of global interdependence. A shimmering pool with fountains circled the base.

It was a 23-hour train trip from Lima to New York City. Mom and Dad took us on a 4-day vacation there. We went with a tour and stayed in the Hotel New Yorker. I had never seen such huge buildings, or so many aloof and unfriendly people in one place.

Our first day in New York we took the subway to the fair. Walking and more walking was all we did. My feet hurt so much I had a hard time caring about anything at the fair. There were foot rejuvenators placed strategically throughout the grounds. You stood on it and put your coins in. It vibrated vigorously and for a short 2 minutes, your foot pain *miraculously* went away.

The Disney Pavilion was memorable. You rode through the darkness in a boat and enjoyed the much appreciated air-conditioning as various Disney characters floated in the air, accompanied by strains of "It's a Small World After All." The experience was ethereal.

Mom took a black and white photo of me in *Dinosaur Land*. I had a distinct look of pain on my face, with my eyebrows pointed upward in the middle and my mouth was obviously in motion as I whined the day away.

I was hot.

My feet were killing me.

This was boring.

The fair was filled with people from all over the world, some wearing saris, some in turbans and I heard many unrecognizable languages. It was fascinating.

Late that day we took the subway back into the city. We stopped at a small sandwich shop near our hotel to have a hot fudge sundae. There was only one other person in the shop. The waitress chatted with him. She finally made it over to us and took our order.

"Yeah, whadya want?" she asked as she loudly cracked her gum. I could see the wad in her mouth.

I had never seen a waitress who was so rude. Waitresses didn't act that way in Ohio.

She was a large African-American, and she wore a dirty, white uniform. Dad gave her the order. 25 long minutes later she brought four small sundaes, which cost as much as an entire meal would have cost at King Burger at home. She did not place them in front of us as I had always seen waitresses do, but plopped them down and scooted them in our general direction.

She wouldn't last 10 minutes in Ohio, I thought to myself.

A policeman came in while we were finishing our sundaes and he was swinging his billy club. We left shortly after. Trouble seemed to be brewing. The policeman kept glancing out the open door as if he was watching someone across the street. My imagination didn't require reality to confirm what might be out there. I was happy to return to the hotel.

"Dear Diary," I wrote, 'We are really in NYC!!! I can't believe it."

I recounted what happened at the sandwich shop and how much my feet hurt at the fair.

"Tomorrow we are going to go see the Rockettes at Radio City Music Hall, then our final day we are taking a bus to the Staten Island Ferry which goes around

Manhattan Island. We will see the Statue of Liberty."
Byeeeeeeeeeeeeeeeeeeeeeee!!!!!!!!!!!!!!!!!!
Diary!"
"Dear Diary,
The Rockettes were really cool!!! Radio City Music Hall is a BIG place!!!! They also showed a movie afterward called The Chalk Garden starring Haley Mills.

Bye

    bye

        bye

          bye

DIARY!"
"Dear Diary,
Today we took the Staten Island Ferry around Manhattan Island, as planned. There was a group of guys on the boat who kept looking at me. Finally one of them came over but he wasn't very cute. Others watched.

Then another guy came over and he was real cute. He asked if his friend could take our picture. The friend took it and I had the friend get one with my camera. Then we talked.

He put his arm around my chair!!! He is staying in our hotel too. He is SO CUTE. He is a soldier from Pakistan who is studying at our Army base in Ft. Eustis, Virginia. After he is done then he will go back to Pakistan.

He likes me. He is Muslim, not Christian.

We arranged for me to call him on the hotel phone after we got back, but Mom wouldn't let me.

She said 'what will people think?'

I am not sure what she is talking about. He is CUTE!!!!!!!!!!!!!!!!!! His name is Abdul Aziz and he is 21.

He came out of the hotel just as our tour group was about to leave for the train station. He came over to me. I could tell he wasn't happy. I explained *that Mom wouldn't let me call. He understood. We exchanged addresses and we are going to write.*

By
    by
        by
            by
                for
                    now
                        Diary!"

I always opened and closed my entries as though my diary was a real person and the endings were geared to fill the page if I hadn't written much. A character in a comic book I once read addressed her diary as a real person, so I thought that was how I was supposed to do it. I also felt like that space had to be filled, perhaps a latent obsessive-compulsive tendency.

Aziz and I were pen pals for several months and after he returned to Pakistan we continued to write for a year. I was so happy to get his letters. I imagined some day we would meet again, that I could travel to Pakistan. Though his letters were romantic and this was the first time a boy had been romantic with me, my hopes of meeting again were dashed when he announced his intent to marry his first cousin. It took me by surprise. We didn't write for long after that. If someone would have asked me if I *really* thought I would meet him again, in honesty, I would have admitted I didn't think it would happen. It was a dream that I wanted to hold onto. It made my teenage world seem bigger than just my own neighborhood. He made it clear that his marriage had been planned for a long time. It was an arranged marriage.

I researched Islam in the reference section at the library. To become a Muslim, all you had to do was repeat three times "I believe in Allah and Mohammed is his prophet" and that made you a Muslim. Of course you were supposed to actually mean it. I said the words just to try it out.

I felt an unmistakable discomfort inside. I knew I didn't mean it and though I couldn't say why, I knew the discomfort was deeper than just about the words I was repeating.

The Muslim religion then was just another religion and held no particular significance to the USA, as it does today due to 9/11, although not all Muslims are so radical, the basic tenants, if followed through, are quite radical. I had always had openness to those of other cultures and religions. It seemed small minded, as well as uncaring toward those in other lands to be otherwise. This is why I couldn't understand why I was feeling deeply uncomfortable. I didn't think long about it since I couldn't figure it out. I now believe my discomfort was spiritual discernment of something much larger than myself.

Post 9/11, I cannot help but think there was some validity to my *discomfort.*

"Beatles Mayhem"

She Loves You, yeah yeah yeah ….

Sunday, February 9, 1964 at 8:00 PM, along with 73 million others, I sat glued in front of the TV set watching the Ed Sullivan Show as the British Rock Group, *The Beatles* performed. They sang *All My Loving, Till There Was You, She Loves You, I Saw Her Standing There, and I Want To Hold Your Hand.* Mass hysteria happened wherever they performed. Beatlemania was created.

At first I thought all the screaming and crying girls were silly. But the next day, when my older friend Sharon seemed to have become one of them, I decided to jump on the Beatle bandwagon.

I had to admit Paul McCartney was very cute, but John was too old and married; George was skinny and homely, and Ringo was old and clownish looking.

To show my new undying loyalty, it wasn't long till I got a Beatle haircut. Then I read in a fan magazine that the Beatles didn't like it when girls got Beatle haircuts, but liked girls with straight long straight hair. Judging from the girls that were always pictured with the Beatles, they also liked girls who were shaped like pencils. I was a far cry from pencil shape so again I was out of step with everything that seemed to be *important.*

Would I ever get it right?

Mom never said a word about my haircut. I can only think she probably supported the age old wisdom of "picking your battles."

I did enjoy the two Beatle concerts Mom and Dad took Dede and I to see. One was in Chicago. It was in the stadium and the Beatles looked like tiny dolls on stage. We could hear them well. The crowd was loud and obnoxious. I didn't like the competition of all those *other* girls. I wanted the Beatles to myself, particularly Paul. My parents didn't say much. They sat, listened and watched.

The second concert we attended was in Cincinnati, Ohio. We were all at the stadium in our seats, but they kept postponing the concert, telling us to wait because storms had been predicted.

I got bored waiting for the concert to start and took a walk.

I meandered back along the wire mesh fencing that covered the outside of the stadium acting as a wall so people wouldn't fall off whatever level they were on. I was on the third level up. Movement below caught my attention.

I stopped and watched.

A van was pulling in a gate and up to the side of the stadium door. The side of the van opened and about 20 feet below me John Lennon stepped out, then George, then Ringo, then Paul.

I could not believe my eyes.

Where was everybody?
I was the only girl here witnessing this. It was a miracle!

I screamed and jumped up and down, shouting, "Paul! Paul!!!"

The boys looked up.

Paul looked up.

They waved, at *me only.*

Time stood still.

I, Cherié Ann, had been *personally seen,* (not just as part of a crowd), and waved at by Paul McCartney and the Beatles. *They looked just like human beings!* I felt as though I should have my name in the newspaper.

In the end, the concert was postponed until the next day since lightening could hit their equipment, but since Dad had to be at work we couldn't stay. Although I was disappointed, at that point, consoled myself with what had happened just to me that the others who were able to see the concert would miss. Paul had looked at me, and all was right with the world.

Now it seems that this was such an innocent time. I was so naïve. Since then it has been reported that the Fab Four had women in their rooms regularly as did and do most celebrities it seems on this level. Though I may have been aware of this then, I was in denial. My world was still basically made up of sugar plum fairies, and all is right with the world beliefs. However, the fringes of the real world had intruded some and were on the increase. Was everyone like this? What did my parents think? I wish I knew. I think if Mom had been asked, she would have preferred that Dede and I would remain this naïve and that the world would be forced to match up. Isn't this what every loving parent would prefer?

I think somewhere inside I knew this was what she wanted. I knew that wasn't the way things really were. I also sensed that maintaining that "innocence" might please my mother, which is good, but that ultimately it would not allow me to successfully function in the real world.

Fighting against the pull of Mommy's "overprotection" seemed to be more and more wise, even though it was extremely painful.

More on Sharon

My older friend, Sharon, was also a source for *cruising*. Since she was older, could drive and she had an old car, we drove to downtown Lima to King Burger at night. This was the cruising spot for the city's teenagers. Some teens would park at this drive in restaurant and actually order something. The carhops delivered it to the car. Others just liked to come in, circle round, be seen, leave and come back a few minutes later to do the same thing. Perhaps someone new had come meanwhile that just might be impressed. I am sure some teens hooked up this way, but we never did. We just watched everyone.

One of those we watched was Rumsey. Most of us had only heard his legend but didn't know him. Rumsey was an older, rich boy who I was only able to catch a glimpse of on occasion. What was unique about Rumsey was his ownership of a shiny, candy apple red corvette, which mirrored the restaurant parking area lights to the point that it actually glimmered. It was a surreal looking luminescence. Rumsey sat at the wheel, driving very slowly, grinning and looking around at the all the lesser males in attendance. He was clearly the Alpha male and everyone knew it. Whoever owned that car would have been the Alpha male.

It puzzled me then and it puzzles me still. Why do both young and older males so identify with their vehicle to define them? If I thought someone wanted me only for my vehicle, it would be a very shallow thing indeed.

Chapter 20

High School
"Shortclutch and Civil Rights"

November 3, 1964, Lyndon B. Johnson was reelected in a landslide victory. The Democrats also achieved large majorities in both the House and Senate.

December 1, 1964, At the Whitehouse, President Johnson's top aides, including Secretary of State Dean Rusk, National Security Advisor McGeorge Bundy, and Defense Secretary McNamara, recommended a policy of gradual escalation of US military involvement in Viet Nam.

By years end the number of American military *advisors* in South Viet Nam was 23,000. Viet Nam was not a declared war.

April 24, 1965, President Johnson announces Americans in Viet Nam are eligible for combat pay.

By now, there were also Anti-American war rallies.

My junior year of high school was a much better year for me than tenth grade had been. I knew the ropes and I was able to take some subjects I liked better. I signed up for Drama.

Some of the boys a year ahead of me had already signed up for the draft. By now, they knew what they would be doing upon graduation. We all watched nightly news broadcasts of scenes from Viet Nam. We saw a man set himself on fire in the streets there. There were semi-clad children running from fires. We saw a Viet Cong man get his head blown off when the south Viet Namese general had him executed.

The unique inhumanity of this war was that the enemy used innocent children to walk up to our soldiers with bombs set to detonate. Who would expect a child to have a bomb? It was insane. Our soldiers learned they could not trust anyone, which meant they would be forced to do things, which would forever provide grist for nightmares, if they lived to come home. There was a never-ending parade of the unthinkable and those of us at home watched much of this on our black and white television sets.

Though I saw these horrific scenes, I did not know what I could do. I couldn't even vote. I tried to insulate myself from thinking too much about it. I had school and my own life.

I liked a boy named David. We not only went to the same school, but to the same church. We both arrived early. This afforded us time before Sunday school started and we had the best conversations. He wasn't like most boys. He listened to what you said and he was just plain nice as well, as very good-looking.

Dan was another boy I liked. Dan was a senior when I was a junior. We had library study hall together at the end of the day. The previous year he had been in my Spanish class. I knew I liked him when he handed me a note right before the bell to start class which read,

"If you have ruffled panties on, smile."

It was unexpected.

Dan seemed delighted when I didn't smile.

I laughed out loud.

A few days later I took a picture of myself to school to show him. I was a toddler with ruffled pants on in the picture.

Lynn, Dan, and I sat at one of the large library tables last period. We passed notes back and forth and Dan did anything he could to get Lynn and I laughing. He usually succeeded. He even resorted to making faces if nothing else worked. The white haired librarian glared the whole time we were there. I hid behind my book trying to conceal my laughter and not make any noise. I would get a firm grip on myself, and then hear Dan snort loudly and both Lynn and I shook uncontrollably in an attempt to stifle ourselves.

It didn't always work.

"Sssshhh," the librarian reprimanded often. Even when she didn't shush, her glares spoke volumes.

She tried to be gruff. I could tell she liked me in spite of our antics.

She smiled broadly at me in approval when I made my way to the center of the crowded but hushed library, one afternoon. I went to the gigantic open Bible that rested on a podium. I wasn't going there for anyone's approval, and was frankly a little embarrassed that she saw me. I couldn't remember where I had seen a certain verse and I was hoping to find it.

This was about the time the Black Panthers gained popularity. I tried to stay out of the fray and just mind my own business.

Stephanie was a petite, black girl in my homeroom, who was also very militant, judging from some of her "honky" remarks. I was reading one of my textbooks one morning before the bell and she accosted me saying,

"You just think you are so smart with your *pink* skin and your *pink* blouse. You think you are better than blacks don't you girl? ..."

Obviously Stephanie was not going to allow me to read in peace and she wasn't going to be ignored. I was nervous and embarrassed.

Where was the teacher, for petes sake!

Other kids began to watch.

She had her black finger pressed on my desk, obviously impatient with my lack of response.

I finally answered, "Let me alone Stephanie!

You don't even know me or know what I think.

I do not feel that way at all!"

Tears stung my eyes. I couldn't believe I was being accused of something that was the farthest from the way I truly believed. She saw the truth of my words, perhaps, or got nervous when she saw tears. Either way, she curtly apologized and let the matter rest.

Such was the crux of the sixties. I had known Stephanie as a classmate for several years. When younger, she was just as "normal" as I, doing homework, liking boys, trying to make her skirt we were sewing come out right for our Home Economics teacher (now called Family and Consumer Science and it is also co-ed). If Stephanie and I had talked then, it would likely have been congenial enough. We were both kids and had things in common.

When we entered Senior High school our sophomore year, she changed. What happened to her? When did the color of her skin become more important than shared years of regular happenings, and inflicting pain become OK on someone you really didn't know but assumed you did for no other reason than that they were "all pink?"

I don't know this for a fact, but Stephanie's home life did not seem to be a bad one. I can only conclude that she listened to and believed black hate dogma or black liberation theology, and interpreted it as somehow fair and just. It was, after all, no more than the way white supremacists operated in the opposing direction. She may not have known it, but she joined ranks with that same mentality. She had not learned to *think,* but only to pursue *not thinking* and to follow, because it was easiest. It allowed her to fit in with those she had chosen as her own *mainstream.*

Hate, regardless of the direction, is the same. I would have voiced this back then as well, and did to the best of my ability to Stephanie.

My favorite subject was Drama. Miss Shortclutch was the teacher. She was in her first year of teaching and newly graduated from Bowling Green State University. Miss Shortclutch was a gangly redhead with thick-lensed horn-rimmed glasses that made her eyes look three times the size they actually were. I thought she was homely but unique, and I liked her very much. My dad had worked with her dad.

She held tryouts for a one-act play, which would be performed in the auditorium for the students at Central Junior High, archrivals in football to South Junior High where I had attended. I wanted a speaking part so badly. We were handed scripts a week early so we could practice at home for the part we wanted.

I knew this was my niche, and that nobody in my class knew this about me. I practiced and practiced.

The play was called *La Infanta*. It was about the Infanta, a ruler in Spain who had an aunt, the Duchess of Albuquerque, who was not nice and tried all sorts of adversarial things against the Infanta. The Duchess was the part I wanted. I was good at dialects so when it came time to try out, I used a Spanish accent. I was the only one who did. Miss Shortclutch read the other part to cue me.

You could have heard a pin drop. I could see the other students glance at each other open mouthed. After we finished, Miss Shortclutch said, "Thank you Cherié," in such a way that I knew she had been impressed, along with everyone else and that I had nailed the part.

The love interest for the Infanta was a "misshapen dwarf." Harold, the boy who was to play this part, was chubby. At one part in the play he falls to his death onstage. This was supposed to bring tears to the eyes of audience members.

When it came time for our performance at the junior high school, all went well until Harold fell "dead." The wooden stage floor cracked loudly upon impact. The young audience erupted in laughter. Harold thought it was funny too and he laid there supposedly "dead," but shaking with laughter.

I was not upset with the audience. It was funny. I was, however, upset with Harold for not staying in character. The principal at the junior high apologized for his students reaction. Even Miss Shortclutch laughed, *the traitor*. *Where was her loyalty?*

Miss Shortclutch had one other flaw. She enjoyed the boys in our English class *a lot*. They were popular, amusing, charming boys, and if they had been in Miss Shortclutch's high school class, they would not have given her the time of day. I knew the superficiality of teenage boys and it didn't require astuteness to know that Miss Shortclutch would not have been a part of her class's *in group*.

I was giving an oral presentation after several others one afternoon, while Miss Shortclutch sat in the back of the classroom chatting with the popular boys. She was enjoying flirting so much it was obvious to me that she wasn't even listening.

I tested it just to make sure by saying something like "the sky is green" in the middle of my report, to see if she reacted. She didn't even notice. I decided to make a bold move. Being bold was unusual for me at the time, since I tried to be relatively unobtrusive to avoid criticism. For me to do this was not only out of character, it exemplified how annoyed I was.

I stopped giving my report in mid report, waited for about 30 seconds in silence, and then returned to my seat. A few minutes passed. Finally noticing that nobody was doing a presentation, Miss Shortclutch finally said,

"Oh! Cherié, did you finish?"

"Yes," I answered.

It wasn't exactly a lie. I presented as much as I intended to for a teacher who was more interested in her teen age male coterie than she was in doing her job.

Another girl in the class, who made the same observation, went with me to the office during lunch. We went to the dean of girls and reported Miss Shortclutch. We told her exactly what had taken place and that this sort of thing occurred regularly. We had reached the end of our rope. We told her we felt that Miss Shortclutch had *a thing* for her male students. The dean listened quietly and asked a couple questions. I was not one to complain and had never done so before and I wasn't a troublemaker. This is likely the reason they listened.

Miss Shortclutch had me give my presentation over, though she looked at me differently from then on. She knew I had reported her, which was likely a surprise. Though, she never treated me unfairly and though she continued her attention to the boys, she seemed to make greater efforts to also do her job.

This whole incident still amazes me. I had never before *bucked city hall* except in my own family. I never told my mother what I was doing. It never occurred to me to ask for permission on this. That also amazes me. This was a time in which Mom knew most of my thoughts or at least the more important ones. I think that I was so certain of my rightful position that I was determined to carry it out, so that justice might prevail and that not only I, but many who would follow me, could possibly benefit. If asked why I had not sought Mom's opinion, I would have been surprised because I assumed her stance would be the same. It was obvious to me that any thinking, fair-minded person would be in complete agreement.

Sometimes there is a lot more there to us just below the surface than is even apparent to ourselves and it takes just the right thing to unleash it. Mom knew about the whole thing after the fact. I don't recall her saying too much about it. I do know, from the way I knew her to be then, that I don't think she would have done it if faced with the same thing. She would have absorbed it and been quiet. The status quo would have remained and though that is *safe*, nothing usually ever becomes better that way.

Fun times...

It was Christmas. I was now 16 so I got to be *Mary* in the live Nativity in the church yard. We even had live animals. This was an annual event and I had started off as a *shepherd* my first year, then got a promotion to *side angel* and then to the *roof angel*.

Roof angel was the year I almost got my fingers frostbit. I was 15. I had to climb a ladder up the back of the nativity building. There was snow on the roof. My bare fingers couldn't handle so much ongoing cold. However, the spotlight was on me and the show must go on. I had to stay in character.

The speakers boomed "Behold! I bring you tidings of great joy which shall be to all people..."

The breeze on the roof was frigid.

My cheeks stung.

I braced myself against the support pole at my back, which was topped off with the star of Bethlehem.

I stood still.

My hands were numb, but they were folded as in prayer.

The spotlight finally turned off, the star remaining illuminated. I carefully made my way to the edge of the snow-covered roof.

As I descended the ladder, I was in tears from pain. Inside one of the the church restrooms, Mom ran tepid water over my hands. I cried in pain. The water felt like it was boiling. I finally thawed. My fingers didn't change color so the episode ended there. When I accused Mom of using hot water, she answered, "No, it is just warm water." She had a concerned look on her face. If I wasn't feeling what was real then that is a cause for concern. She was patient and reassuring.

The only thing required to be Mary was to be in your mid-teens and have participated regularly. I paid my dues each year in the other parts.

I had arrived. I sat there in my blue Mary costume and tried to look serene and holy.

It was a wonderful Christmas.

Mom took pictures. She always did but that year I think she was especially proud. Dad always came to see the Nativity. He must have been proud too. The newspaper came and took pictures. The blurb under the picture gave all our names and the times of the nativity.

These were the fun family years, for me, for certain. I viewed my church family as important and integral to my life. I believe that Mom felt the same way. She had made friends with several women. She seemed happy making dishes for church suppers and the interactions with the others. It was a stable and secure time for me. I do not think my life would have progressed well without this church family. I don't think our lives as a family would have progressed well without this church family. Though no person is perfect and all these people had flaws and made mistakes as all humans do, they were still more kind, more loving, than any human I came in contact with outside that circle.

I am very thankful to my parents for taking the time and effort to find the right mix for our family, though I don't know

that they were consciously aware of all that went into it. It makes me think of a Bible verse, "A man's heart plans his way; But the LORD directs his steps."
Proverbs 16:9

So many people graduated that year that were good friends of mine. I wondered what fun school could possibly be without them.

My senior year, I signed up for Speech with Miss Shortclutch. That was fun. I really found my niche in being in front of a group. I got straight A's.

Tammy was my locker partner. She was a member of Thespians, the theatre group. She wanted to become an actress after graduation. It was later rumored that she went to California and got some small parts, and had a family.

My first real job, other than baby-sitting, was behind the candy counter at the Quilna Theatre as a summer job. The customers were generally very nice, however, the old woman in charge of the counter, and my immediate supervisor was not. She seemed to always be in a nasty mood. She had not been there when I was hired. Her boss, a very congenial woman, hired me. Perhaps she resented not having a say in my hiring.

Another girl quit and they needed a replacement, so I took Rona, Edith's friend, to meet her. Rona needed a summer job. I trained Rona. The old woman treated Rona very well. I was surprised and had warned Rona of her unpleasant personality.

After Rona was trained, the old woman fired me. She falsely accused me of not balancing out the drawer at the end of the day. I was completely crushed. I sobbed to my mom. I was being accused of something not true. How could anyone do that? I was as honest as anyone I knew.

Mom called her.

I was on the phone extension.

Mom told her that what she had accused me of was simply not accurate. She blurted curtly and condescendingly, "Well, can't she lose some weight? She needs to lose the weight!"

Discrimination comes in many forms. This old woman had a prejudice against overweight people. She was small in stature and Rona was petite. Apparently, she was also *very small* in ways other than physical.

Mom was very quiet when she got off the phone. Though I knew that she had suffered similarly from classmates abuse as I had, I had no idea at that time that she may have suffered the same type thing when it came to a job. Now I know that she had. She looked sad, but she had no rebuttal. Perhaps her own experiences, and with having her own child suffer coupled with the real fact of the weight issue, had rendered her unable to respond in such a way that would somehow help the situation. It simply was and you could do little to stop it, so you kept quiet and hurt.

When bad things happen where I have been so hurt, I get through it by reminding myself of the Biblical verse "You reap what you sow." If you plant bad seeds, you cannot get a good harvest. Planting seeds of unkindness or cruelty would not be seeds that I would want to plant for my life.

If I had not been so hurt, I would have felt sorry for her.

Miss DeGrief was my "College English" teacher. This class was only offered to seniors and it was a literature course. We covered both English and American writers. Miss DeGrief was 4'9" and looked and acted like she was 80 years old. She was forgetful, but she knew her literature. I respected that. The boys, however, did not respect anything about Miss DeGrief. They teased her and she was with it enough to know she was being teased at least *some of the time*. Other times, she took them seriously and reacted in such a way that we knew she was simply losing touch with the world. She was a sweet old lady that should have retired much earlier.

Perhaps my school liked keeping much older teachers. Mr. Russler was also ancient, though he was probably younger than

Miss DeGrief. I had Mr. Russler for Civics and Economics. Mr. Russler made no bones about his love for our country. I admired him very much. He was probably a Vet or had a son who was a soldier, though he never shared much of his personal life. I read more about the political scene and world events during my senior year than any other.

I knew the names of all appointed and elected officials on the national level. I was aware of all reported happenings and progress in world affairs. I enjoyed keeping up. I felt more a part of things that way, on the cutting edge. I was an activist at heart even if not in behavior, that is until there was something I could perhaps have an actual affect upon. That day came.

A boy from Denmark who was an exchange student here sent a letter to the editor, op page of our local paper, in which he was highly critical of the USA. He was my age. His criticisms were not political. He criticized Americans on a more personal level. He didn't like our houses were one thing I remember he mentioned, and referred to them as being dull in color and imagination. Well, I couldn't let those insults lay. I wrote to him through the paper and I also sent a copy of his letter along with my own to the Danish Embassy. To the house insult, I told him that pastels were pretty and people have different taste. Not all people like loud garish colors as those I had seen in pictures of houses in Denmark. Actually I thought they were very neat and pretty, but I couldn't let him know that. I repeated the same in my letter to the embassy, along with stating that I didn't think he was a very nice representative of their country.

I actually received a reply from the embassy. I was surprised. They agreed with me and understood my umbrage. They apologized for him that some don't always think before they speak and that this is especially a positive virtue when visiting someone else's country.

However, they had addressed their letter to "*Master* Cherie, ..." apparently assuming that I was male. I thought then, didn't they know Cherie was a female name? Did they think ONLY a boy would be so bold as to write them a letter? Now I think, were they making a passive-aggressive statement to me? Some things will remain a mystery.

Mom's reaction to this whole thing was amusement. I don't think she understood why I got so upset. I wondered why she *didn't* get upset over such things. Why was she so complacent, so willing to let all things possibly controversial to stand?

When I got the letter from the embassy, she grinned from ear to ear. At that point, I think she was surprised and pleased and seemed proud of me. She didn't say that verbally but in her demeanor.

Looking back, Mom and I were either so different or she was, by this time, too beaten down or tired to revolt in any way other than in whatever control she could exert in her immediate circle.

Slumber parties weren't as popular with my friends as they had been earlier. I guess we were growing up.

At church youth group, a male quartet came to sing for us. They were from Anderson College, now Anderson University in Anderson, Indiana. This was where the headquarters to the church I attended, the Church of God, was located. The Gaither's, a very versatile group who not only sang but wrote many popular Christian songs were located in Anderson and were members of this church. Their "Homecoming Hour" is still popular with some. They have also acted as a springboard to many other popular Christian artists.

After the quartet visited the church, I decided I needed to try to get to this college some way. Since it was a private college and out of state, it was more expensive. Since I was also not a very good student, I decided after I graduated that I should work and pay my way. I didn't want to obtain loans and I did not feel right about asking my parents. Thinking back to this now, it was really quite mature of me to want to take financial responsibility.

At some point during my senior year or perhaps it was the year following, I read in the newspaper that Dan Garrison, a local boy who joined the Navy after graduating from Lima Senior in 1965, was killed when he fell overboard as his ship patrolled in the Viet Nam area. It was Dan from Spanish class, Dan from library study hall who was so full of life and so much fun.

The undeclared war was getting way too close to home.

It became ever more difficult to *insulate* myself.

Little Edith was still my best friend.

Our senior class picnic was held at Lake St. Marys in St. Marys, Ohio. Delbert, one of my pals, his friend Richard, Edith and myself, drove together. Delbert was a nerd. He literally had tape around his glasses to hold them together. Delbert also had a motor boat and took it to the picnic. The four of us rode in the boat. All the popular kids stood on the bank watching us. They were grinning and seemed happy for us. It surprised me because I knew what snobs some were and how mean they could sometimes be. Maybe they were changing too. Maybe I just didn't care as much.

The afternoon of June 10, 1966, the girls gathered in white graduation robes and the boys wore black ones. We had an outdoor ceremony at the Lima Stadium where we had attended many football games. We laughed. We cried. The junior class band played Pomp and Circumstance for us, as was the tradition, when we paraded in. Our families watched from the stands. One by one, as our name was called, we marched proudly to the podium to receive our diplomas.

A few weeks prior to graduation, I had lain in bed crying. I felt as though I had been on safe, secure, solid ground and was about to step off a cliff.

Chapter 21

"Steep Cliffs"

Two weeks after graduation, I had a job at the Lima Telephone Company as a Toll Operator (long distance) and worked shift work. I took a bus to work. The company paid for our taxis home at night. As soon as I had enough money saved, I paid for my driving lessons. I continued to save money till I had enough for spring semester at Anderson College.

The telephone company offered many opportunities and temptations that I had not previously experienced. I entered the adult world and was extraordinarily naïve. It was late June, and I turned 18.

We had three weeks of job training in a conference room and then we were placed beside an operator as she worked. We plugged in our headsets and listened. Early the second week, we took a few simple calls, but the regular operator was plugged in with us so no mistakes would be made. She handled it if something came up that we were not yet prepared to handle. Two supervisors were always present.

Some of the supervisors were nice, but there were two who decided that I needed an initiation of sorts. Not since Miss Clark in first grade or Mrs. Stitely in junior high had I encountered such unpleasantness.

Jean and Rosemary looked nothing alike, however, their attitude was identical.

"What's this, Cherié?" Jean asked impatiently as she tapped the computer ticket on the desk.

One call equaled one ticket the operator was to fill out. This was the record of the calls the company kept and filed. When you got one back, there was an error you were expected to correct. I had been out of training less than two weeks. I looked at the ticket. I told her I would correct it. I was in the middle of a call. It appeared that Jean and Rosemary were tied in some sort of *nastiness* competition. That had to be it.

I pulled the key back to mute my voice to the customer and answered her, "I will correct it."

"See that you do" she responded. She glared and walked away.

"Don't let her get to you," the operator next to me said.

It seemed as though Jean, in particular, waited till I was on a call to bring me tickets to correct. Also, when in the lounge during break, she chatted with others and glared at me.

Jean was a short heavy-set, swarthy looking woman with deep lines in her face. She also sported a HUGE diamond. I told Mom about it and she said that when "diamonds" are that big and that sparkly, they are fake. I had so much to learn.

I told Mom about the whole thing, of course. She offered little at the time in the way of advice. She said other things though and her example said many things. Her ways of coping was to do the best you could and ignore any criticism, I imagine, in order to deflect it. Though I tried this, it seemed to incite more abuse, not less. There is a time to "take the bull by the horns."

After a few months of working in constant fear of these women, I decided that enough was enough. I could not continue to function with this much negativity and stress. Come what may, I had to do something.

Not long after my decision, Jean approached me while holding a few tickets. I was on a call.

"Cherié!" she said.

Tap tap tap, the sound of her tickets was very irritating, as she intended it to be.

I was purposely slow in pulling the mute key back.

"Jean," I said, in as uninterested manner as could muster,

"I am on a call. I will handle that when I finish."

I went back to my call.

It wasn't what I said, but how I said it. I used the same tone with her that she had been using with me, one of impatience and condescension.

She looked surprised.

I finished my call.

"Now, what is it?" I asked, somewhat impatiently.

"Here," she answered. "This needs correcting."

No condescension, no attitude, just a simple statement.

I treated Rosemary in the same manner that she treated me as well. She also seemed surprised. They both began to treat me with more respect after that.

I learned another lesson. Sometimes, you have to stand up to a *bully*, even if she *is* your supervisor.

When I shared this result with Mom, again she didn't say much. She seemed pleased that I had somehow solved the problem. I think she was more concerned at my personal life than my work life although they were closely entwined.

A case in point would be that Ohio Northern University in Ada, Ohio is and was a mere half hour drive away from Lima. ONU also has a law school. Some of the other young, single operators talked of meeting up with some of the law students from there. It was against the rules to talk to subscribers on a personal level, but during the later night shift, things relax more and you aren't watched as closely.

It wasn't long before I had begun to chat with some of the law students also. I went on two dates with one 23-year-old law student from Verona, New Jersey. I was dating an older man. I liked his car. It was an MG. It was quickly evident, however, that all he wanted was sex, and I wasn't compliant, so that ended. I had a curfew and I kept it. As I always told Mom, however, what you do after 11:30 P.M., you can do before 11:30 P.M. I just didn't do that at that time.

Even when we didn't meet, talking and flirting with the guys from our boards made it more entertaining at work.

"What's your name?"

"Operator number 94."

"OK, but what is your name operator number 94?"

giggle

"Cherie"

"Hi Cherie. I'm Tony." (I could tell he was smiling by the way he sounded.) "We ought to get together Cherie. What do you say?"

"Oh maybe sometime."

"OK, well, we'll talk again I'm sure. Hey is there an operator there named Connie and your age?"

"Yes, why?"

"Well, she is a wild one I hear. What does she look like?"

If the same male had gotten Connie when he made his call, he may have said the same thing to her about me. MEN! They all seemed to have one thing in mind. How did any woman *ever* get married? All guys seemed to think about or want was sex, not marriage. I really didn't know how to navigate all this very well and to maintain my own sense of integrity. Where is that balance? If you give in then you feel guilty and feel used and he still loses interest. If you don't give in, he moves on to a girl who will. Do you really care if that is all he wants?

I met Tony. He was Italian and gorgeous. We were both with a group of people however, so all was safe. He allowed several months to pass before he called, however, and when I answered I really didn't remember him.

"This is Tony."

"Tony who? I don't know a Tony."

Long silence, which I now know was his disbelief that any female on earth would not know who he is and they would certainly never forget him. I had victory, but then I ruined it. I remembered him.

"Oh, TONY! HIYEEE! How are you?"

Stop it! Well, you blew it!

I knew I had made a mistake as soon as I unthinkingly let him know how flattered I was that he called. I was doomed from there.

I am now very grateful it was doomed.   I have no doubt that Tony was not good news to any woman.

How many Tony's does a woman have to kiss before she finds she doesn't have to kiss them? In fact, she learns over time that just maybe ignoring the Tony's and enjoying who she really is inside brings the most happiness and contentment.

I told Mom about the whole thing. She seemed to think it was funny. Now I wonder if she was thinking about her own Tony's. According to my Aunt Rene, there had been many for them both. I wonder if she had had as much trouble navigating the guy thing as I was having. I suspect she did.

Besides our regular boards, we also had to work the CAMA board. I am not sure what CAMA stood for, but it was tedious because all it required was the operator to say "number please?" These calls were from those who were direct dialing and not using an operator. They had not perfected direct dial technology yet so we had to key in their number for billing, then say, "thank you," then key the red button to drop the call so another could come through. Calls lined up in a que, first one to come in, first one to get through.

I got in trouble one time for folding one of the tickets in half so it would stand up and I wrote on it "CAMA BORED" and propped it on top of the CAMA board. Everyone but the supervisors thought it was pretty funny. It took a couple hours till the supervisors noticed it, but 5 minutes for all the operators in the large toll room to notice and pass the word along.

What did it hurt? It was good for morale.

The phone company covered the price of our taxis home at night, but you had to share the cab with whoever was getting off the same time you got off. When I got home, I needed unwind time.

I watched late night TV. I loved Johnny Carson. My favorite thing was when he had animals on. I laughed till I was sore.

Despite this, I was not happy. What was life about anyway?

Chapter 22

"Turn on, Tune in, Drop out"

"Turn on, tune in, drop out" was a counterculture phrase coined by Timothy Leary in the 1960's. Leary wanted to come up with something *snappy* to promote the *benefits* of LSD.

I learned that he was one of the first people whose remains have been sent into space. It seems *redundant* to me. He was always *in space.*

At Anderson College, Leary was the person I wrote about for one of my English composition opinion papers. The dictionary defines a *hippy* as one who doesn't conform to society's standards and advocates a liberal attitude and lifestyle.

Hippies rejected the 9 to 5 lifestyle and believed that they were objects of ridicule by those whose lives were governed by the clock. They felt that "programmed people" were jealous and resented their freedom. Being a hippy was supposed to be a philosophical approach to life that emphasized freedom, peace, love and a respect for others and the earth. They promoted the notion that there had always been hippies and counted Jesus, Henry David Thoreau, and John Lennon, among their number. They suggested there was a little hippy in all of us, but our socialization process had just repressed it. We needed to find and cultivate *our hippy within.*

I watched as hippies marched across my TV screen. Flower power! Free love! Scraggly clothes, love beads, Height-Ashbury, ...
In stark contrast, I watched our soldiers being killed and I watched the civil rights marches, and the famous Martin Luther King Jr. speech. The hippies I saw on TV were smiling and parading around and dancing as though they were drunk. I thought they were just plain weird. They had "tuned out" and fried so many of their brain cells with drugs that they were incapable of "tuning in" enough to function in life, so they advocated tuning out to others who *were* able to function.

When I compared the hippies to the other much more serious scenes I viewed on TV, the hippies seemed to be complete nutcases who were never grounded in reality. Drugs and free love didn't sound like "freedom" to me, but bondage. Unlike many of my generation, drugs never tempted me. I saw it as a cop out to life, a panacea for those who were not only intellectually dishonest with themselves, but were also in some sort of vacuous la-la land, and who were unable to function or do something worthwhile, much like many Hollywood celebrities today who fancy themselves experts, particularly about political venues.

From what I understood about Henry David Thoreau, he wanted to *live* his life, rather than find out too late that it had lived him, or that he had sleep walked through it. Thoreau's experiment at Walden Pond confirmed his belief that a conscious, deliberately lived life is possible. But how could a person live their life purposefully if they were high all the time? Hippies were simply not grounded in reality.

When the hippies said that Jesus was an *early hippie*, I thought I would choke. Yes, he went against the ills in his society. However, he never used a foreign substance as justification to *drop out* of his society. He paid taxes, evidenced by his comment "render unto Caesar what is Caesar's." He and his disciples obeyed the law of the land. His followers were told that though they were *in the world, they were not of the world.* They did not use this as an excuse to avoid responsibility; it simply served to make them even more responsible.

To me *Hippy* was synonymous with *tuned out, drugged out, and dumbed out*. I can be "snappy" too.

When I first arrived at Anderson, a two-hour drive from home, I hoped I could cope with homesickness. When my parents left after moving me into the dorm, I had a huge lonely lump in my throat. I knew nobody. I had a choice to make. I could hold up in my room and feel sorry for myself, or I could at least go to the lounge and see if anybody was there to talk to.

I decided to go to the lounge. It seemed a little less painful.

There was a sweet-faced blonde girl there who started chatting. She had been attending Anderson for a couple years. I told her I was new. She said, "I figured." I had made my first friend. Her name was Rita.

My roommate, Andrea, lived in nearby Newcastle and she commuted home every weekend. It was a relief. She was critical, and a math major who thought numbers were the greatest thing.

She and a girl down the hall short sheeted my bed sheets, poured much of my laundry detergent into the bed, as well as pins and then remade the bed to look like it was normal. This was during mid-semester exams and I had been up till about 2:30 A.M. studying and had a test the next day, so I was understandably tired. I climbed into bed as Andrea pretended to sleep. I wondered why my feet wouldn't slip in and then I felt the pins and the gravely detergent. I threw the covers back.

Andrea watched as I yelled. I was exhausted and just wanted sleep. I could not believe they obviously hated me enough to do that at this *crucial* time. They used *my* detergent, (not their own), which costs money to replace, and no college student has much extra cash. I thought they could have at least used their own detergent and said so. I was sobbing as I cleaned out my bed. Andrea left the room to visit down the hall and to tell of my reaction. If a reaction was what they wanted, they got it.

I was not alone in my inability to like Andrea. I met her former roommate, a girl who seemed more like me and she had transferred to another room rather than room with her. Her excuse was she *wanted to experience more people*. Right. It was more like what she *didn't* want and that was to have no more experience with Andrea. I couldn't understand it as I had met Andrea's parents and they seemed like nice, regular people.

One girl I liked very much was Debby, or *Nut,* as she was sometimes called. She was a black girl from Chicago. She was funny and smart. I was fascinated with her family pictures and her sweetness. She was not like the black girls I had attended junior high and high school with. They were rough, overall, tactless, and vulgar. Debby's life at home seemed a lot like my life at home.

Debby taught me that black people are just as diverse as white people. This was an eye opener for me.

I hung out with her and a few of her black friends. I asked them some of their black *code language*. They seemed a little surprised I knew about this. *Honky* is the derogatory term for a white person. Most people are aware of this term. *Cracker*, however, was a term they used for a white person they liked. *Boot,* is how they referred to themselves. They made me an honorary "boot." I was tickled. I liked all of them.

Then I got a call from one of the boys, asking me out. I thought about it. I liked him OK as a friend, but I also knew if I went, even in this time of change, that if I wanted to date any white guys, this would kill those chances on that campus. I declined as respectfully as I could. I am sure I didn't handle that very well. When he asked, "why?" I said,

"Greg, you know why. It wouldn't be a good idea for either one of us."

Technically, I was right. At age 18, I was not armed with the necessary courage to buck the safe and established.

I also knew my family would flip. In spite of their acceptance of blacks in general as equal, me dating a black boy would have been the exception.

For St. Patrick's Day I decorated my hair with green "Easter" grass. Though some comments on campus were favorable, others looked at me like I was from another planet. I think I may have been ahead of my time in this regard. I was theatrical by nature in a relatively conservative climate.

This college did not permit students to dance, one of the rules of that church. I didn't really care about that anyway. I think they viewed it as vertical sex. Judging from some of the dances I have seen, maybe they were on to something.

Though I did fairly well in most of my college classes, I didn't feel confident to continue. I was now out of money and would have had to get a loan. I didn't want to take the chance. Looking back, I still feel this was a wise decision.

At the end of the semester, I went back to the phone company till I obtained a job at Teledyne, formerly the company Dad's boss once owned and Dad worked for, a year and a half later. I was hired as a PBX Operator, which also included receptionist duties and filing. I worked four months before I was laid off with several other workers.

Mom seemed sad that this happened and so was dad. I had no idea what I was going to do. I felt lost. I knew *nobody* could help. I had burned my bridges at the phone company. I didn't want to go back there anyway. I wanted to be safe and secure and I didn't know how to make that happen and I didn't really think a person could make that happen anyway. Was I becoming fatalistic, depressed? I hoped not. I did what I knew. I prayed. That approach hadn't failed me yet.

Chapter 23

"Changes"

During the time I had been at the phone company, I took instruction and joined the Roman Catholic Church. That came about when I was going through a rough time breaking away from a man I should not have been seeing in the first place, and we were between ministers at my own church. There was a Catholic Church right around the corner and in walking distance from the apartment where I had been living for a couple months.

Mom had not wanted me to move out, but I wanted my independence and the freedom to be with a boy I liked. I really should have listened to Mom. She was right. Unfortunately, at age 18 or 19, you may fall in love easily and this can be a huge mistake. He was three years older than me and married. I didn't find that out until later when I had already defined myself as being "in love" with him. His wife was also his age and looked me up, as well as talked on the phone to my mother. She said to me, "He got another girl pregnant besides me but he chose me, not her."

When I was back in my hometown recently, I grabbed a snack at a hamburger shop that had been in business there for as long as when my grandparents were younger. It is a landmark that has earned it's way by making the best chili, the best "specials" and the best frosty's I have ever tasted. It was crowded.

I looked up from my bowl of chili and saw a man and woman come in who looked somewhat familiar. The woman was in front and waited with others at the counter. The man's profile looked like it did back then, and he was the right age, but I thought this was just too much of a coincidence to be one. He even had the same haircut though his hair was gray. He turned to pick up something and caught my eye. He held our gaze for a moment then looked away. I knew it was he, the married guy from when I was 18. I also knew he recognized me. Then I looked at the heavyset woman who was with him, though his wife had not been heavyset 40 years ago. I got a glimpse of her face. The mouth was the same mouth; the eyes were the same eyes that stared at me outside at dusk as she told me how he had chosen her over the other girl. They sat near the counter. As I made my way toward the door to leave I had to pass them. I glanced down at her, a pleasant look on my face. I was met with her steely glare. Some things don't change. I thought later how perhaps I should have apologized, but didn't think of it at that moment. The guy made the right decision to stay with her back then though I was temporarily very heartsick. I hoped that they had a good life, as I had during that 40 years.

This was only one of *many* events, in which I know God answered the prayer I prayed when I was 14 to *pull me back* to Him, *no matter what it took*. Maybe seeing them again was a reminder of that fact. God was and always is faithful. He pulled me back to Him under His loving protection.

He has also led me many places. The priest who counseled me back then awakened a latent interest in his church. Though years later I left the Roman Catholic Church, I was initially very active and involved in many outside church activities. I even considered joining a sisterhood, either Franciscan or Dominican as I had several friends who were nuns. I visited convents to inform myself about their way of life.

My mother was not happy about my interest and conversion to Catholicism. She said, "When you and Dede have kids, what will *your* kids have in common with Dede's kids?" When she found out that this argument didn't mean anything to me, for one because I didn't think it was valid and two, because I wasn't going to hold back on something I truly believed in to please her or Dede or her potential kids, she stopped using it. I think she saw my newfound interest as just more youthful rebellion. It wasn't. It was finding my own way in this world and it didn't happen to coincide with Mom's thought. She had proven she had not had any definitive answers for me. I didn't fault her for that. I didn't however, like it that she seemed to begrudge me finding those necessary answers for myself if it was possible. Did she feel threatened by this? If so, why?

As a Mom myself, although I have some empathy for her in this regard, this desire to protect ones children because of what lies out there; I also tried my best not to blunt my own children's searches and explorations for their own identity. I think Mom would have preferred that I use *her* identity. It would have been "safer." I was aware of that even back then as well, and struggled against it. Knowing what I now know about my true parentage and conception, though I have forgiven her, I find it difficult to not have some measure of resentment with the entitlement she exerted. She even admitted when I was in my thirties that she had tried to control Dede and I and our choices. She stopped doing that, to her credit.

I also joined Toledo Council of Catholic Young Adults, (TCCYA) the Lima chapter, a Catholic singles group. Through this group, I attended a singles retreat at the Franciscan Retreat Center in Carey, Ohio, in April 1969. I had just been laid off from my job at Teledyne. Friday was my last day. The retreat started Friday night.

When I got home from the retreat on Sunday evening, Mom was in the living room. I came in the door and announced, "I think I have met the man I am going to marry." Dede overheard and rushed down the stairs cheering. Mom was silent at first, but the look on her face was exuberant. They wanted ALL the details.

Mom was thrilled at the prospect that I was finally walking down her *preferred aisle*, not simply graduating high school and marching down the aisle to get my diploma.

I recounted my weekend for them as best I could.

Friday night I was sitting there in the lobby with many others waiting for the retreat to start. Some were still arriving and registering at the window. While I sat, I noticed a young man come in who was wearing a nice suit. This stood out because the rest of the guys there were dressed in jeans or other casual attire. The young man was smiling and as he got closer I saw his dimples, both cheeks! I was hooked! He registered and I thought, "I would never have a chance with him. He is so handsome and there are so many girls here."

The lobby was so crowded and there were no places to sit. He finished registering and I saw him look around for a seat. The only seat was directly across from me. He spotted it and slowly made his way around people's feet and sat down. I smiled at him warmly and said, 'hello.' 'Hello,' he smiled back. Oh those dimples were simply irresistible.

Just calm down, Chérie. There are a lot of women here who are very cute, as cute as he.

I tried to ignore that inner voice, but also knew it was true.

"My name is Chérie. What's yours?"

"Benjamin," he said.

He added that he was from Swanton, Ohio and asked where I was from. "Lima," I said.

Then we talked about our local parish and about TCCYA (Toledo Council of Catholic Young Adults). I told him I had been in charge of promoting the retreat in my area. He told me he worked for his dad, a truck farmer.

Finally, one of the Franciscan brothers called the group to come to the cafeteria for the opening of the retreat. I didn't want to be presumptuous, so I didn't attempt to engage Ben in such a way that he would feel I expected him to sit with me. Instead, I prayed *desperately* that he would sit with me just because he wanted to.

I found my seat next to the one on the end of the table. He took the seat next to me. I could hardly breathe.

We were able to continue talking during breaks. The Brother instructed us about the events of the weekend. We were dismissed to go to our rooms and told not to be late for our early breakfast.

That night I continued my desperate prayer that Benjamin would sit with me; that he would like me, prefer me to the others. He was clearly the handsomest young man there so it was almost too much to hope for. It would take a miracle.

God answered my prayer when he sat beside me the next morning for breakfast. He continued to sit with me, for meals, for meetings, and during the breaks we spent time together. He listened as I practiced my guitar in preparation for the Mass. He liked it.

He bought me a necklace I had admired in the retreat center gift shop. It was a round pewter pendant, framing the word "Shalom" and hung on a long chain.

That evening we sat in the lounge area where we had met the night before talking, and he kissed me. Of course, I had made it evident that I would like him to kiss me. When he did kiss me, I thought I would *melt*.

Sunday came too quickly. The final retreat event ended with lunch. We sat in his car and talked. We talked about how eventful we both agreed that this weekend seemed to be for both of us. It seemed like destiny. We kissed good by, after we exchanged addresses and we arranged for him to visit me in Lima the following weekend."

Mom and Dede listened with rapt attention to anything I cared to share about my weekend. I knew Mom thought this was the "one" and I simply felt terrified. I had just met this man on Friday. I had not realized how two days could make such a big difference in my situation. I had just been laid off. Now, my life seemed to be taking a whole new direction. Could things possibly happen so quickly? Would God really move this fast? Was I being foolish?

Mom didn't seem scared. That's OK. I was scared enough for several people, but also excited.

Ben was seven and a half years my senior. I married him on the evening of June 23, 1969, two months later. There was also overt pressure to get married from family members, including my mom and his brother, so we moved forward. His brother's reasoning was, "If you know you are going to get married, why wait?" Ben's mom met his father when she was 18 and he was 32 and after a month, they eloped. My mom was nine years younger than Dad. There was precedence for quick marriages and age spreads on both sides.

I turned 21 on June 21.

We had a small nuptial mass at St. Johns Church. My sister was my Maid of Honor and his brother was Best Man. The reception was held at my parent's house, the house that had belonged to Grandma and Grandpa, the one I grew up in. We had wedding cake, punch, mints and nuts and coffee. We opened our gifts as our guests watched.

Our honeymoon was a one-week trip to Niagara Falls, on the Canadian side. I had wanted to see Niagara Falls ever since I saw the movie "Niagara," starring Marilyn Monroe, on TV.

As I look back, I know I was so naïve. I had no clue the nuances and adjustments involved in working out a true relationship. I could not have known since I had never had one before. As my friend Janet used to say, "You can't put a 40-year-old head on a 20-year-old body." So many things in life, perhaps most things, are learned by the seat of our pants. This was no exception.

I am also baffled when I think of how Mom encouraged me to marry so quickly. As a Mom, I have encouraged anything but moving quickly, but to give it at least a year.

Though Ben and I spent most of our honeymoon arguing, as we had since we met the previous April, we believed that *true love* never runs smooth, (or were perhaps just telling ourselves that). We felt that God had brought us together at just the right time and place in both our lives. We met at a Retreat Center, after all! It HAD to be right. No, that isn't anything that someone more mature would accept as *valid* reasoning, but we *made it work* for us at the time.

Though many mistakes were made both by my ex husband and by myself over the years and though we are now divorced, Ben remains to this day a *precious* friend. We still don't get along very well *sometimes,* at least in some topic areas, like politics. However, he is and will forever be the father of my five children. He is a man of integrity. I respect him. I love him. I have no regrets.

I think that regret is a wasted emotion that robs you of life's joys and impedes present freedom. If you need to say I'm sorry, on the other hand, a *valid* thing, then do so. Know that God has forgiven you so forgive yourself, let it go and move forward. Quit wasting life. I learned this lesson from wasting so much precious time doing the opposite.

How could I regret a relationship that produced my beautiful family?

Dad and Mom came up to visit us frequently when I first got married. Aunt Rene would come also and sometimes Uncle John. A couple of times that summer, they brought the ice cream maker and we enjoyed homemade ice cream.

Dad went with me to the grocery on one visit. I couldn't cook, so I bought cans of Chef Boy-ar-dee ravioli. I bought cans of everything. You didn't have to be able to cook if all you had to do was open a can. Dad stood at the front of the store watching as I loaded the cans on to the conveyor belt to check out. I looked at him and he was smiling and seemed quite amused. He later told mom he had never seen so many cans.

However, the look as he watched me was one of pride. I knew he loved me. It was good to see this.

Five months after getting married, I was pregnant with Rebecca, our first child. We visited my parents.

"Mom, I'm pregnant," I said.

"AAAAAAAAAAAAAAAAAA!" she squealed and clapped. She was pleased.

When I was 4 months along I was at her house when I felt my baby move for the first time. I stood still.

"I just felt the baby move," I announced.

Mom was in front of me immediately, her hand on my emerging belly, and she said, "My grandchild!" Mom was happier than I had ever seen her.

My first child, Rebecca Beatrice, (eight pounds, five ounces), was born August 9, 1970. Beatrice was the name Ben picked, after the heroine, Beatrice, in *Dante's Divine Comedy*.

Cara Ann (nine pounds eight ounces) was born July 12, 1972. Sean Benjamin was born February 6, 1974 (ten pounds seven and a half ounces, and was 22 " long, totally natural childbirth), and my fraternal twins, Daniel Paul and Marcus Joseph were born August 3, 1976, also natural childbirth.

Marc, the second one to emerge was born feet first. At that time, I held the record for the largest twins birthed at Flower Hospital in Sylvania, Ohio. Daniel weighed eight pounds four ounces and Marcus weighed eight pounds six ounces. Though they're twins and brothers, they look nothing alike. Marc was always an inch taller than Daniel, with blond hair. Daniel has dark hair like my natural hair color.

When I was about to deliver Becky, my first child, I was sitting with Mom in her carport relaxing with Grandpa and his current and final girlfriend, Olga. Grandpa was in his early 80's. Olga was from Belgium and she had a heavy French accent. She was somewhat plump, about 5'1" tall and had curly gray hair. She didn't hesitate to voice her opinions. I could tell Grandpa thought she was cute and amusing by the look on his face every time she opened her mouth. I agreed she could be amusing at times.

I, however, was nervous about giving birth. It wasn't until my third child that I took Lamaze classes to help alleviate my fear, though by then it was somewhat second nature. I read a few books on childbirth, but that was not the same as Lamaze. I had not yet heard of Lamaze.

Olga was a self-appointed labor and delivery commentator. She told me about giving birth to her two children.

"I was in so much pain!! ... I screeeemed!" she shouted with her thick accent.

I could not believe she told me that when I was afraid anyway and within days of giving birth. Obviously Olga needed some sensitivity training, and she left my terror in her wake.

A few days later Dede, Ben and I went to the mall to see a Hawaiian dance group and musicians perform. Afterwards, we went across the street to a hot dog place that served hot dogs steamed in beer. Ben wanted a hot dog. Dede and I headed for the restroom.

My water broke.
We headed back to Mom's.

Twenty-three excruciating hours and 10 minutes later I gave birth to eight pound five ounce Rebecca. She was mostly bald but had a little bit of blonde fuzz on her head.

I lived through childbirth, but I also learned one thing. There are times in which the body you know so well *will* betray you. Toward the final part of labor, it also becomes abundantly clear that your husband's male appendage is no longer welcome in your life.

Unlike Olga, in spite of the pain, I labored quietly.

Mom was floating. There was another baby girl in our family for her to spoil. She told me that she wished Becky were hers. I loved my baby but I was also scared. Part of me wished it were Mom's baby as well. I felt so inept and Mom was so capable. I also had a bad bladder infection and didn't feel well. This didn't help.

Chapter 24

"Answers & Questions"

By this time, my beloved Beatles had somehow *betrayed* the seeming purity that had been their beginning in 1964 by turning to the drug culture and a fascination with foreign sounds and bohemian fashions. The Beatles and other artists certainly cannot control the influence their songs may have had, but after listening to one of their later *drug use phase* songs, "Helter Skelter," one psychotic "turned on, tuned in, and dropped out" hippie admirer took his *"transcendence"* to another level. His name was Charles Manson.

On the morning of August 9, 1969, (just one year before I gave birth to Becky), in a mansion located within an exclusive enclave of Los Angeles known as Benedict Canyon five people were murdered. Among those found dead was actress Sharon Tate (wife of film director Roman Polanski). I had seen her in the movie "Valley of the Dolls."

Some bodies were strewn across the estate, but Sharon Tate, who was more than eight months pregnant, lay dead with a rope around her neck on the living room floor. Graffiti found written in blood at the murder scene said, "Death to Pigs."

I was married and soon to be pregnant with Becky, by the time these murders took place, so this was particularly horrifying to me. I thought of this often during my pregnancy.

During this time, I went to my doctor, the one who had also delivered me, Dr. Steiner, in Lima for one of my prenatal check ups. Though I now lived in the Toledo, Ohio area, I wanted to give birth in my hometown in order to be near my mother when the time came. I also know Mom was pleased with my decision.

On this particular doctor visit, as I sat in the crowded waiting room I saw a young man heading up the sidewalk toward the door. He walked with a cane and a limp. From the knee down, his right leg was missing. The young man came in and sat down in the only seat available, across from me. I was 8 months pregnant.

When he looked up, I recognized him. It was David, the boy from my church and school that was so nice that I once had a crush on. He was still handsome. I could see by the look on his face that he recognized me as well. We nodded a greeting.

Though the room was too crowded for personal conversation, I knew without saying anything that he had lost his leg due to injury in Viet Nam. We stared at each other. I think that we were both reflecting on how different our lives had gone since our high school graduation and since our youth fellowship days at church.

David was drafted and went to Nam. He had no wedding ring on. I knew he had seen horrors I didn't want to imagine.

Part of what David experienced in Viet Nam became clearer many years later, after talking with my friend, John Henderson, a retired Army Lt. Col. He was a Marine Private First Class when he served in Viet Nam from April 1968 to April 1969.

John told me that prior to going to Viet Nam they were issued a booklet. They were told that they were going to Viet Nam to support the democracy in South Viet Nam so that they would not be overrun by Communist North Viet Nam.

John's job was combat engineer. A combat engineer does many things, from bridge construction and fortification, to other types of construction, but mostly his 11-man unit combed the roads for mines with a metal detector and defused them.

"Five guys would form a line and look for trip wires a couple inches off the ground. The North Vietnamese were good at camouflage, ambush and had good tactical maneuvers. They used terrorist tactics, small unit warfare," he said.

"We would go in by chopper maybe 10 guys at a time. Choppers landed many times and at different times a day at a landing zone (LZ). The chopper would be on the ground in about five seconds and out. You got out and ran for cover as the Viet Cong (North Viet Namese) would target LZ's. There is elephant grass, which is tall and sharp and easy to hide, but then you couldn't see either. You could run right into VC. Many times air power is the only thing to save units that are trapped."

What John found when he got to Viet Nam was that 90% of the country is made up of peasants who couldn't care less about Communists *or* democracy. They just wanted to live their lives without hassle. The peasants would be friendly to whoever was around, either the VC (Viet Cong) or our troops.

"We would find holes under the floor mats in their hootches (huts) with a cache of weapons. It was hard to tell who was friendly or who was not. We had interpreters. Some South Viet Namese were good and some weren't," John said.

"We had to understand how the Viet Cong thought. It was important not to be in the wrong place at the wrong time. Medics were very important in a platoon. There are 33 men in a platoon and one medic. Often medics were targeted, as that would demoralize the platoon if they were hit.

Medics were guys about 20 years old, who were trained to treat all battleground wounds. They try to stabilize you and treat for shock. They use a triage method, dependent on how badly the soldier was wounded.

1. If they could, they would patch them up and they returned to combat.
2. More seriously wounded are patched up and then medivac'd on a chopper as soon as possible.
3. If they couldn't be saved, they didn't tell them there was no hope, but they shot them up with morphine and they were left to die."

A *combat effective unit* as defined in the Officer Candidate School Handbook is "One that will accomplish any mission assigned or indicated for which it has been organized, equipped and trained to perform in the shortest possible time, with the least expenditure of resources and with least confusion."

Proficiency is defined, "the technical, tactical and physical ability that enables superior performance."

Military Leadership is defined as "The art of influencing and directing men in such a way as to obtain their willing obedience, confidence, respect and loyal cooperation in order to accomplish the mission."

I asked John his thoughts about the war. He said, "It is demoralizing to fight a war that we knew how to fight and win and that we were not fighting under the definition of a *combat effective unit*. If we were going to be in Viet Nam we should have gone in forcefully with strategic bombing. LBJ, (President Johnson), said that pilots couldn't shoot a rocket or missile launcher unless there was a missile on them. The whole thing was asinine. From the outset of the war, our politicians were afraid of China, which is why we didn't go in forcefully to win it."

John suggested a few ways this could have been accomplished. "We had the ability to win without sending in ground troops. We could have held the atomic bomb over their heads. We could have blown the dikes around Hanoi (North Viet Nam capital) and flooded it. But, we also didn't want to come across to the world as non-humanitarian."

Though John feels that we won the war, he said, "We let a developing democracy down in South Viet Nam. A couple years after we left, the Democratic Congress cut off all military hardware supplies to the South Viet Namese who had been maintaining up till then. After that, the North Viet Namese came down and took over. Nixon said 'Peace with honor' but there is no *honor* in defeat. We won *every* battle but the history books say we lost the war. So, what does this say about Washington, D.C.? Almost everything in my Army Leadership Guide was and is violated on the civilian management and political side." He feels the same way now about some current events.

I asked him if we should have gone to Viet Nam. So many people protested that war.

He said, "It wasn't a strategic location for anything. The peasants just didn't care. I really don't think so. The real reasons we went there were obscure."

I then asked him, "If the Viet Nam situation were here today, knowing what you know now and with the same people in place, would you go when you were drafted or would you attempt to go to Canada as some did?

"I wouldn't go to Canada," he said.

"My heart wouldn't be in it, but I would do my best to do my duty as a citizen. It would make me very ill at ease knowing I couldn't achieve victory. It's a total breach of political understanding and terrible decisions by Robert McNamara, the Secretary of Defense."

It is obvious John still has the "willing obedience" and "loyal cooperation" segments of the *military leadership* definition. His "lack of confidence" and "respect" is understandable after all he and so many others went through, due not to military leadership, but due to an inept government and LBJ's insistence on micromanaging military strategies which should have been handled strictly by the military.

I have often wondered if LBJ had toy soldiers as a child and he was reliving his childhood games. Human lives up the anti, making the game even more exciting.

How could *"we the people"* have allowed him to get by with this?

I can only conclude that *we the people* were so mesmerized by the youthful John F. Kennedy and his sweet little family, and Jackie's fashion sense, the *Camelot* we thought they exemplified, that we threw away common sense and had not yet recovered. Perhaps Kennedy would have done things differently than Johnson. Perhaps not.

His choice of Vice-President certainly lacked foresight.

However, he was young and healthy. What could possibly happen? Nobody is perfect. That would include *we the people*.

I think that is something for us to remember today, when someone appears to be *so perfect* as did the young Kennedy with all his charisma and physically appealing family. History does have a way of repeating itself, if we don't learn from it. I know that some find history boring. There are many reasons or excuses for this, of course, and most people don't bother to research it, hard facts which could cause us to think and reason more deeply today.

I find this to be *very* scary.

Mom never said much about the Viet Nam War. She watched the news reports. She had lived through WWII. Perhaps by comparison, Viet Nam seemed too remote. Perhaps she didn't identify with it as part of her life in any way. Perhaps by not discussing it, it somehow lessened the reality of it for her. I think it was this way for many people.

On a personal level, of course, this was how she had approached other things in her life as well. She didn't talk about my birth and natural parentage either.

Chapter 25

"Babies and Discoveries"

The decade of my 20's was spent being pregnant and caring for my little children and trying to recover my health. I had three children in diapers at once when the twins were born. My oldest was five and entered Kindergarten later the same month the twins were born.

Going back to when I was three weeks past my due date for Cara, my second child, I was miserable. It was a very hot summer. Becky, my oldest, was a pretty little blonde with soft curls framing her dimpled (like her daddy) face. I really wanted a boy, since I had a girl and this would be the first grandson on my husband's side of the family. I also wanted a dark-haired child since I had dark hair. I remember sitting in the bathroom while Becky napped.

While I sat, I prayed, "God, is this at least a boy?"

I don't think I expected an answer. Admittedly, my question was more of a rhetorical whine. I was overdue and hot and tired of being pregnant. After I formed this question in my mind, not aloud, I sat a few seconds and was about to get up when I heard words, again not audible, but very clear.

"You will have sons.
But this one is a girl and she has dark hair."
That was all there was to it and I was very surprised!
Was that God?
Well, I'll find out soon enough.

Cara was born a couple days later, after a nine-hour labor, much less than my first labor, which sped up considerably after I was again on the toilet in the hospital and prayed for a quicker labor and delivery. She had dark hair. She was beautiful. My *final three children* were indeed "sons."

Of all my children, my third child, Sean, was the most demanding child as well as being the most challenging pregnancy. During my pregnancy with him, I had morning sickness for seven months at any and all times of day. When I was three months pregnant I was admitted to the hospital, because I couldn't keep anything down. I would feel hungry for something, eat and then a short time later, vomit. The one thing I seemed to be able to keep down was Sunkist oranges. I once ate a five-pound bag of them within 24 hours.

Coupled with that, I carried guilt due to articles I read that said if you were experiencing severe morning sickness, it is because you are subconsciously trying to reject the baby. I didn't think that was so, but in my mind if the article said it there *must* be some truth to it.

I carried a pan with me wherever I went in case I needed it. Nausea would hit unexpectedly at any moment. In the doctor's waiting room, other pregnant women stared at me as I held the large pan in my lap.

Sean and Cara were only 19 months apart. Sean required much attention and even as a newborn, he needed little sleep, so this meant that I didn't get much either. He was alert and seemed aware of everything from the moment he was born. This time I had Lamaze childbirth classes. The labor was 4 hours long and I had natural childbirth. He was my only winter baby. I started labor when Ben was at work in the afternoon and he wasn't going to get off till midnight.

The weather was very cold and there were blizzard conditions. I called my mother-in-law to come over to watch my two little girls. I couldn't get through to Ben at work as the phone lines at the plant were down. Then I called my brother-in-law to come get me. I called the operator and explained my situation. She said she would notify the police in the nearby town where Ben worked and they would go tell him. She called back a short time later to let me know that he would be ready and waiting when I arrived. My mother-in-law and brother-in-law showed up. My contractions were going full force by then but I managed to fix an easy dinner for my girls and my bag was already packed, in preparation for the hospital.

When the two arrived, my brother-in-law put two heavy bags of fertilizer in his trunk so we would have more traction on the snowy roads. By now, the snow was getting deep and it was still coming down hard. I said good-by to my daughters and their grandma. We had to drive slowly due to the slippery conditions.

We finally made it to Ben's workplace. As we made our way back into the plant on the long driveway, I could see the blinking lights of the police patrol car. Then I spotted Ben, his lunch pail in hand talking to the police. He was ready to go.

My brother-in-law moved to the passenger side to let Ben drive, a move they would regret since he knew his car better than Ben and in this weather, he should have stayed in the drivers seat. I was in the back seat doing the breathing exercises I had learned in Lamaze to cope with the contractions I was now having very close together.

I was surprised when the patrol car pulled ahead of us, the lights blinking and headed to the highway as an escort. They went slowly but faster than Ben could handle in his brothers car, so at one point, he slid over to the passenger side as his brother slid over the top of him to the drivers side, both sharing the wheel at one point in the exchange. I kept breathing and took it all in. I felt like I was in a movie and watching it at the same time. It was exciting. It was getting dark and I could see the snow in the headlights. All the cars were moving slow due to the weather.

When we came to a fork on the expressway, the traffic was stopped by another patrol car with his lights blinking. The police had radioed ahead and from this point the police in Toledo would take over since the hospital was in Toledo. They continued to escort us through the snowy city streets.

We finally pulled into the hospital emergency room entrance. The hospital staff was expecting us. The police had thought of everything.

The policeman driving the patrol car got out and headed toward me as I opened my door. He looked worried. I assured him that I was just fine, but the contractions were strong and close. I also thanked him. He looked relieved. I got into the wheelchair.

My doctor had been notified, but in the worsening weather conditions he was having trouble getting to the hospital.

I was safely tucked in the labor room bed. However, I was irritable as I tried to cope with the contractions. I was lying on my side. At one point during a hard contraction, Ben made the mistake of laying his hand lightly on my hip. The pressure was too much and made it more painful. I slapped his hand off with no explanation, as I couldn't talk during the hard contraction. Polite amenities were thrown out the window in order to cope and stay on top of labor.

My doctor had still not arrived.

"Get the nurse; I feel the baby's head coming!" I said to Ben.

The nurses rushed in and quickly wheeled my bed to the delivery room.

Now they have labor and delivery in one very nicely decorated room that looks more like a hotel than a hospital.

Sean was born a few moments later in the labor room bed. Labor and delivery was four hours long and I had no anesthetic. It was a completely natural childbirth. The doctor walked in five minutes after Sean was born wearing his still snowy coat. Ben joined us and met his son for the first time.

The nurses kept talking about how big he was. He looked little to me. Ten pounds, seven and a half ounces and 22 inches long is quite large for a newborn. Each of my babies had gone past the due date and he was about a week overdue. When I visited the hospital nursery a couple days later on one of my hallway walks, there were two male visitors looking in the window at the babies. The nurses had the clear bassinets propped up so visitors could view them better. It made quite a *lineup*.

They observed as I did, *tiny, tinier, little, small, HUGE, tiny, little, small*. One of the men said to the other, "Look at THAT one. He is a football player!" They were talking about Sean who dwarfed the other newborns. I was amused.

I breast fed all my babies. Sean's oldest sister, Becky, had a little problem catching on at first to being breast fed, but I was also inexperienced. My second child was a little easier. However, Sean seemed to know it *all* right from the beginning, sheer and accurate instinct, and needing little help from me other than just being there. The nurse would bring him to me at nursing time and he was not only wide-awake, but his lips were smacking the air in sucking motions hunting for his nourishment. The nurses were amused. He was an *eating machine*.

Sean has always been an excellent eater. As a boy, he enjoyed watching me cook and even joined in on occasion, especially if it was baking Christmas cookies. He is now a 6'1" man with broad shoulders and a muscular thick body. Some things do contain continuity.

Besides caring for my babies, I also spent my 20's dealing with my health problems. I had been having gall bladder attacks. Childbirth *pain* seemed tame by comparison. The nerve endings in the chest area where gallbladder pain is felt are the same nerve endings that are affected when you have a heart attack. Every time I went to the ER, they checked to see if I was having a heart attack.

When Cara, my second child, was eight months old, I had to have emergency gall bladder surgery. They told me if I hadn't had the surgery right then that I would have been dead within 48 hours.

I thought the surgery would end the attacks. Unfortunately, sometimes stones would be trapped in the duct. It felt like I had never had the gall bladder removed. When I had an attack, Ben took me to the ER and they would give me medication to stop the attack, along with pain medication.

On one of my visits to the ER, one doctor not only put me on medication, he also put a tube down my throat and into my stomach. I was told to "keep swallowing and quit whining." The attending nurse looked sympathetic and angry with the doctor's demeanor. He also told me I had *pancreatitis*. When I spoke another time with another doctor, he asked why I thought I had pancreatitis. I told him that is what the other doctor said. He responded, "You do not have pancreatitis." A few years later, I learned that the first doctor who had been so impatient and nasty was dismissed from the hospital. Apparently he didn't have valid credentials.

While I was going through all these health issues, I truly thought I might die. I prayed, "God, am I going to die young? Am I not going to be able to raise my children?"

It was during this challenging time that I met two women who would become lifetime friends. I was 25 years old. Janet and Lois were both quite a bit older than me. They had been friends for several years when I met them. Janet was nurturing to me. Sometimes, when I experienced these attacks, Ben was at work, so I called Janet and she came over to see me through and pray for me. The hour didn't matter. I could call her at 4 AM, or even when Ben was home but needed to sleep. I don't know what I would have done during this time if it hadn't been for Janet. She was a great comfort in a time of great need.

Lois was more of a spiritual mentor. She taught what she knew and she seemed to know quite a bit, from a Biblical standpoint.

Sometimes Lois and Janet would invite me along when they went to the hospital to visit and pray with someone. It felt as though I was in some sort of *training* when I puppy-dogged along with them.

Both Janet and Lois died the same year, months apart. That was a rough year for me, as 2003 was also the year my mother died.

Lois was in hospice care in her home. I finally understood what the death of a true saint meant. She had a visit from her ex-husband, who I also knew. While visiting he began to cry. She brought him up short with "Hey! Quit it now. This is what it is all about you know."

Lois prayed for healing from the cancer. She spoke with me the summer before she died that October. She said, "Cherie, I pray that I will be healed from this. BUT, if God chooses to take me to heaven now, I don't want *anyone* saying God isn't good or that he didn't heal me. This may be the way he chooses to heal me. I am at peace." I believe she told me this so that my own faith would not be in any way derailed by her death and so that I could repeat this to others as needed. I told my daughter, Becky, what Lois told me. Becky said, "Wow! She is really handling this well. She is handling this the way a true Christian should handle it." I agreed.

On October 1, 2003, Lois penned this poem.

Here's my Lord, my Shepherd, my Guide,
We skip across the clouds; on His shoulders I ride.
With my arms around His neck and my hands in His hair,
He says,
"Hang on Lois Ann, we're almost there."

She died October 24, 2003.

Spending time with Lois and Janet and others who were praying for me due to all my physical problems was the best thing I could have done. I had also developed what is now known as agoraphobia, technically "fear of the marketplace." This was before they knew about agoraphobia however. I became reclusive because I thought I would have a panic attack. The long dealings I had with the gall bladder pain and continued pain after the gall bladder removal had set off the panic attacks. My heart beat wildly as I sweat and trembled. I was terrified. I felt I was either dying or going insane. I tried prayer. I knew what the beginnings of an attack felt like. When I felt this coming on, I tried behavior modification with a spiritual slant. I talked out loud to myself that I am a child of God and that nothing can by any means harm me that God is in control of my life and He is supreme. There were several truthful admonitions I spoke besides these. After awhile, I seemed to calm and it would pass till the next time.

One time when the attack began, I headed to my bedroom and lay on the bed with my eyes closed and whispered my prayerful and positive statements. I was quiet for a moment and while I lay there I thought perhaps Ben had come into the bedroom. I felt his hand on my head; the spread of the fingers and the warm pressure so I finally opened my eyes to see what he was doing, assuming he was checking on me.

When I opened my eyes, I was surprised that he was not there. Nobody was there. I lay there for a little longer, the symptoms completely gone.

What had happened?

I felt the hand, the pressure from the hand and the fingers spread on my head very distinctly.

I concluded that it must have been an angel that touched me. How do we explain that which is inexplicable, other than through our faith in God. The Bible says that the only way we can truly reach God is through faith, even faith as small as a mustard seed. I figured I had enough faith to qualify on the mustard seed scale anyway.

Shortly after this, the panic attacks stopped completely. Sean was a one-year-old when I had my *last* attack. I was healed.

Mom later told me that she wished she had simply come to my house and stayed with me when I was going through these rough times. She admitted there was really nothing stopping her. She said she didn't know why she didn't come. She seemed baffled. It never occurred to me to ask her, because I knew she would say that she didn't want to leave Dad that long and I knew she preferred her own house and bed. If Mom had thought more about this, she may have even remembered saying this to me. There had been precedence. When the twins were born and she stayed at my house to help out for a few days, for one example, she seemed to be biting at the bit to leave. She simply stated, "I am going home." I felt lost because I so needed her help. I also loved her company and I felt rejected. I couldn't help but wonder that if my sons had been female, would she have felt differently?

I also knew I had no right to ask her to give up her "life" to "mother" me. God provided the others to meet that need, regardless. And it *was* a *need*, not just a *desire*.

Chapter 26
"Sons"

Twins

The holidays were approaching. As usual I was on top of it doing my shopping early. I was healthy. My family was healthy. All was right with the world.

Ben and I had considered having another baby but three small children were a handful. We didn't want to cross off the possibility of another child at some point so we chose a simple method of birth control. Condoms had always worked for us.

One amorous night while using condoms, I "heard" that still small voice inside that I had heard just prior to Cara's birth, about her having dark hair and that I would have sons. This time I was *asked* one question.

"If I wanted someone to be born now and I wanted them to come through you, would you do this for me?"

My mind sped.

I knew I had a choice to say *yes* or *no*.

I also knew that I couldn't be who I thought I was and claimed to be and say "no" to God, whose voice I thought I was hearing.

"Yes," I said in silent answer.

A few minutes later, Ben and I discovered the condom we had used had a tiny hole in it. He knew it was possible I could be pregnant. I said nothing to him at the time, but I knew *without doubt* that I was pregnant.

Ben slept.

I looked out the window at the backyard. The moon shown brightly outlining the children's swings set. I pondered what had just happened. Then I heard the still small voice again.

"You are pregnant. You will have a son; you will name Daniel Marcus."

At the time I knew I would have a son, but I didn't know about twin sons, although I was given two names. I thought it was a first and middle name. Sometimes perhaps we don't hear clearly and also God only gives us what we can bear. I don't think I could have handled the knowledge that I was carrying twins at that moment.

Toward the end of my pregnancy, it was a hot last week of July. I was huge. I was miserable.

"God, please let this be the last of pregnancies," I prayed.

My obstetrician had ordered me to stay off my feet the last few weeks of my pregnancy. Fortunately, the summer Olympics was on so I entertained myself watching the events.

One morning as I was partially asleep and partially awake, I had a dream. It was just one word repeated over and over.

"Twins. Twins. Twins."

I awoke. I realized that I had this dream a couple other times but had not remembered it upon awakening till now.

Why am I having twin dreams? The doctor didn't say anything about twins.

It wasn't common at the time to do a sonogram unless something was thought to be wrong. My pregnancy had gone relatively smoothly.

A couple days later, I started labor.

I directed Ben to the hospital as he drove. I was doing my Lamaze breathing. When we got to the hospital they told me I was already in transition, the last and hardest phase of labor before birth. My obstetrician had been waiting for me.

My son cried loudly before he was completely born. The nurses were busy cleaning him up, when the doctor said,

"Is there another one in there?"

I looked up at Ben who was beside me and asked, "Is he kidding?" Then I looked into the round mirror positioned so I could see the birth. I saw a tiny foot drop into view.

I was in shock but too excited to dwell on it. I knew I had to get that baby out so I started pushing again. The doctor said nothing. I think he was more shocked than I. He had not had the benefit of twin dreams. Likely he was also concerned that this was breech and he had not been prepared. Breech births are most often C-section births. The babies had been in there like shoes in a shoebox.

I could feel my hipbones parting to accommodate this more difficult birth. It scared me. I thought they might break.

Don't think about. Keep pushing!

It was only two minutes between births, but it seemed much longer. Pushing was much harder.

The doctor grabbed the baby and they began to work, as there had been no initial cry.

"Come on baby!" I heard him say.

I looked at Ben.

I was scared.

Ben looked scared as well.

"WAHHHH! ..."

The baby finally squalled loudly.

I was relieved. It was a boy.

I remembered the two names.

I said, "The first baby will be Daniel, since I had *heard* that name first and the second one is Marcus."

Ben didn't disagree as he liked the names, but was unsure who would be who. He came around though.

The doctors prepared to examine the sacs and placenta to see whether the babies were identical or fraternal.

"They are fraternal," I said. "They don't even look alike."

"Well, just wait to see," the doctor replied.

The tests confirmed what I already knew. They were fraternal twins.

The staff was amazed at how big they were as were the doctors.

Daniel weighed eight pounds four ounces and Marcus weighed eight pounds six ounces. I broke the size record at the hospital for twins.

I also knew the middle names. It was simply there in my head and seemed to be *their* names. Ben was agreeable.

He told me later with tears in his eyes, while in my hospital room, that this was quite an experience.

Daniel Paul and Marcus Joseph were healthy boys. We were blessed.

I now had my "sons."

Labor and delivery had lasted only four hours. I had no anesthetic other than a local, for the episiotomy.

I also had a tubal ligation that same afternoon. Condoms were now banished.

Mom came up to stay for a few days to help. I knew she didn't really want to be here. It was a bittersweet time. I think she came because she saw it as part of her "role" and because she knew if her mom, Mae, was in her place, she would have helped. Though I have no proof of this, other than knowing the type of person she was and from all the stories I have heard about her, Grandma would likely have had a different attitude altogether from my mom.

When the twins were three months old, they caught chicken pox from their siblings. It seemed to be one thing after another. When I look back at this time, I often wonder how I got through it. Yet, when my mother-in-law visited when the twins were a month or two old, she said, "Chérie, you seem happier than I have ever seen you." I was a little surprised but after I thought about it, I knew she was right. Part of it may have been hormones working their magic. I was also spending more time talking to God. He was my companion. How could I not be happy? Ben seemed happier too. He commented to me during this time, "When I get off work, I really look forward to coming home. I just really enjoy being here."

I also had Lois and her husband over during this time as well as several guests and family and they officiated at our baby dedication. How could I not dedicate Daniel and Marcus to God after their conception had been so remarkable? Obedience comes in many forms. Perhaps that was also a key to the simple joy I felt and it had rubbed off on Ben.

The "football player" ...

Sean was an adorable and intelligent child, as all my children were.

The twins were a couple months old and Sean was 2 ½ years old. Sean emerged after his nap one afternoon from his bedroom, but this time he could barely talk and was choking. I reacted quickly. I called his pediatrician. Since he could breathe, I was told to get him to the pediatrician rather than the hospital. We rushed him to the office. I was frantic. Then they told us to take him to the hospital. He had swallowed some sort of quarter-sized piece of metal. We assumed it was a coin from the way the x-ray looked, but it proved to be a plug from an electric box. He had to have been in the basement and brought it upstairs.

After arriving at the hospital, a surgeon was called. The surgery would be very simple. Under general anesthetic, the surgeon would go down the esophagus with instruments and pull the plug out. Though the surgery wasn't complex, when the surgeon was called it was late. He was at a party and said he would be in early in the morning to do the surgery. Since lying down could dislodge the plug, which could mean Sean would choke to death, the staff propped him in a little wheelchair tied in with cloths to sleep for the night. He could also not drink anything or it could cause the plug to dislodge. I stayed with him all night. The nurses had concerned looks on their faces and the one who told me what the surgeon said looked disgusted. I didn't realize it at the time, but I think she was hinting that I could pursue this legally if anything happened to my baby. She hinted that he was drunk at the party. Another doctor should have been called in. On hindsight, I should have insisted on this. I was still naïve in many ways. At that time I thought a person could usually trust doctors.

Sean slept fitfully in the chair and begged for a drink. His lips became chapped he was so dry. I rubbed ice and a cold wet cloth on them to help. When he cried, it caused him to choke, which scared him. It was a miserable night for all. The surgeon finally showed up and did the surgery. It took less than a half hour. When Sean finally awoke, all he did was drink. After a few days, he was discharged.

If this had happened today, there is no way I would be so complacent thinking the hospital staff knows what they are doing. I would more than erupt until I had my child taken care of in the proper way. Hindsight is always 20/20.

Another overly exciting afternoon, I discovered my active, curious little boy had swallowed some flavored children's aspirin. I called the poison control center.

Sean seemed lethargic, but it was also close to his naptime.

"Do you have Syrup of Ipecac?" they asked.

"Yes," I said.

His pediatrician recommended having that on hand in the medicine cabinet.

"Give that to him and watch him closely. This should take care of it."

The ipecac syrup induced vomiting. He vomited hard and I hated having to give it to him but I couldn't take any chances that he had only taken a couple pills. By that evening the crises had passed.

One thing Mom always told me that I agree with completely, "parenting is not for wimps."

Chapter 27

"My sons and Grandma"

I was very proud of all my children. Mom, however, continued her dislike of boys even after I gave birth to boys. She was overtly partial to my daughters and much more harsh when correcting the boys. My girls usually spent a week at Grandmas in summer visiting. Sean wasn't allowed this at as early an age as the girls had been, but eventually he was allowed.

My sons grew up hearing disparaging remarks about men from both my mom and my sister, who had developed her own brand of *hatred*. The word *hatred* is the correct word. When my sister was asked about this she would always reply the same way, "I don't hate men. I am afraid of men and don't trust them, so that is why I react the way I do." Perhaps Mom could have said the same. All I knew was I didn't appreciate the *man bashing* conversations my sons heard regularly when we visited, and said so. When they got old enough to voice their opinions, they told me they hated the way Grandma and Aunt Dede did that. They would be men some day, after all. I told Mom I did not appreciate it. She was neither defensive nor offended. She was, if anything, dismissive. I don't think she saw it as any problem. I can only think that she still thought as she did when I was still living at home, that if she believed something, then I would eventually be persuaded, regardless of what I saw with my own eyes on my little boys faces, which was both shock and pain. This was simply unacceptable. Perhaps she felt that only mothers of little girls could have empathy for their children. Was it OK for little boys to feel bad about themselves simply because they were male any more than it was for girls to feel that way about themselves for being female? It may sound as though this is overstated. I only wish that was true. If I could do things over, I would object even more strongly. It is a fine line between respect for your parent and emotionally protecting your child. The latter has to take precedence.

I know Mom loved her grandsons, in spite of these issues. She told me once that she had corrected Sean about something and later saw his little wallet, which contained pictures. He had turned her picture face down in the plastic window, after her reprimand. She was amused. So was I. He didn't talk back. He employed his own brand of quiet rebellion.

By the time they were men, the boys recalled the times at Grandmas and still expressed resentment. They also knew Grandma loved them, in spite of this.. I explained some of her reasons to them for her feeling the way she did and why she said some of the inappropriate things she said. I told them it had little to do with them. Their relationship with her steadily improved, as they grew older.

Grocery Store Shopping

Ben worked shift work. He worked in quality control. If he worked all night then he needed as much quiet as possible to be able to sleep during the day, so even if he was home, he really wasn't home. I provided almost all childcare.

Shopping for food for seven people was no small achievement. It took forethought and newspaper shopping supplements to both grocery stores in town. If there were big enough bargains at both stores to make it worth my time, then I shopped two stores. I also clipped all the coupons I could find for items we used. I didn't clip coupons for extraneous things, which bit too big a bite into the budget.

Before heading for the store or stores, I carefully made my list according to the layout of the store and noted by the item if I had a coupon for that item, with a "(coup)" note beside it, so I wouldn't forget to use the coupon. I organized my coupons by the layout of each aisle to be more efficient. After I finished all my prep work, I made sure all my children were wearing clothes that were clean and that they were dressed for the weather. The twins were bundled in winter and put into car seats. In summer with less clothing, it made my trips much easier.

The children all liked going to the grocery store, but I didn't like whining crying children in the store. They all knew from experience that if they wandered or put up a fuss that there would be consequences. The consequences usually meant that I would wait until such a time that their dad was available and that child would be left home. If that wasn't practical then it may have been something else they enjoyed or liked to play taken away. Regardless, they knew my rules, and we all enjoyed this outing.

When we arrived at the store I got two carts. Daniel and Marc were placed into the second cart. I pulled this cart as I pushed the other one for the groceries. To ensure the others wouldn't wander, they knew they were to have one hand on the grocery cart at all times.

We started down the first aisle, chatting as we shopped. Occasionally, I would take their suggestions on cereal or some other favored food. I also told them that if all goes smoothly I would get some sort of treat for them.

I checked my list and as an item with a "coup" beside it was checked off, I put that coupon at the bottom of my pile. I was very organized because if I hadn't been and I had to drag two carts and five children all over the store looking for something missed, it was too much of a hassle.

Dan and Marc may have fussed sometimes, which only caused me to work faster as well as to try to calm them. Occasionally I ran out of room in the overloaded grocery cart, to the point where things were falling out and their cart got some of those extras. I had to be careful what extras went in there because if there were items the twins liked, they would begin opening boxes or packages. This is amusing now, but it wasn't then.

People would watch as I made my way around. Some commented. If a child acted up, they got a warning that I would take care of this when we got to the car, if they kept it up. I learned early on that a child knows when you're grocery shopping that you are at their mercy, unless you have a plan. We have all seen a child throwing tantrums in stores while the helpless looking parent is embarrassed as they try to drag the child out. It is the same as when you are on the phone. Children think you are busy and won't make the effort to deal with them. My children were shown differently. I would tell the caller that I would have to call them back. I would hang up and deal with my child. My phone calls were usually peaceful. If we were in the car and somebody decided to pick a fight in the back seat, which also makes it more difficult to concentrate and thus more dangerous, they learned that I wouldn't just yell and that would be it. They had one warning and if I had to pull over, they knew they were not going to like it. Follow through and consistencies eliminated most negative behaviors. They were happy and so was I.

Finally, we were ready to check out. I loaded the groceries and handed the cashier my coupons. My check was always made out ahead of time, except for the amount, to save time.

When we got home, if Ben was available, he helped bring the sacks in. If he wasn't available, I got the children inside first and got them occupied with something while I brought the sacks in. In summer, I used the children's wagon so I could cart more sacks to the door than I could carry without it. Putting everything away took about 15 minutes unless I bought hamburger, since I made that into patties. It saved prep time at meals. I am relating this minutia to emphasize all that was needed all at one time. It was quite a juggling act.

Ben often complained at the high cost I spent on groceries, but I truly didn't see how I could do more than I had been doing.

I got my vindication when a salesman stopped in who tried to sell us a "grocery" plan. He claimed, especially with our large of family, that he could save us "big bucks." We listened. He took our information down to analyze with accuracy.

"How much do you spend a week?

Do you use coupons?

How many gallons of milk do you use a week?"

We used four gallons a week but we sometimes ran out and I had to ask Ben to pick some up.

The questions went on and on. Finally he added everything, and calculated what it would cost from him. He looked surprised, then dejected as he honestly admitted to Ben,

"Based on this, I can't save you anything."

He looked at me.

"You are really doing very well with this, very efficient."

There was a baffled admiration in his voice. He looked at Ben as if to cement what he had already said, "She is really doing a good job."

Ben looked at him, then me.

Ben said very little after that about our grocery expenses.

Looking back at this now, I realize that God truly is our defense. I absolutely believe He sent the grocery salesman to our door, to advocate for me to Ben.

"Thank You, Daddy for Your faithfulness in all things, no matter how seemingly small to everyone else."

Grocery shopping was very different for my mom while I was growing up. If Dad was away on a business trip, Grandpa drove Mom to the store for groceries, since this was before she had learned to drive. When public transportation is adequate and cheap, as were our city busses, unless Mom was grocery shopping, we really didn't need to take a car. When Dede and I were little, we went along and either waited in the car with Grandpa or went in with Mom. After I could read, I sat at the magazine section and looked at comics while Mom shopped. When she got back, I had picked out a comic I wanted. She usually bought me one if I had behaved well.

If Dad was home then he drove and they shopped together for groceries and both put the things away when we got home. This was a weekly routine. I grew up thinking all men helped with these types of things. Imagine my shock when I learned otherwise.

Understandably, I don't think Mom had a full grasp of my daily life as a mom. It was very different having two fairly well behaved, (most of the time) little girls than it was having five mostly noisy very active children close together in age. The latter may be healthier, as well as more the norm for most. I remember when Mom called and she could hear the background sounds, she commented, "Boy your house is noisy!" I hadn't noticed. I was used to it. For the most part, that noise was happy noise.

By the same token, I lived near a larger city than the one in which I grew up and I lived well outside of town. There were no city busses that would come out this far. Not having a car would have been ridiculous. Although Mom got her drivers license after I was grown, one time when she was with me on the expressway belt where I lived and I was driving, she commented, "There is so much traffic! If I had to do this, I would just pull over to the side and wait for somebody to come and get me." I laughed and said,

"No you wouldn't. You'd get used to it." She had a look of fear and doubt on her face.

Chapter 28

"My Three Most Embarrassing Moments"

At age 28, several months after the birth of my twins, I decided that I didn't want to be fat anymore. I was lying on the couch and I felt an inward "nudge" I knew by then to be God. I also knew what it was about. I had to do something about losing weight and I really didn't feel like it. I wasn't willing. I didn't want to do what I knew it would take to lose so much weight. So, I prayed, "Lord, I am willing for You to make me willing to be willing to be willing." That is exactly how far *away* from the task I felt. A day or two later I knew I was willing to be willing to be willing so then I prayed to be willing to be willing. I am sure you see the pattern. Finally, I was willing. I joined Weight Watchers with my friend, Janet.

When I was pregnant with my twins my weight soared to 295 pounds, but six weeks after they were born I had lost 60 pounds. Toxemia was also a factor at that point at the very end of my pregnancy, causing much water retention. I weighed in with Weight Watchers at 275 pounds. Almost two years later I reached my goal weight of 150 pounds but I eventually got down to 144 pounds.

I became a lecturer for Weight Watchers. I worked for them for a year.

While working with them, I had one of my three most embarrassing moments.

1.

It was the Christmas season. I wanted to make the last meeting before Christmas a special one for my class. I wanted them to feel encouraged that they really could make it through the holidays without gaining weight. While I was losing weight, I had been able to lose ten pounds during the holidays.

I baked a festive Weight Watcher refrigerator cake for them to sample. Since I had my class in the back of a lo-cal bakery, I had access to refrigerators for the cake. I also wore a bright red suede-like dress, (which I had sewn myself), with slits along the side and red heels that matched. It was party time! It may have been a little too much *party*.

After I finished the class weigh-ins, I went to the bathroom and then headed out to the bakeshop to get my cake. I was putting it on the decorated table in front of the room and placing things just so, when I overheard one woman to my left behind me whisper to the woman sitting with her, "Well, she must have gone to the restroom." I had a bad feeling. I looked down my left side.

When I had gone to the restroom and pulled up my panty hose, the back of the slit had caught in my pantyhose. I could see my entire exposed leg and knew there was more than that exposed.

I turned around quickly and sat on the table edge, facing my class. Fortunately, there were no men there that night. I wanted to crawl in a hole and disappear. They all laughed. One woman graciously said, "I thought it was a new style." I extricated the entire back of my skirt, which was inside my panty hose, realizing I had been out in the bakeshop to get the cake in that same condition.

We laughed about it and had our meeting and they loved the cake. I am quite sure their holiday was made much merrier every time they repeated the story to friends and relatives. So was mine.

2.

It was this same holiday season and Ben and I decided to take our five children to a Christmas movie at the mall. Since festive clothing can make you feel more Christmassy, we dressed that way. I again had on heels.

Any Mom will tell you to always make your children go to the bathroom before leaving home or before going into a movie, for obvious reasons. I took the girls to the restroom and Ben took the boys. The girls beat the boys since they were younger, and we stood in the lobby waiting for them.

A couple people passed me and grinned but I thought they were just being friendly.

Cara tugged on my dress to get my attention. She was about eight at the time.

"Mommy," she tugged harder.

I looked down. "Yes, Cara?"

She pointed downward toward my shoes. I looked. I saw nothing amiss. She shook her head and pointed behind me. I looked down behind me.

There was at least four feet of toilet paper caught on my heel that I had been dragging ever since we left the restroom.

Another woman looked down and grinned as she passed. "I am living Erma Bombeck's life," I grinned back.

Erma Bombeck, for those who may not know, was a popular humorist at the time that focused on her family for most of her humor.

3.

It was a hot summer day and the company Ben worked for had a special family day planned. All were invited. There was not only plenty of food, but also beer kegs.

The fire brigade had been specially trained for safety at the plant. Ben was part of the group. We got a demonstration of their skills. There was a large pool with water in which to dip their buckets for the bucket brigade, one man passing the buckets swiftly to another to douse the fire they had set for the demonstration. It was impressive. All five of my little children in their cute little shorts outfits were attentive while watching daddy and others put on their show. I wore pink gauze pants with straps and a pink striped t-shirt under it. The six of us stood on the sidelines with everyone else as we watched.

All applauded as they finished.

I noticed one young man I had met previously go over to Ben to talk and I saw them look my direction but I didn't think anything about it.

Then I saw a group of four men that Ben worked with head my direction. They looked determined. They also grinned. It finally occurred to me that they were after me. I could not abandon my kids nor could I outrun them plus I didn't want my kids to be scared, although I felt true fear, even though I knew they wouldn't 'hurt" me.

I had no option left except to sit down as securely as I could and try to bolt myself to the ground. It didn't work. Two guys grabbed my ankles and two grabbed my arms. I screamed but again, I didn't want my children alarmed, which they would have been had I acted truly frightened. I gave up. They carried me to the pool and threw me in.

OK, be a good sport, Chérie.

I sat there a moment and then stood up dripping. I let it drip a moment before stepping over the side of the pool. Onlookers had been amused, but some were now looking down or away. Although that should have set off some alarm in my head, it didn't.

I climbed out and headed back to my kids as they watched. I told them we were going to the car. They came with me. The car was a fairly long walking distance away and I noticed men who passed us would either look away or stare.

By the time we got to the car, Cara said, "Mommy. You can see your underwear through your pants."

I looked down. I was horrified.

GAUZE! NO! NO! Oh NO!

I had the t-shirt on the top so that was ok.

However, my underwear was slightly askew below and there was a little more visible than just underwear, as Cara also pointed out.

She seemed concerned but also smiled.

I don't think I have *ever* been so *totally mortified* in my *entire* life.

I found out later that the guys had gone over to Ben to *ask his permission* to dump me in the pool. He gave his OK.

I am certain they realized Ben is a little naïve, but they were not. They knew gauze would respond to water the way they hoped.

None of them had looked away when I climbed out of the pool.

I was mortified.

Doing my usual comparisons with my mom, I have asked myself if Mom would have ever allowed herself to be in any of the positions above. The movie theatre event would perhaps be the only one. My mom limited her world purposely. She would not have been in front of any group on purpose. She certainly would not have attended any type of work related event with us that Dad's work may have had. He would likely have gone alone, if there had been any such thing. It would not have been questioned but assumed. How could I be so different from her? How? Those questions always followed me.

Chapter 29

"Camping, Clothesline, and Community Theatre"

Camping

We had a pop up camper, which slept eight people, so just the right size for our large family. All of us enjoyed camping most of the time. Sitting around the campfire on a balmy July night roasting marshmallows and simply sharing each other's company was wonderful.

We usually went to central Ohio to Mohican State Park and the trip included canoeing.

When Dan and Marc were about four years old, we took them with us canoeing for the first time. All riders wear life jackets and the water the time of year we were there wasn't over a foot or so deep. The river does have a couple spots where there is relatively mild whitewater. Ben had one canoe, and he had the back control position, with Becky in front and Dan and Marc rode in the middle. I was in the control seat in back in another canoe with Sean and Cara.

We were in whitewater and Ben's canoe went sideways so it was horizontal to my oncoming canoe. I could not get around him. We headed right for the middle of his canoe where Dan and Marc were riding. At first they were just watching us come toward them and watched the swirl of the water. As we neared, Marc's little face crinkled into to one of real concern and he reached his chubby little arm out motioning me off repeating, "Stop! Get away! Stop!" As soon as we bumped them with a mild jolt it moved them around so they were then going the right direction.

I admit that I was a little nervous, but amused at the same time. I didn't think we were in any real danger. We all laughed about it back at camp.

This was the same trip, however, that I jumped out of the canoe in an attempt to keep the canoe from crashing into the trees along the bank. It was stupid, but I was trying to protect my children. Although I managed some control of the canoe, I also banged my knee hard on a rock in the bottom of the three-foot turbulent water. The knee bothered me for some time afterward.

Sean was always at the mercy of his older sisters, whether on a camping trip or at home. They would hold him underwater until he said "uncle" then they briefly pulled him up for air.

They would also tickle him till he said "uncle."

Mom didn't even like to take us to the drive in when we were children since it was outdoors, let alone considering camping. I loved the drive-in and begged to go. We didn't go on a true family vacation until I was in my teens. I was so envious of families who got to travel and see things. I cannot imagine that camping would have ever even made Mom's radar. Camping was something other families did in movies.

I know people and families live differently and like different things. However, I view childhood as a time to explore, and as a parent, to expose your children to different and safe environments, within the family budget of course. Mom and I obviously held divergent views on this.

Clothesline

I had a clothesline and the girls helped me hang out clothes. Sean liked to run between the clothes. Becky and Cara got exasperated with their little brother after warning him to stop running and he didn't. They tackled him and took off his clothes, which they put on the other side of the road.

I looked out the front window to see my spidery-legged little boy, totally naked, gingerly walking across the stones at the edge of the road to cross over to get his clothes. Sean was always doing something to make life interesting.

For example, one day I heard what almost sounded like thunder outside, but I knew it wasn't thunder. I looked out and there was Sean, who was about eight years old at the time, on his bike pedaling as fast as his little legs could move and he was leading a herd of cantering horses. There were probably about 15 horses. This was the "thunder" I heard. He headed his bike into the pine trees lining the side of the drive. The horses wouldn't follow him in there. I was afraid for him but it did look funny.

I asked him about it and he said he was minding his own business taking a bike ride and saw the herd heading right for him, so he quickly turned around and pedaled as fast as he could. If the horses had been galloping, they would have run him down. I didn't even know any people around here had horses, but they had gotten out somehow and the owner eventually showed up to collect them.

One time we heard the bellowing of cows and it was the same thing. I looked out the front window and there was a small herd in our front yard milling around. Though they were not likely dangerous, as a precaution I would not allow my children to go out. The farmer finally arrived and collected them. I was glad Sean didn't have to experience this like he did the horses.

I remember running through the clothesline when I was small and getting reprimanded for it. Occasionally, I helped hang out clothes after I got older. For the most part, however, all things involving housework or laundry, Mom handled. Dad vacuumed and washed dishes when he was home. Though I did not have oodles of siblings, I played with other children in my neighborhood. I never had to deal with cows or horses though.

Community Theatre

With my new weight loss, I had the confidence to try out for a community theatre production of *Camelot*. I was terrified, but excited as well.

I got the part of Morgan Le Fey, aunt of Mordred, nemesis to King Arthur. The part involved little challenge as far as singing. Since I was also in the chorus, there was dancing but it was fun dancing, not a challenge. My costume as Morgan Le Fey was black with a red draping. I held a black cat puppet, which seemed real to the audience as I held it.

This was a dinner theatre. Mom and Dede came to see one of the performances. Mom said she overheard one young woman in the audience telling of her theatre experiences, apparently extensive, and during the performance she made comments to her companion. Some of it was not at all favorable. When I came on, after I was finished she turned to her friend and said, "Now SHE is an actress!" I was flattered.

Some in the play pointed her out as a well-known community theatre actress. It is known in theatre circles that most who are good singers couldn't act their way out a bucket if their life depended on it. Conversely, those who are better actors usually are not as proficient singers.

The woman who did our costumes also acted in many plays when she was younger. She told my Mom, "It is fun to watch Chérie slink across the stage. She is good."

Being in this play was one of the most fun things I did outside of my family activities. It was also a vehicle to edge my way to "independence."

Although Mom would never have desired to do this sort of thing, she seemed to respect my individuality and draw to do it. Mom had finally *allowed* herself to allow me to be grown up. I was 31.

Chapter 30

"Back to School"

After Daniel and Marcus entered school, I decided I would go back to college. I prepared my children by teaching them how to do their own laundry. They caught on, for the most part. I knew that going to school would eliminate much of my time for home tasks.

I applied at Bowling Green State University for spring semester. They replied by sending me a letter asking, in essence, why I wanted to attend since my grades had not been very good so many years ago. They required an essay from me stating my reasons. My comments included an acknowledgement that though my grades were not the best, this was a long time ago and I did not believe the grades indicated my abilities. I was not very motivated then, however I had gained maturity and was now motivated. I received a *conditional* acceptance, in response.

While Dan and Marc were in Kindergarten, I took one class only for spring semester. I took a class in which I figured I would do well. Since I had done well with speech in high school, in particular oral interpretation, I signed up for oral interpretation in the theatre department. I wanted to start out slow as I hadn't been to school for several years. I also declared my major in theatre.

My sister-in-law decided to go to college as well. She took an English composition class. We car-pooled that semester. She went into elementary education.

I was 33 years old. There were not many non-traditional (older) students at that time, but there were a few and I was able to make some friends. I also looked young for my age.

Oral interpretation proved to be an excellent choice. The older graduate assistant teaching the class took me aside after class one day well into the semester.

He said, "I have to grade you on a *completely different* scale than the others. You are so good at this. I like the others to see and hear you because you are an example for them because then they know this is how is it *supposed* to be done. You ought to see the woman who heads the oral interpretation area and tell her I referred you. Next fall, you could do a demo in front of her oral interpretation classes."

I thanked him. I could not believe I had received such a wonderful compliment. I was floating.

He had, however, suggested I take a writing class if I intended to continue college studies. I was *comma* happy. I had to take comp anyway to graduate from there. It was required of all majors.

I received an A for the oral interpretation class, and my *conditional acceptance status* was changed to a full acceptance.

I was determined to redeem my academic past.

If asked, I am sure Mom would have wondered why I felt the need to return to school at this time of life. I don't believe she would have condemned me for it in any way, however. I think she and Ben both had a wait and see attitude. They weren't alone. So did I.

The following fall when Daniel and Marcus were in school for full days, I signed up for a lighter but full time load, and took classes that I figured I could handle OK.

Since I had had an English class at Anderson College at age 18, I was able to defer part of my requirements in English 112. They waived the long research paper since I had done that at Anderson, the one on Timothy O'Leary. I did have to do the several essays, both in class and homework. My writing improved. We had to do a blue book essay for a final. If this didn't pass, then we could possibly flunk the course. I got a B+. One must think and write linearly to do expository writing. I was more of a creative, circular thinker at that point.

I also performed a selection in front of the oral interpretation lecture hall. It went very well. The students applauded. They didn't do that too often. I was beginning to gain a reputation as a *born actress* in the theatre department.

I was also taking Acting I. I received straight A's as I had in oral interpretation, including my final project, which involved directing others and taking part in an approved selection for the class. I chose a scene from "The Burning Bed," a play involving a woman who was almost raped, exacting her revenge on her assailant. It was a challenge most would not have attempted for Acting I. I got an A.

I also made the Dean's List. If I could do it, I am convinced that pretty much anyone who wants it can, regardless of past academic failures. Go for it! What are you waiting for?

Second semester, I tried out for and got a part in Treehouse Troupe, a traveling children's theatre troupe. We went to area elementary schools and performed as well as conducted workshops for the students and constructed our own props. We also received academic credit for this. I was only able to take two other classes along with this one for a full load.

We did a performance of "Pinocchio" and I was *Candlewick*, Pinocchio's friend. For our performance of "Blue Horses" I played *Captain Mercury Wonderstar,* a superhero of sorts. My costume was blue satin boxer shorts with tights, and a tight fitting top with a huge blue satin star trimmed with sequins on my chest. I jumped in at various moments with great aplomb and drama and proclaimed, "I am Captain Mercury Wonderstar!" They children loved it. It was so much fun seeing their star struck faces and giving them autographs as requested.

This was the second semester in a row that I had made the Dean's List.

I was also invited to join the Honor's Student Association along with Alpha Lamda Delta and Golden Key Honor Societies and I could now sign up for honors classes.

I took many honors classes as an undergraduate. They were always more interesting than regular classes. I was like a proverbial sponge with learning. I loved it.

I also decided to change my major to Interpersonal and Public Communication, which has since been changed by the college to Communication.

That summer I decided to take Speech 103 as an independent study. I had hoped I could just test out of it, but it didn't work that way. It was a required class. I had the independent study with the professor who ran the English 103 area, which was extensive. He had written the text for the class.

I met with him on three occasions during the summer. He gave me assignments and then I was tested on them. I had no trouble with this. I got an A.

However, on the final meeting with the professor in his office, I was wearing shorts over my leotard. I had just come from aerobic dance class. I was also eliminating one of my required PE credits in as pleasant a way as I could that summer.

He made sexually charged, inappropriate comments to me, which I am sure he thought were complimentary. I heard after that, that this particular professor had a reputation for hitting on his female graduate assistants and others he worked with closely. I was glad our meetings were complete.

On another occasion, the department head of Communication Disorders, a professor in the speech therapy area of communication studies, was making his way up the stairs as I was going down one day during fall semester. He stopped me. I knew who he was, of course and he asked my name. I answered, "Chérie." He responded, "What a beautiful name! How appropriate for you." I thanked him. He took my elbow. Why don't you come up to my office for a visit," he said, almost gushing with lusty congeniality.

I did not have this professor for any class nor would I ever have him for a class so there was no reason for me to *visit* him for anything. I knew what he had in mind. I told him, "Well, I was just on my way down to the card shop so I have to get going." It was the truth, but he took it as the rejection it also was. He looked as though I had slapped him. The smile disappeared. I made my way downstairs quickly.

Any people in power positions always have the temptation to abuse that power in some way, regardless of the area in which they work, from business to ecclesiastical to academia and all other fields. Some could hold the same position and never be tempted in this way. Humans are very imperfect creatures and those imperfections can sometimes show up in the most unexpected ways. I had learned by this time, not to be at all surprised at the darker side of people.

When I told Mom about my grades she seemed truly pleased. Again, I don't think she could understand my desire, however, to pursue all that I was pursuing, but she tried to be very supportive. I appreciated her support immensely.

Whether you have "support" or not, if you have a dream, it is wise to pursue it fully. Isn't that what life is all about, living fully?

There were so many things always going on, on campus. It was fun to see everything I could squeeze in.

Brother Jed was an evangelist and Sister Cindy was either his sister or his wife, and she accompanied him. She was a sedate young woman who never said anything as Jed spoke. He made his annual appearance on campus in the fall. He drew crowds on the quad that came to listen and to heckle him. He always had an answer for the ones who heckled. I walked up to join the outer circle of students listening to him. I could not understand why he would put himself through this, what I would have considered torture. I also didn't view it as being a successful vehicle to reach his audience in the way I thought he hoped. My perception was that they thought he was silly, over zealous, and a nut case.

I watched him closely. I caught his eye. Perhaps, since I was a little older than the other undergraduates there, he thought I was a plain-clothes campus police there to keep order and to see what he may be up to, interpreting my eye contact to be a warning. Perhaps he recognized something else. I held his gaze. He nodded at me in acknowledgement and continued to preach.

In class events were just as interesting as those outside of class.

Speech class was one of my favorite classes as an undergraduate just as it had been in high school. I consistently earned A's for each of my different types of speeches. Our first speech was a *demonstration* speech so I took my electric pan, whisk, eggs, milk, cheese and not only showed them how to make a French Omelet, but also told them how, using a French accent the whole time.

The professor wrote in his comments, "What verve! Vive magnificence! Voila! An A of course!" I was truly in my element.

For our final speech of fall semester, it was to be a two minute long entertainment speech. The goal was simply to entertain with humor. The more the class laughed, the higher our grade.

After giving it some thought, I knew that the thing college age students are basically most interested in is sex. I decided to tailor my speech around that area knowing the shock effect would bring laughter.

There was a popular TV commercial at that time where a woman sang, "Bring home the bacon, fry it up in the pan, and never let you forget you're a man cause I'm a woman, W O M A N…." Woman was spelled out.

I dressed in my red dress with heels. I remembered to check my back after I went to the restroom this time. I had learned my lesson in front of my Weight Watchers class when this same dress was the one that caught in my panty hose.

I took a frying pan with me as a prop and spoke the words to the song as I gave the class a seductive look.

From the looks on their faces they seemed to be in the expected shock mode. I played the room.

I threw the bottoms to a pair of pajamas that I had bought as another prop on one boys' desk. He jumped back. The class was already laughing. His reaction made it louder.

I stayed in character.

I took out the roll of clear plastic wrap, another prop.

"Meet your hubby at the door wearing nothing but this and the lint in your belly button," I oozed.

One boy was standing up laughing and looking around at the others with a look on his face like "Can you believe this?"

The professor always sat in the back of the room taking notes and writing his critique. At one point his mouth was hanging open. I don't think he could believe it either.

I saved my best for last. Since it was near Christmas, I tucked a candy cane down the top of my dress secured in my bra.

I strutted back toward the professor.

The class was howling by this point, bordering on total pandemonium. He had been looking around at the fun everyone was having but when I started to walk toward him he looked scared and ducked behind his arm.

I waited patiently by his chair till he finally looked up. When he peeked up at me, I reached into my top, and delicately pulled out the candy cane, offered it to him, and said with the sultriest voice I could muster,

"Merry Christmas, Carl."

He took the candy cane and I sat down. One boy was literally on the floor laughing.

The professor's note to me regarding my grade read, "What can I say! A+++++"

Later that week, when I passed him on campus, he stopped me and told me word had gotten around. A colleague teased him about losing control of his class. Many were teasing him. He told me he would keep the candy cane on his desk, as a souvenir.

I asked him later why he had looked so scared when I headed back to him during my speech. He said, "Chérie, I didn't know you as well then. I thought to myself, 'this person would do anything.'" I was amused. By that time, he knew what I already knew which was that I had taken it as far as I would take it, all for the humor.

Years later I ran into him and asked him if he still had the candy cane on his desk. He replied, "It burnt a hole right through the desk. I put it in the drawer."

I was flattered.

All that is necessary for evil to succeed is for good men to do nothing...
Attributed to Edmund Burke

I took *Human Sexuality* one summer session from the Psychology department. It was held in a large tiered lecture hall and there were two graduate assistants in the room, a male and a female, though the male is the one who taught it more so than she and the professor would also teach.

The class covered several things including sexually transmitted diseases (STD's) and social issues. I was sometimes amused by the naiveté of some students' remarks in social science classes, although social sciences were a favorite area of mine and I always did very well. My favorite was sociology and since I was able to take honors classes, it was even better.

One topic that this class covered was abortion. They covered different types of abortion as well as different reasons some women may choose to get an abortion. They covered Sickle cell Anemia, Tay Sachs disease, Downs Syndrome as well as situational reasons a woman might choose abortion. One young female student stated that if she got pregnant she would get an abortion because she just wasn't financially ready to care for a child and she wanted to finish her education. She went on further to say how she envied guys since they *don't really have to think so much about this.*

I sat there listening carefully to each one who spoke for what they thought were good reasons for getting an abortion. I grew more and more uncomfortable. Nobody was saying anything about reasons *not* to get an abortion.

It got down to the last few minutes of class. I was sitting about five rows up from the bottom where the professor stood, so I was close to the front. The lecture hall held about 300 students and it was full.

Dr. R. asked if there were any more comments or questions before the end of class. I had to raise my hand, although I was very uncomfortable being the probable minority in the filled room.

Dr. R pointed to me to speak. I finally found my voice but my throat felt constricted with the emotion that began to increase with every breath. I spoke not only to the professor but also turned around to address the mountain of students behind me.

"I am upset," I began and tears filled my eyes as I tried to regain composure. A pin would have echoed in that room it was so uncharacteristically quiet. There was no movement, no coughs the entire time I spoke.

"I am a little emotional about this but please ignore the tears and listen to my words. I am the mother of five children, the 4th pregnancy being twins," I continued.

"I have listened to all these reasons put forth as viable ones for getting an abortion. Well, gee, before you write off those children born with those diseases, maybe you should talk to some of the parents who have had those children to see if they thought their child's life was valuable regardless of how short of a time they had them rather than assume worthlessness. I am also *pro choice.* To those who have educational commitments or something else you wish to fulfill, perhaps you should be exercising your *right of choice* and be very careful to use efficient birth control. You *do* have *choice.* But once you have exercised *your choice* to have sex, an adult choice, and whether you used birth control or not but became pregnant, that is where your choice ends and the baby's life takes precedence. Part of being an adult is to take responsibility for your own adult choices. Otherwise, perhaps you best choose not to engage in adult activities.

To you, (I looked directly at the young woman who spoke earlier), who envy males their reproductive role; I am proud that I am able to carry a human life and give birth. It is a gift, not a curse.

The closest I have come to heaven on earth is right after the birth of each of my babies. I have two daughters. I hope they don't get pregnant before they should. However, if they do, then I would hope that I would love and support them in such a way that they felt they had the best choice, the unselfish choice to allow their baby its life.

Your choice ends where the baby's life begins.

I am always amused in classes such as this where you are in this little safe haven, this little academic world where you think you have all the answers. This is *not* the real world. This is insulation. Wait till you get out there for a while and deal with making crucial life decisions. This is an artificial world. Don't assume all will later fit neatly in with your preconceived little notions."

I finished. Though tears were streaming down my face at least some of the time that I spoke, my voice held strong. I looked at the professor and mouthed to him "I'm sorry." I was referring to the tears. I saw him watching the class as I spoke. He had a slight smile as he looked at the sea of young faces. He seemed pleased with whatever expressions of thought they wore. The female graduate assistant looked angry. The class filed out at the end of class. The loud noise of conversations and scuffling feet was missing that day. It was total silence.

Both the professor and the male graduate assistant thanked me after class, for speaking up. They both said something similar that the students needed to hear that, needed to hear that living real life and making real decisions can greatly change perspectives. The female graduate assistant continued to look angry, gathered her things and stomped out.

I knew I had done the right thing in speaking up. It was one of those times when though you may be the sole voice of reason and doing the right thing, perhaps you were planted there for that very reason. I felt as though I had passed some *significant test* with flying colors.

I had no clue at that time that some of my words that day would be put to the test later when my teen-age daughter became pregnant. Even if I had known, it would have made no difference. I also learned since then that early feminists (suffragists) were very pro-life. They considered abortion as I do, a convenience for men among other things and that it seems more logical that it would benefit the man. They also believed as I do that it is a privilege to be able to give birth, not to denigrate it as some do. I would think that feminism, to be true to *itself,* would embrace *all that womanhood* offers, not the proclivity to become more asexual and to value traditionally more masculine characteristics as somehow superior. Something somewhere really got turned backwards. Personally, I believe this may have started with more modern day feminists in the sixties who asked not just for equal pay for equal work, a fair request, but took it many steps further toward complete self-absorption. *Finding oneself* became a national past time. The decade of the 80's culminated and fully dotted the collective "i" of me me, more me for many. Abortion, at the bottom line, and statistics will show this is convenience in one form or another. Yes, there are some circumstances that are much weightier; however, the vast majority of abortions are performed due to the *inconvenient result of an unwise decision.*

The summer I took this class, Mom and Dede took a road trip to California and back. Dad stayed home to watch the cats and take care of the house. This was adventure plus for Mom. Mom said that by the time they were on the way home, although she liked the slot machines in Las Vegas, she didn't like non-green landscape. She said until they got back to where things were green again, she had forgotten how to sing. This was literal, not figurative. I was amused. She may have forgotten how to sing, but she finally gave herself permission to go and do, to see what could be seen someplace else. Not since she and Aunt Rene were single and in their twenties had she traveled so well. I was pleased for her. I would really have liked to go, but I liked what I was doing more.

I finally graduated with my Bachelor of Arts degree in communication in August 1986. My family came, including my Mom. I had already been accepted in graduate school. I mean who would ever have thought it? Me, going to grad school? Wow!

"Grad School"

During my graduate year, I moved to Bowling Green and rented an apartment close to campus. Being in close proximity in the winter was a plus as well as being able to be more available to my students and my professors alike as well as the library for research. Daniel and Marcus came with me, and Cara came right after Christmas. Rebecca and Sean chose to stay at home.

I elected to write a thesis rather than simply taking some sort of test on my communications knowledge. The professor that I had given my candy cane speech for as an undergrad was my thesis advisor.

The new professor to the department greeted us in our research methods class with, "Welcome to graduate school, where instead of absorbing knowledge, you will generate knowledge for others." I was impressed.

I call my graduate year, "hell year," for good reason. I took a full load and the papers we were required to write were 10-i5 pages or more per class plus exams. I was teaching 3 undergraduate classes both semesters of Speech 103 as a teaching assistant.

Second semester I had to write a grant proposal to get funds for my thesis research. I got it.

Prior to Christmas, the professors in our department asked all the graduate students to meet at a local restaurant for dinner to celebrate. It was nicely decorated for the holiday in our reserved banquet room. Dr. W., in his late 40's, had been my academic advisor as an undergraduate, as well as teaching my undergrad interpersonal communication class, announced to our table that he had only two students in his entire career that impressed him with their intelligence. "These two women are sitting at this table." He referred to myself and another younger woman. All eyes were on us. I thanked him. I was nothing short of astounded, flattered and embarrassed. His attention only served to raise jealousies from a couple other women in my department. Neither was smiling. They gossiped unceasingly.

Dr. W. had always seemed arrogant. I had dubbed him "peacock" due to his strut. He was also flirtatious with me, so I was always on my guard, but dutifully respectful. I remember one time when I met with him in his office, I said something, in response to a remark he made, about my faith in God. He quickly looked at me and said, "Do you really believe in that?" His question sounded incredulous, but it also had the ring of a true desire for my honest answer. He listened very attentively. I shook my head and answered, "Yes." I was truthful. I may not always have lived the way I feel that a person should live who is attempting to live the right kind of life, but I had no doubt about my beliefs.

Years later, I heard that he had become a sincere Christian and had died after battling cancer.

I decided to do my thesis on "The way males/females, females/females, males/males groups/dyads communicate and empathize with each other." This was an exploratory study, which meant the results might simply indicate criteria for a more official larger study. I used qualitative research methods, which involved hiring several people to do participant observation research and take field notes for me. They received a small stipend for their efforts from my grant money. I gave them a simple training session on what I was looking for. They did a good job for me. My thesis was over 80 pages long. My daughter Cara was a fast typist, so I hired her to type it for me and I paid her what I paid the field workers.

I had no idea that when it came time for my oral defense with my thesis committee that it would be such a grueling two hours on the hot seat, as I proved to them that I truly was the researcher and writer of this thesis. I had chosen the department head and my undergraduate academic advisor, the one who had so complimented me at the holiday party, to be on my thesis committee. My thesis advisor and friend told me after the meeting, "I have no idea what was going on in there." Even he thought it was unnecessarily brutal.

I thought I had it at least partially figured out. The professor I liked, my thesis advisor, was not a popular professor in the department. The students tended to like him, but his colleagues didn't. Unlike others in this department, he was not arrogant; he was genuinely friendly and seemed to care about his students more than simply putting on an appearance of it. This was purely political and there may have also been some *professional* jealousy involved. All this is conjecture of course, but this is what it appeared to be. The other two resented the fact that I had chosen him as my advisor. How dare I prefer this *inferior* guy to them as my thesis advisor? Though I cannot prove it, I think my time on that hot seat would not have been quite so grueling if one of the other two men had been my thesis advisor.

I received my Master of Arts degree in August 1987. My family came, including my mom and sister. We had a small gathering to celebrate. Mom seemed proud. It made me feel happy.

Chapter 31

"Back to Family"

Daniel and Marcus lived with me in Bowling Green, as I stated earlier, while the other children elected to stay at our house. I enrolled Dan and Marc in third grade.

They were outside exploring where they shouldn't be at one point near our apartment. Our landlord came to the door later that night and told me about it. He also told me that my son used some cuss words. I thanked him for telling me.

I went to the boys' bedroom. Marc was in the top bunk. Daniel was already asleep. Marc was leaning up in bed and he knew why I was there. He spoke before I had a chance to reprimand him.

"I know, Mom," he said, talking very fast, "I am sorry I did that. I shouldn't have cussed and don't worry about it. I already washed my mouth out with soap."

His face was full of concern and sincere remorse.

I almost laughed but choked it back. I said, "OK. I am glad you told me that and that you have learned your lesson. Don't let it happen again." He assured me that he wouldn't.

I left the room quickly before he could see how hard it was for me not to laugh. How many children would wash out *their* mouths with soap?

He likely did it to prevent me from doing something. I am also certain, because I knew my son that he did it because he knew he deserved it and was truly sorry.

For second semester, Cara, now age 14 and in ninth grade, decided to move to Bowling Green with us. I enrolled her in her new school and she liked it much better than her old school. I had encouraged all three of my older children to come with me if they wanted, but they had a choice. Cara was having problems with boys at school treating her badly and she seemed to be under much stress and I knew she needed her mother. She did better in

Bowling Green schools. So did Dan and Marc. It was really unfortunate that they had to return to their old school the following year.

Becky had learned her own method of coping at home, she told me. She said that as long as she kept to herself, did her jobs and stayed out of her dad's way, she could pretty much do as she pleased. Ben spent most of his time downstairs in his den doing whatever he wanted, usually working on some project for his job, which is what he did and had basically done since we got married.

Sean preferred the familiar, though he also hated his school and suffered as well from bullies. Due to the fact that he chose to be a good student and chose not to be involved with football, a "sin" at this village school to not choose to be a jock; he was not part of the *in* crowd. He played drums in the band and eventually became head drummer. It was fun going to the games and watching him lead the band out on the field. He had a true talent and flair for percussion and showmanship.

Our marriage had suffered much while I was in school but not directly because I was in school. It had begun long before that. Some might say it had begun when we met.

Ben was an introvert and loved working on his projects. Sometimes he chose to spend time with his family. I know he believed that he loved me. The way he chose to show it or not show it was something I could not comprehend. I felt terribly neglected, alone and unloved. When Ben did talk, he was critical much of the time and had a bad temper. Part of the reason I went back to school was for this reason.

I also wanted to be able to do something more with my life and if something happened, to be able to support my family and myself. I wanted to provide a good academic example to my children. I knew that if I got a degree and went on to get a graduate degree that my children would be more likely to have the confidence to do so. I felt it was giving them a leg up to improve their lives, their future.

Regardless of my reasons, both seemingly viable ones at that time and not so, due to my loneliness, I made some mistakes, totally wrong personal choices of which I regret and have tried to amend as I am able Again, God in His faithfulness *pulled me back.*

Time and a larger perspective have a way of healing some things. Today, Ben and I are true friends.

Mom appeared to be very proud of my college graduation and MA degree. Ben took Mom and my photo together on campus. She had her arm around me and mine was around her. I think she had a hard time understanding exactly why I might want to do it, at least at first. I had, after all, married and had children, so why bother. I believe my suspicions of her *undercurrent* attitude *are a part* of what spurred me to embark on my academic journey. I didn't like and was so wounded by her attitude and comment when I graduated from high school (i.e. "I'll be even happier when you go down another aisle"). She was, however, *always and only* very supportive of my studies once she saw how much I enjoyed them and how well I did. She was mom. I miss her very much.

Chapter 32

"The Girls"

Rebecca

I gave all my children what I term an affectionate name or *play name,* and one which just came out of nowhere but was used to show love to them and tease them. I had done this same thing with my mom when I was an elementary age child. I called her *mom-be-bor-lassa-tiki.* No, it made no sense whatsoever.

My children seemed to like it, or at the least took it in stride, when I used their own nonsensical name. Rebecca's play name was Becky B bug tug-a-lug-dug-wug or Becky B for short.

Becky was in first grade when Ben and I took her twin baby brothers to school for her *show and tell.* Not only did the teacher seem to enjoy it as well as the other children, but also, I shall never forget the look on little Becky's face. She was positively beaming with joy. Little children can be so cruel to each other. They called her "Rooster" at school. She was a quiet little girl except at home where she felt more secure. This was one school day, however, where she got to be *princess* for a while. I still cry when I think back to this time.

How many moms do this, I wonder? I want to turn back the clock, scoop her precious little body into my arms and reassure her of just how much she is and was loved. Having several children sometimes precludes as much individual attention as one might like. This is possibly my largest regret, the lack of individualized attention for each of my children, but possibly more her since she was older and didn't seem to require as much.

Becky suffered from eczema, a skin condition causing a rash and redness, which we had to get crèmes for from the time she was just a few months old. She also eventually had to have an inhaler for asthma. This was much of the reason she did not enjoy camping as much as the others, though there were a few camping trips she did enjoy.

As a toddler to pre-schooler, she called the Maumee River, which is near our house, Big Waa, for Big Water. She had the cutest most airy sounding little voice and when she used her "mature" reasoning ability, she sounded more like an adult than a little girl. We have a tape of one of her conversations with Ben and I. Her daddy asked her if, when we went outside to pull the wagon, she would pull him. She was very matter of fact when she answered the obvious, "No dad-dee I can't do that. I too little."

In the background of this tape, you can hear her one-year-old brother Sean, who was in his high chair and had finished his dinner, yelling "All duh...all duh..." (i.e., all done). He kept getting more adamant. When I talked to Becky on the tape about starting Kindergarten soon, her three-year-old sister, Cara, or Annie, (as I called her by her middle name often), not to be outdone, piped up "I go kinergaten tooo," in her little sing song voice.

Teen age Becky had not been without her *challenges* with boys, as have we all. She, however, didn't get pregnant. She dated a few boys through high school and right after, which I didn't like in any way. They were disrespectful and lived lives I didn't want Becky to be part of. I didn't like them mostly because I didn't like the way they treated her.

Finally, she brought home a young man just out of Marine boot camp, and then a Marine Reservist. Larry was polite to me and seemed to be much nicer to her than any of the others she had dated. This was the first one I liked. I told her this. Her dad liked him as well.

When they decided to get married, she was only 19 and he was 21. That was my only concern. I had a little talk with her about this prior to her wedding. I told her that statistics were against them making it by marrying so young. However, she was of age and there was nothing I could do to stop her and wouldn't anyway. I said that I loved her and said that I hoped she and Larry would be one of those who did make it. I also said that if they didn't, that she was always welcome at home.

This is when I learned that moms who cry at weddings are not just crying for their child's happiness, but also, and perhaps even more, about the child leaving home. Things would be forever different.

As Mom used to often say when she witnessed my challenges, "Parenting is not for wimps."

I asked Becky in recent years about that time before Larry arrived on her scene and the frogs she felt she had to kiss before she found her *prince*. I was feeling very guilty for the time I spent away from home while I was in college, time I could have been more on top of her life. Ben was home physically, but that is not quite the same thing as actual *involvement.*

When I was home, I spent as much time with she and Sean as I could since they chose to stay at the house. She said that even if I had been home more, she would have most likely made the same choices. She was in a rebellious stage. Admittedly, she has always been very hardheaded about almost everything. She comes by that honestly. She hadn't gotten the best grades in school either. She went back to college years after she and Larry were married, earning her degree in Social Work. She worked for a few years, but with the babies coming, she chose to be a stay-at-home Mom. She is now home schooling. She is a dedicated mom and wife. I am very proud of her.

Yes, she followed a similar academic path as I, as far as marriage first but put the children off till after college. She also made some unwise choices.

During this time, Mom was very concerned for her. So was I. It simply was not in any way a path my mom would have chosen, Becky's path or mine. It is difficult to see your child make some of the same mistakes as you have made. If I had been asked at the time whether I thought my mom could ever have lived in such a way as to truly understand first hand any of this, I would have probably laughed. Though I knew she had suffered due to her father, I felt she had not only been a good student, and had a good work ethic, but had been an exemplary young woman in every way

Cara Ann

Cara was a bright, very affectionate little baby and child. She learned how to walk at the age of one and it took me only two weeks to potty train her at two. She wore her heart on her sleeve so I had to be very careful in how I approached her. While potty training her, all I said when she had one accident in her panties was, "We only tinkle in the potty." If only potty training was always that easy. I have pictures of my son's slumped sitting on the potty chair asleep. Becky was also easy to train since we were on a trip and she liked her little yellow travel potty seat.

My play *name* for Cara was *Carbel Annie* most of the time, but it was also lengthened to Carbel warbel weebel wabbel, and for her middle name, Annie, wannie, wing wong dong kong. She thought this was amusing.

Cara was a born leader. My mom once said she thought that Sean would do anything Cara said to do. Cara climbed trees and was the tomboy at school as well as home. Boys chased her at recess and she told me she would gouge their arms with her fingernails to the point where she got skin under her nails. She didn't put up with anything in elementary school. For sixth grade field day, a time parents were invited to watch the events, Cara got first place in every event, beating out all the boys and she got an award. Apparently this doesn't happen too often. It made the village newspaper.

Cara also got the lead in a play the sixth grade performed. I was told that there wasn't anyone in the class better for the role. While performing, her picture was again taken by the village newspaper and was on the front page.

She was a good student throughout school. She also enjoyed playing flute in band.

In seventh grade, she tried out for and got to be a cheerleader. She was a cheerleader for two years. She was physically slow to develop so was very thin and boyish shaped those years. Ninth grade, however, things changed for her. She became subdued. Boys teased her very cruelly about her appearance. She was sad and very stressed. This was when I brought her to live with me in Bowling Green. She did much better there. Perhaps things would have been better for her emotionally if we hadn't had to move back.

Things really started to change. Cara changed from a relatively happy little girl, to a subdued teen. She was troubled. I didn't know what to do except to love her.

Her sophomore year was when she started to hang out with tougher kids, probably in order to ward off teasing. She started to smoke and she drank and became more secretive. We had a wonderful relationship prior to this time. Peer pressure is a very real and negative thing. Her older sister had her own very nonproductive way of trying to survive this time as well. They hung out together. It was a very stressful time for us all. Then everything changed.

When Cara was 15-years-old, her best friend was Tammy. Cara told me that she wanted to spend the night at Tammy's, but that there was a party at a different house first. I dropped the girls off there and I told them to have a good time. We waved good-by.

Later that evening, I had a strange feeling that I needed to check in with Cara. I called Tammy's house. Her mom answered.

"May I speak with Cara? This is Chérie"

Silence.

"Tammy is spending the night there!" her mom said nervously.

Silence.

My stomach clenched.

"I think we have a problem" I said.

We agreed that I would call the police.

The police took a report, Cara's physical description and other pertinent information. I was told that if they showed up, I should call the police department back to let them know.

Cara told me before I dropped them off that Tammy's mom would drop them off at home in the morning.

I sat in a chair in the living room, lights on all night. Becky was in her bedroom but she knew this was trouble with a capital *T*.

I felt sick to my stomach. I wanted to escape this reality but there was nowhere to go. I had to endure. I prayed, of course, and deep down, I just knew she was OK and all would be OK, but until I had her safely home, an element of fear and concern remained as a constant. It was a very difficult night.

It was around 5:00 AM. We heard Cara coming into the yard, walking. I waited. Apparently she didn't question why I was up so early.

"Hi!" She greeted me as she ascended the steps. "Hi!" I answered. I played it as cool as she.

"Tammy's mom had to go to work early so she dropped us off down the road a little ways."

I allowed them to go back to her room. I called the police to let them know she returned and then I called Tammy's mom. She said she would be over to pick her daughter up.

"Girls!" I said. Becky had already spilled the beans so they knew they were in trouble. We waited until Tammy's mom arrived. They left.

"I wanted to go to a party and we knew you wouldn't let us," Cara said in her defense.

The house I had dropped them off at wasn't even the place where there was a party. They walked from there after I drove away. After the party, they had most of the night to kill. There was a pick up truck in front of a house that had been left unlocked. They spent the night in the pick up and then walked home.

"Do you know the police have been looking for you? Do you know how worried we have all been? Do you know how much danger you could have been in? You are grounded for a month. By grounded, I mean you will not only not see Tammy or anyone else; you will not be permitted to even accept a phone call from any friends."

I wanted her to get it that this would not happen again.

Tammy told Cara that her mom talked to her about the incident, but that was it. No grounding. Cara was not happy, but she knew how worried I had been and seemed to know I loved her and that this really was for her own good.

It was 7:15 A.M. The school year had just begun. Cara was a sophomore. She was getting over the flu so when she said she felt sick to her stomach I surmised it was residual flu symptoms. So did she. Almost before I had the thought, it was out of my mouth. I said it teasingly.

"Gee, Cara, if I didn't know you were still a virgin I would say you're having morning sickness." I laughed.

Perhaps *something* in me just knew. God prepares you for what you need to know.

A couple weeks later, with her grounding long over, Cara was going to spend the night at Tammy's.

Tammy's mom was taking them to town to get pizza and a few things at the store after she picked Cara up, then they were going back to Tammy's house. She had been gone a little over an hour when the phone rang. I answered.

"Hello."

"Mom?" It was Cara.

"Yes."

She began to cry.

"What's wrong?" I said, now alarmed.

"Can you come to Swanton to pick me up?"

Swanton is about a 15-minute drive from my house, and where they had gone for pizza and to the store.

"Yes of course I can. Where are you?"

She started to bawl.

"I was arrested. I'm at the police station."

My knees buckled. Cara had never committed any crime. This was not like her. I felt there had to be some mistake.

"What were you arrested for?"

She bawled, "I don't want to tell you!"

"Cara, I'm going to find out anyway. You may as well tell me and I'll be right there."

"I was caught shoplifting at Rite Aid."

I was stunned.

"What did you take?"

More loud weeping.

"A pregnancy test."

We hung up. I hurried to the police station. The policeman was very nice. There were no charges. He said, "If she took a pregnancy test she may have more problems than this."

On the ride home she told me she took the pregnancy test at the drug store, because she didn't have enough money for both the pizza and the test. She was scared and very embarrassed.

We talked at length. Her father overheard us. He was very quiet.

"Mom," she said, "when you teased me that morning about morning sickness I got scared. I had already missed a period. I decided to find out for sure. If I had not gotten caught, I would have taken the pregnancy test and had an abortion. You would never have known about it."

At that time, abortions were available for minors and they did not have to notify the parents in any way. I told her that we should not cross any bridge till we come to it. Let's find out what we are dealing with. We both cried. I held her and told her I loved her. I tried to stay calm, for her sake. Although she was scared, she was also relieved. She was no longer carrying her burden in the same way. Mommy was sharing it with her.

I called her pediatrician and they made an appointment for her at the hospital for her to have a pregnancy test. It was positive.

Cara thought she wanted an abortion. I scheduled an appointment with a family counselor. Cara, her father, and myself went.

The counselor questioned all three of us. It was difficult and wrenching for us all. The counselor suggested to Cara, "You have known about your possible pregnancy for some time now. Your parents just found out about it. You are in the earliest stages of your pregnancy and you have time. Give this a week. Allow them to get used to this. Will you do this?" "I will wait a week," Cara answered. It was also a way for Cara to step back and evaluate options rather than having a knee jerk response that she would likely regret the rest of her life. Some things cannot be undone, no matter how much you may want to do so. I knew my child and at 15, she was still a child. I did not want her to agonize in the long term over a wrong decision, made under duress. "It is too important a decision to take lightly," I told her.

There was a teenage girl a few years older than Cara, who lived across the road. She had a baby boy at the age of 15. I called our neighbors to see if she might meet with Cara and I about her own experience.

We sat outside on lawn chairs. The young mom, Yvette, told us that she had never considered abortion. She said, "I had friends who had them. What I noticed after my son was born and these friends would visit is that they would leave in tears. They regretted the abortion decision they had made."

Cara had two forces pulling at her. Her friend Tammy had had an abortion and was urging her to do so. Then there was

Yvette. She was doing well, with her parents support. The father was not involved.

Cara had already broken up with the boy who fathered her baby. He drank and smoked pot. She had made a wise choice. Cara also knew that her father and I would be there for her every step of the way. I also offered to adopt her baby if that is what she would prefer.

She decided not to have the abortion.

RELIEF!

I made an appointment with a counselor at a home for unwed teen moms. They offered childbirth classes there even if you were not a resident and I thought this would be a better class atmosphere than to go to a regular Lamaze class with mostly couples there who would likely be much older than she. I wanted her to be as comfortable as possible.

The counselor showed us around and told us where the class would be held when Cara was further along. We went back to her office. She told us that most of the girls living there had parents or guardians who wanted them to get an abortion and they didn't want to go that route, so they were thrown out. They had much fewer options than Cara. I admire those girls for making this hard choice to allow their babies to live whether they intended to keep them or not.

There are also other pro-life agencies that will assist girls in Cara's position. In my own area is The Pregnancy Center geared to this very population. Concerned people may donate money and supplies. Hospitals and other facilities also have a *no questions asked* drop off of newborns. This helps alleviate some of the anguish and pressure of a girl who has given birth on her own and doesn't know what to do with her baby. She now has this wonderful option instead of some trashcan choice she may have made otherwise.

The counselor at the home also told me that I was a most *unusual mother*. At the end of our session with her, she said, "Congratulations!" as she smiled sincerely. We thanked her. It was the first time someone had said something truly positive to us and I hadn't fully realized until she commented how tense I was. I felt immediately more relaxed and felt a flood of joy surged at the warmth of her words and smile. It was as though God smiled His blessing on what we were doing and us.

Cara seemed happier also after this. It was not going to be the end of her world. She was loved and she knew it. Most of all, she knew she wasn't alone.

She asked me to be her labor and delivery coach. I agreed.

Cara was in her junior year of high school. The other students were supportive of her. The school counselor was supportive as well. During the second half of the school year, however, we arranged for her to be tutored at home so that she would not have to navigate the stairs and all the commotion on those stairs and the hallways when she became more ungainly. Her tutor was also a wonderful support and Cara seemed to thrive being at home. Ironically, it was a wonderful time for everyone.

I gave a baby shower for her in the spring. We enjoyed shopping for a special dress for this event. I bought her a dress at Sears, which was styled with room but was not a maternity outfit. It was a navy blue and white georgette dress with ruffles at the bottom and she wore pearls. She looked truly lovely and seemed happy and enjoyed the shower. Mom and Dede came up for this event. I had no idea, of course, at the time, how much this resembled Mom's own story although Cara was much younger (a child herself) and Cara's pregnancy was unintentional.

Cara told us about the natural father of her baby. I had met him a few times during the month Cara dated him. She broke up with him before she knew she was pregnant. He drank and drove and he smoked pot. He was also very possessive of her. In many ways, he was not different from other boys she had dated and that Becky was dating during this time. Due to his negative habits and immaturity at age 18, she concluded after we had discussed it, that it would be best if he were not informed at this time about the baby. He was not aware she was pregnant.

Mom had some input to this, which, in light of her own decisions about me probably seemed like déjà vu for her. She said, "You would be worried every time he took the baby for a weekend." She was right, of course.

Months later Cara and I attended Lamaze classes at the home for unwed teen moms. It was the right decision. Most of the class consisted of black girls. Since the area the home was located in had a high African-American population, this is likely why. All were friendly to us. We all seemed to be in the same boat on the surface, but I knew differently and I know they knew.

I noticed that some of them looked curiously first at Cara, then at me. They knew I was her Mom. Initially, they were a little tentative with me. Honestly, I don't think they knew what to make of us. Their situations were so vastly different.

I have no way of knowing this, but I felt it a few times there. They looked at me with sweet little smiles, children themselves, and I knew they wished either that I was their mom or that their mom was there and felt the same as I.

I never said anything to Cara about this. I wanted to cry, and to hug them and tell them that somehow, some way, it would be OK. The only thing I could do was to be nice to them and do right by own child. They were certainly doing what they felt was right by theirs. What a helpless feeling, just one more lesson that life is not fair. And you can only do what you can do.

My baby girl gave birth to her baby girl in early May 1989. The nurses commented how well she did especially considering she was only 16 years old. She labored better than many 30 year olds. It was difficult for me watching her go through childbirth. At one point toward the last part of labor, although she had had an epidural, she looked up at me with tears in her pleading scared eyes, and said, "Mommy."

She had not called me *Mommy* since she was about 5. I almost lost it. In seconds I traveled through a maze of thoughts arriving at our Lamaze training versus being a Mom, and I knew that if I lost it at that point, she would as well and it would not be good for her. I quickly pulled it together.

"You can do this. It is going to be OK. Lets' breathe," I answered her.

I saw the look in her eyes change from fear to a new resolve of confidence. I told her she could do this so she could.

Victoria was born minutes later.

We were jubilant, ecstatic, and joyful. The celebratory atmosphere was so very welcome after everything that brought us to this point.

What comes to mind is the verse in scripture that what the devil intends for harm, God turns to good. Cara had been on a road, which could have ended in tragedy. She was drinking, as many teens do. Her schoolwork was suffering and she was not happy. She was running from life. Through this time, this experience, she was reassured of just how precious she is, how loved, and her schoolwork improved. During her senior year she continued playing her flute in band, including at the football games. What a fun time those were, along with the band shows we attended. She also had a major role in the school play. I wanted her to enjoy her senior year. Basically, Cara's life got on track.

I cared for Victoria, but I made sure Cara took responsibility as well. She breast-fed and used a breast pump to fill bottles in her absence. We had some challenges. It was difficult for me as an experienced mom not to try to take over. It was a difficult balancing act for her as well. Strangers thought the baby was mine, naturally, and that Cara was the sister.

My own reward was when I saw her "senior book." On the page titled "My Best Friend" she wrote about me. I cried when I saw it. This Mom stuff can be challenging sometimes. Then you have moments like this and the challenges recede. They are not so important after all. Love is all that matters, in everything.

Cara is now happily married to her high school sweetheart. Prior to her marriage, we continued our routine of alternating care for little Vickie while Cara completed her degree in education at Bowling Green State University. She is a middle school social studies teacher. She loves history. She was married after her college graduation and after her fiancé got out of the Navy.

When Vickie was five-years-old, Cara had dreams of Vickie's biological father and in the dream all went well. We talked and I supported her decision to tell him. My mother did not.

I said to Mom, "Cara feels it is the right thing to do now. I agree. He has a right to know and Vickie has a right to see him if she *cares* to do that."

We went round and round on this. Knowing what I know now about my own beginnings and how all things were kept a secret by all to my mom's grave, for her to feel any differently when it came to Vickie, would probably have forced her to rethink her own decision. That would have caused her much cognitive dissonance, and I don't think she could have handled it.

Cara contacted the young man. They met at a park. He came and bluntly asked, "Did you have a boy or a girl?" What else would an old girlfriend want to meet with him about, after all?

We had a big family picnic at a park shelter house, his family and ours. They were a friendly group. Vickie got to know her grandparents on his side and liked them, as well as several cousins. He wanted Cara to change Victoria's last name to his, but it was decided she would keep Cara's name.

We thought it was going to work but it wasn't to be. As she got older, Vickie shared that her "father" was still drinking and smoking pot. He was once arrested when she was with him. It was a terrible time for her. Finally, when she was in her mid teens she refused to go for visits though he still lived with his parents. He tried to persuade Cara to force her, but she refused to allow Victoria to be put into that position ever again.

Life has been more peaceful for all ever since. My mom, to her credit, resisted saying, "I told you so." During the years prior to the upheaval, she said on more than one occasion that Allen, Cara's husband, is Victoria's *real* father. Again, Mom's attitude was much more understandable now that we all know how she handled things for herself and my adoptive father, who she chose to lead me to believe, was my natural father.

I only wish she had been open and honest with me. My daughters have told me that they wish that as well. Becky said, "I feel as though we only knew one little part of Grandma." I think it is safe to say that the three of us would have felt much less *soiled* had we known Mom's true story. The three of us have made unwise choices about males. I think we all may have unconsciously compared ourselves with Mom and found ourselves so lacking. It could have helped us all to learn she really was human and made her own errors in judgment regardless of the motivation. I also think we would all have had a better relationship with her to have known, or perhaps I should say a more honest one, especially me. As it was, I think we collectively felt that Mom could only empathize from a lofty position of moral superiority afar, but not in reality. How can a person feel "right" or "good" about who they are, next to someone who did it all the "right" way in spite of having a father like Grandpa?

Chapter 33
"The Boys"

Sean Benjamin

Sean or my *affection play name*-Sean-taunawaun don taun, was the only one of my children who enjoyed baking Christmas cookies, as well as decorating them. In fact, he was interested in cooking in general. Many times, he stood watching while I was at the stove, but never more than for Christmas cookies. White Velvet Cut-Outs were our family favorite, sugar cookies with cream cheese as one of the ingredients. It still remains as the single best sugar cookie I have ever tasted.

Decorating the festive shapes of stars, reindeer, wreaths, candy canes, Santa's and Christmas trees was something all enjoyed. I bought tubs of white frosting and used food coloring to make red and green. I also bought red and green sugars to top them off. The cookies were spread over the top of our large table and on the counter on paper towels. The children were pretty good about taking turns with the colorful tubs of icing. After the decorating was complete, Ben liked to take a picture to commemorate the yearly event. Each child got to sample some cookies and I stored the rest in containers and put them in the refrigerator. The cookies, though we made several dozen, didn't seem to last long. My now adult son, Marc, laughingly calls them "crack," exemplifying his continued inability to resist them.

One early December day, Sean was moping and when I asked him what was wrong he said, "I'm bored. And Christmas isn't as fun as it used to be either." We had not yet made cookies that year and it was close enough, so I said to him, "Do you wanna make Christmas cookies?" Immediately his face brightened and he was eager for the task. His boredom vanished and all was right in Sean's world once again.

Looking back, I think much of his seeming moodiness was due to stress on the school bus and at school, cruel teasing. Home was his haven. He could be his intelligent self without fear of criticism.

As a baby, he was absolutely delightful and funny. He was smiley and happy most of the time, but did not hesitate to let you know if there was something with which he was displeased. He never required much sleep, not even as a newborn. He gave up two naps a day early. He loved to eat as much as anything else. I nursed him till he was ten months old. I quit when he was cutting teeth and tried to use me for teething.

He also required much attention from me and by the age of two, I often walked with him hanging on to my leg.

I remember one time while visiting my parents, Sean was probably about eight months old and he wanted my attention as usual. I was tired and wanted to just sit, relax and not be bothered. However, when he fussed I held him. I also started playing with him. Mom observed and said in a disapproving tone, "What are you doing that for?"

I responded, "Well, I may as well enjoy it."

Right or wrong, I don't believe she would have reacted the same way if my baby had been a girl.

At the age of three and four, Sean was fascinated with little square colorful wooden people made by a popular children's toy company. I got tired of having those all over the house and it also hurt when you stepped on one. I remedied that by giving him one of my old large purses. He balked at the idea of it being a purse, at first, so I told him it was his "briefcase." This was acceptable to his burgeoning male ego. He was rarely without his briefcase wherever we went and it skimmed the floor as he carried it with the straps on his little shoulder.

When he was four years old, he and his sisters were sitting at the kitchen table as I cooked dinner at the stove. My back was to them. Part of the food was already on the table. My "mom sensor" told me it was too quiet and they were doing something they shouldn't. I took a stab at it and said, "You guys stay out of the food." There was a pregnant pause and little Sean asked incredulously, "How did you know we were getting into the food?" I decided to play with him. Well, Sean, I have eyes in the back of my head. All moms do." This wasn't entirely untrue. My mom told me the same thing and I always sort of believed it.

Of course Sean immediately came over and wanted to see them. I told him, "They are invisible." He looked at Cara. It seemed like he was skeptical but also admiring, just in case.

That same day he asked, "Mom, what was I when I was a black boy?" I answered, "Gee, Sean, I didn't know you were ever a black boy. Was I your Mom?" He seriously thought about it, his brow crinkled with the effort, and answered, "A black mom was my mom."

When I asked if that was I, he wasn't sure. Some will say that is evidence for reincarnation. Others are more likely to think it is the vivid imagination of a wonderful little boy.

Sean was a generally happy little boy although he took everything very seriously and became less happy when he started school.

When Sean was in first grade, as the school bus drove up one morning to pick up the kids, the girls were already out the door, but Sean adamantly refused to go to school. No matter how much I talked he was adamant in his refusal and I could see how torn he was. He wanted to obey me, but whatever was bothering him was greater than this. I allowed the bus to leave without him and called his teacher to make an appointment. This was serious.

I told her what was going on at home. She looked genuinely concerned. She admitted some of the kids had made cruel remarks so she decided to move his seat and had a talk with the class about how to treat others. I hoped this would work. She told me to call her right away if anything else came up.

Sean learned things the way his dad and his uncle learned things, slowly. He wasn't satisfied to know facts; he wanted to understand those facts and all behind them. I am sure he appeared slow to the other children who were more immediate by nature, more social, talked more and had less need to analyze things. I think most of us are like this; more surface-oriented most of the time. Sean didn't know how to be a surface person. He was deep and intelligent from the time he was born. I saw it in his eyes.

I shared with his teacher about Ben's brother, Sean's uncle. Uncle Joe had two majors from The Ohio State University in mathematics and civil engineering. While getting his degree, he not only worked a job, he also graduated at the top of his class. He wanted to be a pilot in the military and Astronaut/Senator John Glenn put in a good word for him, but due to childhood asthma, he wasn't accepted, though there had been no recurrence as an adult.

Apparently his IQ was high enough that he has to fill out paperwork from time to time for the government and they have tracked him all his life. Additionally, Ben had been valedictorian of his high school class. He also was and is a very scientifically minded person. Sean inherited those talents.

I gave it some time and asked Sean if it had improved. He said, "Yes." At the teacher's recommendation, he also began seeing the speech therapist twice a week, not because of any impediment, but so he could communicate with her and perhaps improve his social skills.

I also spent time with him each night and we read from his book. I had him read to me "with expression" and this seemed to improve his reading and communication skills, though he didn't like reading till he was in 5th grade.

When I went for Open House when Sean was in fourth grade, his teacher took me aside.

"Sean is very good at math."

I thanked her.

She looked serious and repeated, more firmly,

"No, I mean he is REALLY good at math! Genius level."

She wanted me to *get it*. I *got it*.

This was the reverse reaction of the initial teacher he had in third grade who, because he was quiet and took longer to express himself in reading and English, she deduced he was not intelligent enough to keep up with her advanced level class, so she recommended we put him in a lower level class. Though I knew he was intelligent and perfectly able to do this work and then some, I also knew this was a personality clash, and that this teacher was not open to different learning styles. This woman reminded me a lot of my first grade teacher who put me in the lowest reading group. I placed him in the middle level class. He got straight A's. When I met with this teacher she said, "He is so intelligent and way beyond this level. He should be in the higher class."

This was something I already knew and told her so. She shook her head. She also agreed it was probably better for him emotionally not to have to endure put-downs from the other teacher. The following year he was back in the higher-level class and got his usual A's.

For all parents who have concerns about their children in some way when they are small, know that if you do your part with them, love them and respect their uniqueness as human beings, whether they get A's or F's, they really will be OK in the long run.

By the time Sean was in the older primary grades and upward, he had saved his money and if his siblings borrowed from him, he charged them a high interest rate and even insisted on collateral. He was business minded from the start.

He also tracked the weather like a meteorologist and kept the information on his bulletin board. Each day his markings would change.

I think Mom learned by now to appreciate her grandson's uniqueness. She didn't say much, but from the way she conversed with him, I could tell she was impressed.

Sean started a latch hook project when he was around eight years old from a kit I bought him. I thought it would be a good learning tool. It was easy enough to do but it took time to complete. When completed, he would have a small latch hook rug with Snoopy, the dog from the Peanuts comic strip, riding a scooter.

Sean began the project but after a half hour he said, "This is hard." He meant it was going to take awhile.
"I'll never get done," he added.

I suggested that instead of trying to do so much at once, which would make him get tired of it and then quit altogether, that he should just do two rows a day, no more. Eventually, the project would get done. He decided to take my advice. He was persistent and he did get done. He was as proud of finishing, as he was pleased with the rug, I think. He had learned a valuable lesson. Persistence pays off.

Later, this lesson likely contributed to him persisting in getting his college Business degree that normally takes about five years to complete when going full time. Instead he had to work, go to school, got married, bought a house, took time off, both he and his beautiful wife working all the while, and then went to school some more. He persisted for about fifteen years to reach this well-earned goal.

Once when he was about nine or ten years old, I spent a few days in Lima at my mom's, along with my girls, while Sean, Daniel and Marc stayed with Ben. I think Mom was having garage sales and I wanted to be involved.

After a day or so, Ben told me Sean asked him how long it would be till I got home.

Ben answered him and then Sean asked, "Dad, do you love Mom?"

"Yes, Sean, I do."

"Do you miss her?"

"Yes, but she will be home very soon."

"Boy, I sure do too. I sure will be glad when she gets home," Sean answered.

There are no words to express how wonderful it is to be loved and to be missed.

The Twins:
Daniel Paul and Marcus Joseph

Daniel and Marcus were two very different little boys right from the beginning. They also looked nothing alike, though they had shared the womb.

Dan, older than Marc by two minutes, was a sweet, good-natured baby. My play *name* for him was *Dandie.*

Marc (Marky, play name of Marky Naks) was also a sweet baby but he got into more things than Daniel. I am aware of studies done on identical twins, if not also fraternal, where they have their own twin language. The only thing I witnessed which was a form of negative communication was when they got angry and bit each other. It was quite serious after a time. They would be bruised. I did everything I knew to do. When I took them for check ups at their pediatrician they looked at me as if to say, "what are you doing to these poor babies, mother?" I explained that they bit each other. The pediatricians were of little help in this, no real suggestions as to how to stop it. I did what I could to separate them, and admonish them not so gently. Eventually, they got old enough to get it and remember it and the biting phase passed.

We attended a grade school performance that Becky was in, at the high school Little Theatre when Daniel and Marc were three. We sat in the cushioned seats waiting for the performance to begin. I dressed my small sons in trousers, a nice clean shirt and little vests. They looked like the adorable little men that they were. Ben held Daniel and I was holding Marc. A man was sitting next to me. Marc watched him and when the man glanced his way, Marc said in his most amiable and friendly business like voice, "Hi! My name is Marcus. What's yours?" The man was amused, as I was. You would have thought Marc was a 30-year-old public speaker he spoke with such poise. The man replied "Well, hi Marcus. It's nice to meet you." He held out his hand for Marc to shake, which Marc did without any hesitation. Sometimes you wonder, as a parent, where your children pick this up at such a tender age.

This was also the age Marc was when I was awakened in the middle of the night. Dan, Marc and Sean slept in the bedroom downstairs. My bedroom was dark but something woke me. I thought I saw and heard movement near my bed, so I concentrated on trying to see what was there. I thought I glimpsed blond hair in the darkness.

I said, "Marc? Is that you?"

"Mom," he answered in whispers but with a concerned tone. He didn't want me to be angry with him for being there and he had waited patiently on the floor till I woke without saying anything.

"Mom," he repeated. "You know my room down there?"

"Yes," I said.

"Well, my room down there; there's a lotta dark down there."

I was amused and touched. "Marc, would you like to crawl in bed with mommy for awhile?"

I saw him shake his head and he crawled into bed as I held the blankets open for him. I covered my little boy up and cuddled him. I could tell he had gotten cold and I wondered how long he had been sitting there. I also wonder if he had planned to just sit there all night if I hadn't gotten awake. Regardless, he cuddled in and seemed relieved and comforted. He fell asleep within a couple minutes. I enjoyed holding him close. All was right again with his little world, and mine.

When Dan and Marc were four-years-old, I began *learning times* with them. I painted colorful shapes on the basement floor to help them learn both colors and shapes. We worked on several little projects. For Valentine's Day, we decorated shoeboxes to look like mailboxes. They seemed to enjoy these activities but it also showed me that I lacked the patience necessary to continue this. Home schooling was just beginning at that time, and it did not receive the quality support that it does today. Due to this, although I would have liked to do this, I didn't feel confident that it was the best for them. Their birthdays were in August and this was considered a late birthday for school. Kindergarten Clinic was held in the spring to determine whether the child is ready for school. They weren't. So, I enrolled them in a pre-school held in a Lutheran Church. They went three times a week and seemed to enjoy this experience. At the end of the year, the school held a little graduation ceremony with the children wearing miniature white caps with tassels and received a scroll stating they completed nursery school. It was held in the high school on stage. The little children looked very cute. More importantly, they obviously felt positive about themselves. If only that self worth could have been maintained, things may have been smoother..

At age five, Dan and Marc took a camera I had laying out. I didn't know about it as it had been carefully returned. When I got the film developed, there were some unexpected ones there. There were extreme close-ups of Dan's smile, of Marc's smiling face, of the corner of Dan's eye and partial smile, of Marc's fingers and more. They had taken pictures of each other and of themselves. I showed them the pictures and asked them about it. They could hardly deny it with this proof. I just told them not to do it again. They didn't. However, those pictures are now precious mementos.

Unlike Sean, Daniel and Marc not only hated school overall, but they also didn't do well academically. They were the antithesis of Sean academically. I had more than one teacher tell me that Marc loved to daydream. He stared out the window. He was not motivated. It was similar to what the teachers had said about me.

In junior high they caved in to the pressure from this rural school and joined the football team. It was brutal. They dropped football. They dropped band early on. I think they had been so beaten down by the other kids and even some teachers that they gave up. They managed to graduate and I was frankly very thankful and relieved.

Again, no matter what end of the spectrum your child is on, as a parent, respect their uniqueness as people. No two children from the same set of parents will be the same. Love them. Train them up in the way that they should go, as the Bible says, and when they get old they will not depart from it. They will also be OK, regardless of the way it looks sometimes. Don't ever give up on them and let them know it.

More than once I heard from them, "You gotta feel that way. You're my mom!" To this I replied, "I don't gotta feel any way because I am your mom. Many moms don't. You are very special and God has big plans for you. Don't ever forget that."

Say this sort of thing to your child often. Say it to yourselves if you don't quite believe it, until you do believe it. It is the truth.

My children loved performing for us. Of course, Cara usually ran that show, complete with choreography. Sean, Becky and Cara made up songs and dances to go with them to perform. I have an adorable picture of the five of them in their pajamas in the living room. Dan and Marc were still in diapers and were wearing only that, at less than two years old. All either had their arms high or on their chests since they were out of sync, their mouths open in song. I remember that performance. Surely nobody has ever had more talented and creative children than I. And nobody has had more talented and creative children than you. Believe it. It's good for all of you.

Cara and Sean in particular liked making up songs. They would even do medleys of these songs together as well as by themselves. Sean used the medley while sitting on the couch singing and bouncing his body off the back of the couch in time with the beat, as a form of comfort as well as enjoyment. The songs were songs about their daily lives and reminded me of the types of songs in operas, but without the grand operatic arias. They were *slice of life* songs. No, they weren't "country" style either. I am also certain that both Cara and Sean, if asked, could still sing the medley of those songs today.

Cara was outgoing and in charge of her siblings at this age. If Becky thought she needed to have her younger brothers reprimanded, she called Cara. I have been told that Cara would hold Marc by his thick hair and twirl him around and then let go and he landed outward from the centrifugal force. She told me that Dan's hair wasn't thick enough for this. I did not know, at that time, that this was happening. When the girls got rough with their brothers, I warned them that someday their little brothers would likely be taller and larger than they and that they could decide to get even, so they had better treat them well. So far, they seemed to have kept their "retaliation" minimal.

Mom once told me that Sean would jump off a cliff if Cara told him to. I think she was just a little secretly pleased.

When Marc was a pre-teen, he *encountered* the mailbox in a way most don't. He was playing one of his super hero games brandishing his sword, looking the opposite direction, and turned just in time to run smack into the mailbox. His eye was black and swollen for several days and his nose was twice the size it should be.

Later, as a teenager, he was scared of the neighbor's rooster, who liked to chase him in the yard. Marc was the only one the rooster picked on. Perhaps that was because Marc reacted to him. It was very amusing to see Marc run out of true fear from a chicken.   One day he said it finally dawned on him "Wait a minute. I am running from a chicken. I am bigger than he is." So, he stopped and stood his ground.   For the first time, the chicken was the one who retreated.

Daniel was sparkly-eyed and so sweet from the very beginning. Other than his biting fights with his twin, he was very easy. Almost everything delighted and pleased him and he tried hard to please others. He was the most genuine, pure-hearted little child, however, as he grew, whenever a backyard game took place he never failed to get his feelings hurt and stomped away angry. I think the others felt he wanted special treatment, which they refused, and this is what ticked him off.

Telling my then 12-year-old sons and Sean who was 14 years old about their sister's pregnancy was interesting.   I sat them at the kitchen table and told them I had something to tell them. I had to be careful how I presented this, as I didn't want to appear that I thought this was OK to do, but at the same time, I wanted to be sure Cara was supported and the baby fully accepted.

After I explained it to them Daniel said, "Wow, you mean she is really going to have a real baby?"

The look on their faces was priceless.   They had half smiles and I could tell they were concentrating and taking the whole reality of it in.   The older children had gotten to see me pregnant so it wasn't so hard for them to grasp.

From slumber parties my girls had, where we played volleyball or badminton in the backyard where I joined them, to autumn bonfires and roasting hot dogs and marshmallows, we had so much fun. Mom and Dede and sometimes Dad came up for those.   There were so many good times and it offset anything negative that may have happened along the way.

All three sons got into their own brand of trouble as teenagers and I had to separate fights by standing between them when they were all tall enough to look down at me.   That was interesting and I am sure it looked like a precarious position to be in, but I didn't hesitate in assuming that position to keep them from hurting each other.

Sean would crash parties as a teenager, but when he was found out, the hosts usually liked him so well they allowed him to stay.

He once took the blame for an auto accident and it was his friend who was driving but the friend would be in greater trouble than Sean who had no infractions. The friend was too young to drive. I am not sure what temporary lapse in judgment, caused Sean to allow him to drive but he did, probably peer pressure, wanting to be the nice guy. It was a quiet street and they likely thought it would be OK. The boy hit a mailbox and the owner came out screaming at them. We got it corrected however, and I think Sean learned that there are some things we don't do to "protect" someone else. It did show what a loyal person he was, however, loyalty cannot be allowed to block common sense.

Sean worked as a delivery driver for a local pizza shop while in high school. After high school he decided to join the Navy Reserves before college. We had visited several recruiters. I was particularly unimpressed with the Marine recruiter. He came out to the house. I found him to be a stereotype *gung ho* type, and I am sure he thought he was convincing me to support Sean to join. He was wrong. He emphasized how *nice* the uniforms looked for one thing. *Did he really think I was that stupid?* He also told a story of how one mom was against the Marines and she ended up baking him a pie before her son left for boot camp. I found his goals and his recruiting method to be very transparent and sexist. I was also amused that he actually thought he could dupe me.

While in high school, Daniel and Marc tried football and baseball. They liked both games but found the overly competitive spirit and the over zealous coach to be so negative and nasty that it outweighed their love for the game. They dropped out of sports, something akin to great sin at their small rural high school, as I have mentioned before. Those events notwithstanding, Marc and Dan finally made it through high school. I enjoyed stopping by after school to watch them play baseball, while it lasted. Marc also joined the wrestling team.

After they graduated, we paid for driving lessons as we had for Sean and the girls. We didn't think it necessary to drive previously when they could take the bus to school. It seemed to offer more opportunities for trouble. Daniel and Marc both had their clips with the law, as Sean had, as it was, usually due to speeding.

Marc decided he wanted to join the Army Reserves, a decision he would regret later. I was against it at that time. The world was in flux, very unstable, and as a mom, it was a big concern. My mom didn't have to face that, although the Viet Nam War was in full swing at the time I got out of school, since she had no sons. By this time, Mom was very proud of not only my girls, but also of her grandsons. She just looked at them like she really liked them. She had not ceased man bashing, but it was tempered. Man bashing came mostly from Dede. Mom tried to avoid it when they were in earshot. She seemed to begin to understand that these young boys were, partially at least, influenced by the way they were viewed and treated, including by her. The older they got, the better she was able to see them as people, people with feelings. She tried to be more patient with them. Her words became less harsh and if she did reprimand, she tried not to do it in such a way as to undermine their gender. Obviously, I appreciated her efforts.

Chapter 34
"More Travels"

Cedar Point

We went to Cedar Point Amusement Park in Sandusky, Ohio every summer. The company Ben worked for provided either the full price ticket or later, partial payment, so this was a true perk for our large family. We all looked forward to this event of the summer, only a two-hour drive away. Sean, in particular, was enthusiastic.

We normally started our day there with a picnic in the picnic area. This saved dollars since the park charged twice as much, at the least, as it would cost outside the park for the same thing. Later in the day, we would buy one food item and then perhaps an ice cream cone or funnel cake to end the day. Nobody felt deprived.

We rode the coasters, the biggest draw for Cedar Point as it had more coasters than almost anywhere. The big treat was getting to ride the year's newest coaster. The fact that the lines for the newer rides were twice as long didn't seem to dissuade the children. We waited as long as two hours for a favored ride. As the children got older, pragmatism kicked in and we decided not to waste so much time for one ride. We could always hit that ride the following year when lines would not be as long.

One year we took our pop-up camper and stayed in Cedar Point Campground adjacent to the park. This allowed a less harried day, by stretching it to two days with one day spent relaxing at Cedar Point beach and playing in the surf of Lake Erie.

Next to the coasters, we enjoyed the water rides when the temperature rose to 90 degrees or more with high humidity. Yes, we looked stringy-haired after the drenching and yes, if jeans were worn, it took awhile for them to dry out, making the wearer regret their choice when the harsh material sometimes rubbed the flesh raw, not to mention we all smelled like the Lake Erie carp the rest of the day. Also, I learned early on that tennis shoes were the best choice of footwear. Not only did they remain comfortable throughout the day of walking, but also when wet, they dried out and were still comfortable. I learned my lesson from my mistake of wearing sandals and getting blistered so badly that I could not walk.   I stopped at one of the medical stations they have throughout the park. They bandaged me and I was at least able to function and with less pain. Thinking again of all this, you might wonder why it was so much fun.

Cedar Point employees were always friendly and helpful. The only drawback, particularly for families, was the increasing preference of young women for wearing the scantiest shorts and tops they could find. Public displays of affection while waiting in long lines were also disconcerting for caring parents.

The year the twins were one, we got around the park with them in the side-by-side type twin stroller. My parents and sister accompanied us that year. They received lots of attention as twin babies do when out in public. It poured rain that year and we sought out shelter under whatever makeshift roof we could find. Mostly we attended the indoor shows and waited for the older children to get off rides and we viewed the 20-minute movie at the giant IMAX theatre.

We also had the twins identical "train blankets," made as a gift from a relative. They were colorful blankets covered with cute trains, befitting baby boys. Danny and Marc loved them and wanted them no matter where they were. Those two blankets and our thin jackets were our only source of warmth as we huddled under a sheltered area.

Cedar Point closed near midnight during summer weekends, with fireworks at a set area to draw the crowds nearer to the exits. After one such closing, we stood waiting for Ben to bring the car to pick us up. Usually we all trooped out to the car somewhere in the huge, lighted, parking lot. I stood in the light of the roof above where they sell tickets, the booth long closed and dark inside, with my children. Sean was probably 11 years old. He scowled his worst scowl. I knew we were all tired and somewhat grumpy, but I saw no reason for this extreme face.

I asked, "What is wrong, Sean? Why the big scowl?"
He answered, "Well, it's all over. No more fun for a year."

I said, "You mean to tell me you think you only have one fun day a year? What about Christmas?"
He acknowledged that Christmas was fun. I was both amused and baffled, but was glad he enjoyed the day so much. I

just wanted him to be able to see the fun in *many* things. He was obviously still too young to appreciate all of life's many nuances.

I remember Mom and Dad taking us to Russell's Point when we were children. It was our version of Cedar Point, but *much* smaller. I was a teen before I ever heard of Cedar Point. I am not sure why they didn't take us there. This made me more determined that when I became a mom that my own children would get to do more "out there" kinds of things like I always wanted to do. It is nice to allow enough *large places* so that we can appreciate the home fires, rather than feeling somewhat trapped by it. Again, Mom didn't like traveling on even shorter trips very much. Our fun was going to movies regularly. We went to the county fair once a year also. I think for Dede and I, the things we did as children were simply on a smaller scale and something Mom could accept. We also ate out on a relatively regular basis. When we went to the fair, we got to ride almost as much as we wanted, even when the rides cost an "expensive" 75 cents, costly then. When I spent my week or two in the summer with Aunt Rene and Uncle John, we rode go-karts and jumped on trampolines..

Sea World

Victoria was about a year old when we decided to go to Sea World and to a nearby campground. Cara and the boys also went. We tent camped in a two-room tent, boys on one side and the girls on the other. A zippered flap separated the two rooms. We used air mattresses with our sleeping bags, so it was very comfortable.

When we camped we always bought firewood at the campground and had not run into any problems. This campground had no wood. We looked everywhere and nobody had any wood. There had been a drought so this might have been part of the reason. Instead, we bought some logs in a grocery store. These were fireplace starter logs. It was only after we used them and roasted meat over them and ate it that we discovered that the fumes could be carcinogenic, so one would assume that the black tar which fires generate from these logs could also be. We joked about "glowing in the dark." It wasn't very funny, but what could we do at that point.

The night became chilly even with our makeshift campfire. I decided to fetch my jacket from the back room in our tent. I went into the tent and the flap that separated our room from the front was partially unzipped. It zipped from the bottom up. I could see my jacket in the other area and squatted down to reach into that area and retrieve it.

I grabbed the jacket and then realized that my hair had caught in the zipper. I had to do some fast analysis. If I just sat down it would pull out my hair. I couldn't leverage myself to stand nor could I untangle my hair.

By the time all this had passed through my mind, I teetered, lost my balance and sat down hard. Yes, it hurt when I felt my hair rip out. I looked up and there was a long clump of my hair hanging in the zipper.

I sat there for a while thinking and realized the others would probably never let me live this down.

I made my way back to the campfire and told them what had happened. Sean, especially, always found slapstick humor to be hilarious. They all made their way to the tent. They looked in and there hung my hair in the zipper. The site of it caused uproarious laughter. Sean could barely stand he laughed so hard. It reminded me of the time when we lived in Bowling Green when I was in college and he saw me (head down) walk into my bedroom wall, missing the door by an inch. He rolled on the floor (literally) for a few minutes and burst out laughing several times throughout the rest of the week, without provocation other than the thought of the way I looked when it happened.

As I have mentioned, I think now that the lack of vacationing when I was small was the main reason I wanted my own children to have vacations. I thought family trips were the best thing, even as a child. Classmates went on vacation and I heard about it. People in movies vacationed. I begged to go. I think if I had known Mom turned down going to Florida with Dad at the time, I would have been hysterical. I am glad we finally did a little vacationing when I was a teen.

In fact, before we left on a three day trip to Washington DC, I didn't know it but Dad had a very bad gall bladder and was in pain. We went anyway because he didn't want to disappoint us. As soon as we returned, he was put in the hospital and packed in ice to bring down the fever. He had emergency surgery. This was the wonderful man he was.

Two Weeks On The Road

The summer of 1991, we decided to take a road trip south. We had our Ford Aero-star van packed, with our two-room tent roll on the top rack. Becky did not go along with us. Camping had never been too much fun for her, partially due to asthma and partially due to her attitude. Cara was now in college and again dating Allen, her high school sweetheart.

The van was packed and we were buckled in. I still remember the excitement I felt as we started out of the drive on our adventure. We didn't know exactly how long we would be gone. We estimated perhaps a week or so. Sometimes things change.

Our initial destination was Cherokee, North Carolina, an Indian Reservation. We stopped the first night at a campground in Tennessee. The Smoky Mountains were beautiful. We took the Blue Ridge Parkway, which is very slow driving with much scenery. Ben seemed to have a need to take pictures of everything. He had always been a camera bug, but his borderline obsession drove me crazy. We bickered. I knew we had to make better time in order to be at the campground in Cherokee at a relatively decent hour. I lost this battle.

We wound our way in the van up the side of the mountain toward Cherokee in pitch-black night. There were no lights but our car lights as we drove slowly for safety. All were quiet. It was late. We were tired and we were nervous, or perhaps I should say that I was nervous. One wrong turn could mean death.

We finally made it to the campground. All the other campers had long since gone to bed. It was chillier on the mountain.

Ben and the boys got out and began to put up the tent, not the easy kind of tent like today. It took awhile. Push this pole in here, thread that string around here, pound in the stakes.

"Hey, Dan, quit it!"

"Shut up!"

"No, you shut up!"

Ben mumbled something and I heard them all laugh. They were not being very quiet.

Cara, little Vickie and I waited in the relative warmth of the van till the tent was ready. We all hurried inside and got into our sleeping bags as quickly as we could.

We slept well, until about 5:30 AM. We had been asleep about four hours. One of our campground neighbors with a fifth wheel camper was attempting to leave and was backing up so we heard the loud beep beep as he backed. That wasn't what woke us though. What woke us was the couple talking loudly. I heard a man's voice saying, "Yeah well, they got here real late at night and woke us up they were so loud so I don't really care. See how they like it."

It wasn't just the boys and Ben who made noise the night before, but when Cara, Victoria and I got out of the van and we made up the inside of the tent, I guess we were louder than we thought. The couple finally left and after the rest of the campground began to awaken and make more noise we got up. We would just have to get to bed earlier.

While in Cherokee, we went in various shops that sold "authentic" Indian pieces. We also attended an outdoor play at Unto These Hills outdoor theatre, with live horses. It was a play about *The Trail of Tears*, the story of the forced relocation of Native Americans from their homelands to Indian Territory (present day Oklahoma) in the Western United States.

We also watched as Indian artisans did their work in the Oconoluftee Indian Village and explained the culture and history of their ancestors.

I watched Vickie while the rest went tubing in the very chilly Oconoluftee River. I liked tubing and although it was hot, that was a very cold mountain stream. They had a ball, although they emerged from the river with blue lips.

The campfire was especially welcoming that night.

After a few days we had seen as much there as we cared to see. After some looking at the map and discussion about whether to go to Asheville, NC, a very scenic area or to go east across North Carolina, we decided to go east and head to the ocean. Virginia Beach would be our second destination.

On our way out, however, we made a stop at Mount Mitchell, the highest point east of the Mississippi. The gentle mist of low-hanging clouds surrounded it. We took family pictures from the deck at the summit. This provided an awe-inspiring view of the breathtaking Blue Ridge Mountains. Even in the heat of the day along with all the climbing, we enjoyed ourselves. I was disheartened to see all the bare trees, erect and stark, apparent victims of acid rain.

Teen age Cara was allowed to drive part of the time. This lacked foresight on our part. We were on the expressway and she was driving down a mountain. There are signs on the expressway picturing a truck heading downhill indicating warnings to them. Between watching her own downhill driving, along with all the traffic, especially the semi's, Cara panicked. I was in the passenger seat.

"Mom!" Cara began to cry.

"I can't do this! I need to stop! Take the wheel! Do something! I'm going to let go of the wheel."

I remained calm and told her that I could not take the wheel right now.

"You can do this," I spoke reassuringly.

"We will be at a place where we can trade drivers soon. You *have* to drive. It is OK. All will be OK. Do NOT let go of the wheel."

Everyone in back was completely silent watching us.

Cara continued to weep softly, but she did not let go of the wheel. When we were able to change drivers, we did and she said, "I never want to drive in mountains again!"

I think we all concurred with this. We never wanted her to drive in mountains again, especially if we were with her.

We stopped at a campground half way across North Carolina. The man at the campgrounds was friendly. I remarked to the kids that he didn't even have an accent, which had been very noticeable up to now.

They laughed. "Mom, he did too," Cara corrected me. The boys agreed. They also accused me of starting to sound like I was from that area.

Ben went to the restroom while the rest of us were in the tent. We had purchased a new lantern, which ran with a battery or electricity if you had that, for this trip. Ben had warned about knocking it over as it would likely break.

I giggled along with my children as we chatted and told funny stories.

I was attempting to move from one area to another, and knocked over the lantern.

The glass broke.

We all froze.

We looked at each other.

We knew what this meant.

Benjamin.

I think I was as scared as they. I told them, "don't say anything when he gets here." I felt like a child myself who knew we were in trouble. They knew I was scared. *Quit it! You are an adult*, I reminded myself.

We heard him coming.

All were quiet.

"Hi Ben!" I greeted him. "Please don't get mad. I accidentally broke the lantern."

He was livid. "I told you so!" he ranted.

He finally got over it after ranting for the better part of 20 minutes and we slept. Ben did have a very bad temper.

When he was truly angry he would stand over me, red in the face, veins popping on his neck and yelling so that the spit flew. I would sit very quietly and hope it would soon pass. I was afraid to move until he finished and walked away. No, this was not the best way to handle things. He is aware of that now.

There were no other incidents the rest of our vacation.

Virginia Beach was an interesting experience. The loud jets fly unceasingly overhead, due to the Naval base there. There was no let up. I have since met a Virginia Beach native, and she said that you get so used to them, you don't notice. She added that the jets are the "sound of freedom." The campground there was very nice. Shimmering pools, including one for toddlers Vickie's age were inviting. Vik loved it and so did the rest of the kids.

We also walked the beach and the kids played in the surf. It was their first time to see the ocean.

Leaving that area proved to be more challenging. I was driving. I got out of Virginia Beach just fine and thought we were on our way. Not so. First we came to Chesapeake, and one city melted into the next one with no demarcations other than a sign to indicate you had gone from one city to another, then to Norfolk. At one point I made a circle and was in Virginia Beach again. Ben couldn't figure it out either. We had a map. It looked simple on paper.

Let's try this again.

Chesapeake again, Norfolk.

"I just want to escape!" I ranted to my family. I felt similar to Cara on the mountain, except this was a closed in feeling of panic.

It occurred to me that I needed to do something different or we could be circling that area forever, caught in some sort of highway *Twilight Zone*.

I have no idea what different route I took, but we knew we were finally headed toward Richmond. I drove around Washington DC. Even with the traffic there, it was less stressful than getting out of the Virginia Beach area.

We stopped for the night at a campground in Frederick, Maryland. We had already made the decision to travel to Gettysburg on our way home. It would be educational for the kids and Ben and I both wanted to see it. We had never been there.

Gettysburg was everything we thought it might be. Pennsylvania's beautiful rolling landscape was peaceful, a stark contrast to the battle that had taken place there a century before.

The battleground seemed to have ghosts. I could see the men who fought there, hear the cannon fire, the yells and the dead bodies. In all the quietness, the area was alive with activity long past and the heartache. I felt the pain. Even my children were quieter than normal. How could anyone not be impressed with this area. I wished we had a personal historian with us to give us more detail, but we had to settle for the car battleground tour.

Our campground at Gettysburg kept the period theme by using lanterns from the Civil War era as lighting along the path. Cara seemed to be most affected by this stop. Perhaps visiting Gettysburg helped cement her love of history, which she now teaches.

After a few days there we were finally on our way home. We made our way east around Pittsburgh and back into Ohio.

Upon arriving home, I played the messages on my answering machine. We had been gone two weeks. I told Mom before we left that I didn't know how long we would be gone, and that she shouldn't worry. I called her once during those two weeks to check in.

I played my messages and heard things from Mom and Dede, like "Where are you? Do you know how long it's been?" There were at least seven or eight messages. On a few of these messages they even sang songs. I knew we had been gone for awhile, but I thought I had made it clear that I didn't know how long we would be gone and that it could be awhile. I called Mom immediately, of course, to let her know we were home. I had always thought of Mom as a "worry wart" and this was simply more evidence. Did she sit around and borrow trouble? Was there something else going on besides her own overactive anxiety? Did she want me to feel guilty for going to begin with, thus making her worry? I will never know.

Looking back at this longest vacation we ever took as a family, although we had some scary times, some exciting and educational times, as well as some bickering along the way, almost like a Chevy Chase "Vacation" movie, it was a memorable vacation. Perspective is a large part of everything in life. I am fairly certain that all who were on this trip would not have traded the experience together as a family for anything.

Chapter 35

"Daniel's Accident"

When Daniel was 18 years old, he became involved with a girl that he met at the church I then attended. This proved to be a big mistake. She had been involved with Daniel a few years before, but then dumped him for an older guy and left. She had a baby and then returned to our area. Her mother, who also attended the church, gave her Daniels number without asking me first if I thought that was a good idea. I would have told her not to give her daughter the number. She later apologized and acknowledged that it was a bad idea.

Daniel had been relatively *innocent* until he met this girl. When she reentered his life, they moved in together. It made me heartsick when he moved. My instincts were right. She dumped him again for another guy, plus they were experimenting with drug use and drinking. He was devastated when she dumped him.

He didn't feel he could share all of it with me, though we had a good relationship. He became convinced nobody could do anything for him.

One morning Cara dropped off two of her children for me to baby-sit while she went to a doctor appointment. The sun shone brightly over the foggy mist covering the fields across the road in front of the house. I heard the chop chop sound of a helicopter. As I watched out the front window, the chopper landed in the field. I saw that it was a life flight helicopter from an area hospital. They loaded someone in. I realized they probably had to land where they could, due to the fog. I had not seen a chopper this close before. I watched as it took off. Then I went back to playing with my granddaughters.

A few minutes later the phone rang.

"Hello," the man on the phone said. "I am the chaplain at St. Vincent's Hospital."

"Yes?" I answered.

"I am sorry to have to let you know this, but your son, Daniel, was involved in a severe car accident. Could you come to the hospital as soon as possible, please?

"Is he all right?" I panicked.

"He is all right at the moment but that is all I know. Could you come?"

"I have my granddaughters. I will come as soon as I get someone to take them."

I called Cara on her cell phone. She had not yet reached the doctors office. I told her about the chaplains call and she said she would come back immediately.

I called Ben.

Cara picked up her children, and I left for the hospital.

I called the pastor at my church, a dear and wonderful friend and confidante. He agreed to get to the hospital as soon as he could.

Daniel's thigh had been crushed like cornflakes, his orthopedist told us. His lower leg was broken. He was scheduled for surgery to insert a steel rod into his leg. The surgeon said that since he was so young, the bones would bind back together. This was good news.

Daniel had been driving at a relatively high speed for the foggy conditions and had run into a tree, which flipped his car upside down. A motorist found him and called 911. He was conscious the whole time. The rescuers had to use the Jaws of Life to pry him from his car. They said that if he had not been wearing his seatbelt, he would have been killed.

Little did I know at the time, but the chopper I had watched earlier that day, had not been able to land further down the road due to fog so landed at the nearest place they could to the accident and this was across my road. The person I saw them loading was my son.

My pastor arrived shortly after I did at the hospital. He talked to Dan and prayed with him. Dan later told me that Bob, the pastor was so positive and faith filled, it seemed to be infectious. Love oozed from him. Dan decided that he wanted what this man had.

Dan was operated on the following morning. My pastor visited him again. Dan was very receptive. He had a long road ahead to recover, not just physically, but emotionally and spiritually. He also had to face legal charges.

My mother was very defensive of Dan during this ordeal. She was angry and in denial of some of the things that were indeed accurate about her grandson. I am certain she couldn't bring herself to face the reality of all that was happening. I didn't want to face it either, but I had no choice. None of us did. Ben was quiet throughout this challenging time, and he had a worried look on his face constantly.

Dan's operation was successful. He used crutches for awhile and eventually went to a cane. He was indicted and had to spend two months in jail. He was charged with a four-point misdemeanor, reckless operation. His license was also suspended for a year. I visited him frequently. Spiritually, he was healed. He prayed. He had faith that all would be well. God kept him alive through an accident that should have been fatal. He wanted to get out of jail.

There was a hearing in the fall, at which time the judge would ascertain whether she thought he should be released. We were hopeful. I could not see any reason for him to remain in jail. He was a changed person, and for him to be kept longer, seemed to be injustice.

Dan's lawyers pushed me to the front table in the courtroom.

"Say something to the judge," they insisted. "It will help. You are his mother."

The female judge apparently fancied herself to be like the erasable "Judge Judy" on television. She even sounded like Judge Judy.

First she addressed Dan. She asked him a few questions and he shared that he was now a "Christian" and "had changed." He also elaborated that he knew what he had done, and was sorry.

Then his lawyers asked if I could speak on his behalf. She agreed.

"Who are you?"

"I am Dan's mother, although I know this doesn't carry much weight here." I began.

The judge interrupted me and quipped, "Well," she grinned, and looked at her *audience,* "it's good to hear you know your place here."

Her comment stung. I could tell she thought she was being witty, but I wasn't on trial here and I thought her comment was uncalled for.

She continued to grin and looked back at me.

I held her gaze, never changing my expression, and paused as if to say, "Are you through being cute yet?" I kept my dignity.

I continued.

"I have known him longer than anyone and I know him very well."

I never broke eye contact with her.

"I assure you he is not the same person he was a couple months ago."

She looked somewhat skeptical as she returned eye contact.

"Well, I am not sure what you mean." She glanced at his papers on her desk. "He hasn't been in any trouble before looks like."

I answered her with a sideways grin, and a *please, I know the whole story; I'm his mom,* look on my face and continued my eye contact.

Though the papers may not have shown any record, I knew he just hadn't yet been caught before this. She seemed to *understand* my look and the message. I also know she believed me.

When she asked, I told her that Dan would be staying with me at my house.

A few minutes later, she turned to Dan and said, "I am going release you to stay with your parents. You are on probation. I don't want to see you back in my court, because if you are, it will not go so well next time. Good luck to you."

Dan was free. We were jubilant.

He came home and seemed relieved and happy to be here. He now walked with a cane. His doctor told him that in a few years he may want to have the steel rod removed as this could then cause him some discomfort and by then, his leg would be healed and next to normal.

Dan went to church regularly. He was baptized. He also received disability for a time. A few years later, after getting back to work and with his leg healed, he walked with a slight limp. He had the steel rod removed. He still walks with a limp, but it is much improved.

During this time, he visited a new church. He met Karen there, the girl who became his wife. They share the same birthdays so now there are three in the family with August 3 birthdays, plus their anniversary. They got married in an outdoor wedding at the park, one very hot August 3, day. They now have a scrumptious little girl named Alison, my sweet, exuberant, smart granddaughter, and recently also baby Darlene. Life has had its ups and downs, but they are happy. Daniel is a dedicated family man. God is faithful. Daniel's family is truly blessed.

Mom remained stalwartly loyal to Daniel the whole time. She defended him. She loved him. I was so very pleased with her loyalty.

Mom knew she had been blessed with two easy (by comparison) children. God knows what we can bear. I suspect this would have been more than she could have borne had it been Dede or I. She said as much.

Chapter 36

"Snatched"

Marc joined the Army Reserves soon after high school and an unsuccessful semester at a community college. His MOS or job description in the Army was to drive vehicles, including trucks as well as smaller vehicles. In war time, this is one of the most *unsafe* jobs. He also didn't care for some of the men who he had to work with at the Reserve Center. Marc was in a four-year college at the time, and he was increasingly dissatisfied with his military duties. He then made it to IRR (Inactive Ready Reserves), who almost never got reactivated.

However, because I knew things were escalating in the middle east, I suggested he try Air National Guard since I had heard rumors of IRR being reactivated and sent there and it made me nervous. The rumor proved true. Since we lived near the airport and they have an air base there, the air guard would also be convenient and would likely suit his personality and desires better. He investigated and made the contacts, and filled out paperwork to transfer to this branch. The Army gave him written permission to transfer.

We thought all was in motion, however, the man handling the recruitment in the Air Guard was new on his job, and he also did not seem very motivated; he procrastinated on many things and was difficult to reach. Marc felt he was recruiting himself and was doing all the work. I agreed. The recruiter was not thorough or detail-oriented and neglected to send all necessary materials with Marc when he was transported to Columbus for his physical and written test. This delay, due to the nonchalance of this one man, was about to end Marc's chances to enter the Guard and almost got him sent to the Middle East. During the time he had arranged to go back to Columbus to complete whatever was missing, the Army notified him by mail that he was to report to Ft.

Leonardwood, MO for his transition from IRR to active duty at the end of August, and then he was to be sent to Iraq. These orders superseded any previous orders or permission they had given. To say he was devastated is not an overstatement and frankly, I was ready to send him to Canada. I told him not to panic, to just enjoy his weekend as there was nothing that could be done till Monday. It was a Friday. He had to wait all weekend before he could call when they were back in their offices.

He was told that in order to appeal, he would have to fill out paperwork which they would mail to him immediately. They did so. The Army representative on the phone tried to talk him out of it however. During this appeal process, all his orders were suspended until some sort of board dealt with his appeal.

He filled out the applications and also had to provide a letter stating his reasons for his request. I helped him write it. In the letter, he explained the whole situation, including the permission that the Army had previously given and that if the new Air Guard recruiter had provided all the need paperwork, there would be no need for any of this and that he would now already be in the Air Guard. He asked them to allow him to continue his path into the Air Guard, a path more fitting with his abilities to serve our country. He sent the materials off to the Army Headquarters in St. Louis.

Both of my sons-in-law who had been in the military, as well as my friend, John, Army Lt. Col. Ret., told me there wasn't much hope they would decide in his favor. Allen, in particular, told me that for an order like this to be overturned, it would literally take a miracle. "It just doesn't happen," he said. The officers at the Air Guard said similar and their hands were tied.

I had everyone I knew praying and I prayed continually. We were on pins and needles. I knew God could make a way where there was no way. I prayed that he would find favor with this board.

It was the first part of July and Marc and his dad went on their annual retreat to Kentucky at a monastery. He had his cell phone in case the Army tried to reach him for the results of the appeal. He called me the second day there and he had a message on his cell to call them. He called and they told him that they would work with him on this. He only had a certain amount of time to get all the things needed to get into the Air Guard however, and if they weren't completed by the date they gave, then the order to report to Ft. Leonardwood would be back in effect.

As soon as he returned home the following day, he went to the air base and explained all to them. The base Commander was there and though the recruiter was about to set up an appointment later the following week, the Commander took charge of Marc's case and said, "No, he is going tomorrow. The Army just doesn't change their minds like this. I mean this just doesn't happen. It is some sort of miracle. The Army could rescind this *break* at any moment. We aren't going to lose this, by taking any longer." Others there echoed the Commanders assessment that this was very unusual. I also think the Commander realized what a sloppy job the recruiter did and was doing and how this was affecting Marc's life and likely the lives of others. They provided the needed information and he drove himself to Columbus this time. The Commander also made sure he could reach him if needed while in Columbus to answer any questions they might have. It was a good thing since there was a question and he did have to call him once for answers. He got through all the requirements in Columbus then drove directly to the base when he got back with the paperwork, to be immediately processed, as the Commander had directed. The Commander was there to meet him, swore Marc in and said "We are faxing the Army with this right now." They sent the fax and got receipt of confirmation. "The Army can't touch you now, Marc," the Commander said.

Marc was not just relieved, but positively exuberant. So was I. We said a *thank you* to God. All knew this was indeed a miracle, including Allen. He was flabbergasted, as were Larry and John. Military men know just how rare this happens, if ever.

Marc has enjoyed the time in the Air Guard, has been promoted a couple times, and it has indeed been a better fit for him. It lengthened his stay in the military, but it was certainly worth it. He even elected to stay in longer and now enjoys the military very much. He has also risen through the ranks.

Marc not only received favor from the Army decision-making board, but also received favor from his Commander in the Air Guard. God answered my prayer in an overwhelming and wonderful way. We still marvel at this miracle.

I look back to so many scary events in the lives of my sons and I marvel at all they have come through. There was a time I thought to myself, *if they can just make it to age 23 or 24 alive, then there is a good or at least better chance that they will live and survive to live their lives.* The things they got involved with or that happened due to lack of wisdom and immaturity seemed to always be laced with danger to the point that I truly felt they could end up dead. My girls got into negative situations which were more relational, and difficult to deal with for certain, but they were not like the directly life threatening situations of the boys.

Though Mom was still living, she was also getting frail and her mind was not as alert as it once was. She was pleased for her grandson and this news and agreed that it was a miracle.

Chapter 37
"Church"

My experiences with churches, in general, over my life have been positive or at the least an intermingling of experiences. One would expect that is as it should be. It is when the converse happens that it, naturally, gets one's attention.

The church I joined in winter, 1994, was one of those intermingling experiences of both positive and negative. At the time, I would have viewed it mostly positive. In hindsight, it was not so positive, as it was very stressful, but it was positive in the sense of a learning experience.

My long time friend, Janet, had been with this particular church body for several years. She invited me to go with her. I had been going through a particularly difficult time and I decided to go. I hadn't been to any church for a while at that time.

The first visit was very positive for me. I received unbelievable encouragement from the Associate Pastor (Bob) who proved to become an invaluable friend and confidante. He was the pastor to which I referred for helping my son Daniel after he had his accident. This man was possibly the single most loving and humble man I have ever met. The Senior Pastor, Gerald, was almost the polar opposite.

Pastor Bob had been so helpful to me as I watched his boldness in his ministry on a consistent basis over the five years I was a member of his congregation. The very first time I attended, he told me things that he could not possibly have known. I had been going through some very rough times, culminating that previous week. Due to this, I had prayed while sitting in my car the previous Tuesday night.

I was basically pouring out my heart to God. I said that I felt that I was possibly not capable of a strong walk in God, and that I seemed to fail over and over.

I said through sobs, "What is wrong with me? Am I like seeds that have fallen on rocky soil?"

I was referring to the *parable of the sower* where the seeds thrown on rocky soil are shallow and cannot be sustained. I continued in prayer.

"I feel like I am on the palm of your hand."

I put my palm out in front of me to illustrate to my Father just what I meant.

"There I am, and it is like there is another hand coming down at me and there are no handholds on the palm so I can hold on. I feel like this hand will pluck me off. Unless you close your hand over me to protect me, the hand will take me. Please protect me."

I shared this prayer with no one.

The following Sunday, January 9, 1994, I visited Janet's church. Toward the end of the service, Pastor Bob approached me. Though I had met him perhaps 20 years before on a couple occasions, he did not recognize me till after he started to talk to me.

"I have a word for you," he said. Though he hesitated when he recognized me, I told him, "go ahead." If he had something he felt I needed to hear I certainly wanted to hear it. I could make my own decisions about it later. He proceeded. Bob had no idea what these words would mean to me.

> "The Lord would say to you that you've been on an incredible journey throughout your life. My hand has been upon you and I have watched over you and your family, but I am now at the beginning of a healing process. I'm going to take the broken relationships that have been so meaningful to you in your life. I'm going to bring them back together in newness and freshness of life. For the day of new beginnings has only begun. For one would think that this had changed and that had changed, but I have made changes from the beginning of time, changes that I have meant for a purpose and for the perfection of my people.
> For I have called you to maturity, and I've called you to that place to walk therein. Many would try to snare you away and take you away, but I will not have it, for I have made a snare for him. For I have deposited a great richness, and as you once again

begin to speak, a newness of life and a newness of heart shall flow from you, my daughter, and many hearts shall be changed and challenged, for I do not change circumstances roundabout, but I change them from within. For you are good ground; you are good seed and my hand has done much, and I will not allow all the years of the plowing and the planting of seed to go to naught. For even now will the newness begin, and the changes radically take hold. No longer will the abuse go on, but a new day is coming. Believe my word and stand upon it and see if I will not even change the hearts and hands of those that are stretched forth to bring destruction. I will set a standard before them and deliverance shall come to your house, because I am for you. And I shall stand with you, for you are mine. I shall not let you go. No one can take you out of the palm of my hand."

His last few sentences were said with emphasis on "no one." I was in shock.

Nobody could have known what I had prayed alone in my car less than a week prior, except for God and myself.
I stood there with tears streaming down my face.
There were no words.
Bob asked, "Does this mean anything to you?"
I shook my head.
"You have no idea what this means to me. Thank you."
I told Janet about the whole thing later. His word for me had also confirmed that I was indeed good ground, the parable of the sower to which I had referred in my prayer the previous week.

I think that most churches have standard-bearers, pillars, people of love and true compassion. Pastor Bob was one of those people. I would also imagine most organizations and churches also have cliques and factions, those who run things on several levels both formally and informally and there are usually unspoken rules that you learn only through experience. This church was no exception. If you were on the worship team, for example, and the in-group became *disgruntled* with you in some way, your microphone might be turned off. Of course you were not told the accurate reason for this. This happened to more than one person on different occasions.

When I started attending this church, they didn't allow women to hold any key ministerial positions, except for the worship team or as one of the members of the prayer team. Elders were only men. Some would say this is scriptural, which they also thought at the time. Since that time, they now have a female serving as an associate pastor. I am not sure what her ministry focus is. I guess their stringent position was amended due to pressure from sister churches allowing women to serve as pastors and they wanted to stay current, as well as possible discoveries in scripture not viewed the same way as before. Scripturally, Deborah, for example, in the Old Testament was very active in the ministry of her time.

Scripturally, as far as Elders being only men, it also states they are to be a husband to only *one* wife. In Biblical times, men could sometimes have more than one wife. Men can go through divorce, but these men are still able to continue to occupy positions as elder. So, just what does this scripture mean? I am not going to delve into those issues here. I am simply stating what went on and the obviously transient views held by this leadership at that particular time.

Another question regarding "Elder" is that the very word would indicate someone not only more mature in years but in Christian service, a long term, committed believer, not a novice. To ensure the future membership of this church, they began to develop very young, committed men to be Elders. Though I have no doubt these young men were dedicated, there are certain things a person gains from just living, which is likely why scripture indicates "Elder" to mean just that. The young men were barely past 19. It would seem to be an oxymoron to call these young men "Elder."

The leadership had ousted, on more than one occasion, someone who was mature (30's-50's) and in charge of some program or ministry, out of the program and one of these young men were put in their place. Again, I would imagine this was needed in order to retain the young ones. Making a person feel useful and needed ensures retention. My friend Janet used to talk about this. It bothered her.

I would have thought that it would have made more sense or be more logical to have the younger man (or woman) as a type of apprentice, so that they could be groomed for the position and learn it thoroughly. They would also have to learn the virtue of patience. Knowing the "I want it *now*" mentality of today, I can only conclude that this virtue was considered secondary to "future membership security."

These were only some of the issues, which concerned me.

I was standing in the hall one evening while the Senior Pastor was conducting a class with married couples with families. I do not recollect the name of the class, nor the reason it was held. I generally remember what I overheard, though this is a paraphrase.

"If you will just hand over your decisions about your marriages, your finances, and about your children to me, things will go smoothly for you. You will be successful. If you would just 'submit' yourselves to me, it will all be well."

Was I really hearing this? Surely not.

I felt my arms chill.

This sounds like a 'cult.'

I had heard this church referred to that way from outside sources, mostly disgruntled extended family of those who had left their family's traditional church. I began to wonder if perhaps they had been correct.

I attended one class, which was broken into smaller groups. We were to pray for someone in the group as part of spiritual development. If, during prayer, we became aware of some impression that could help this person, we were to share it with them. Sometimes, this proved quite accurate and sometimes not. We were in the learning stages.

I had been in prayer for a woman who was also well respected, and part of this church in-group. I was a little nervous. While praying for her, the phrase from "Star Trek" about "going where no man has ever gone before" kept floating across my mind. I tried to ignore it since it seemed silly to me and made no sense. I finally got up enough courage to speak.

"I know this is silly and it makes no sense to me, but this line from 'Star Trek,' the one about 'going where no man has ever gone before' keeps playing over and over in my head."

The woman looked at her friend (also part of the in group). The woman stared back at her.

"That is the very phrase we have shared in jest and yet we are serious as to what our goals are spiritually, to go where no *man* has ever gone before."

I learned then that sometimes it pays to be brave and bold, like Pastor Bob.

I became friends with Bob's younger sister, Belinda. Though she was a decade younger than I, we had several things in common. We got together frequently on a variety of occasions. She was a member of the worship team, and played guitar. She was also the most *Martha Stewart-like* woman I have ever met. She came up with recipes and decorative nuances in her home that would not be outdone in *Better Homes and Gardens.* We both liked the Victorian era for decorating ideas.

She had also been in this church since she was a young teen and had served in a variety of ways. There was one thing, however, that made her vulnerable. She was naïve. She believed she was more secure in this church than what she was in reality. She also trusted people more than she should have and she was too open with some of her conversation and the things she chose to share with others. It could and did end up being used against her.

The church encouraged home groups so all could feel a part of the whole and get to know others better. I went to a home group in a nearby suburb. The homeowner was on the worship team, but the head of the group was a church elder, a man in his 40's or 50's with grown and almost grown children. One Tuesday evening after we got started, he started to gossip about my friend Belinda and her actions that he perceived as being out of line in church. I was stunned. I sat there and didn't say much of anything.

On my drive home, I prayed and I cried. I was angry. I could not believe someone in his position would do such a thing. I decided to just pray about it for now.

Because I was in charge of the church newsletter at that time, Bob liked to meet with me on a somewhat regular basis though meetings were not prescheduled. I got a call from him to come meet and I assumed this was one of those meetings.

We always chatted and had a good time in our meetings and usually made some interesting discoveries. I always enjoyed them. I think he did as well. This time he asked, "You are going to the home group at Mark's house aren't you?"
He knew I was.
"How is that going anyway?"
It sounded as though he was asking a simple question. I hesitated. The last home group was the one in which the elder gossiped about his sister and my friend. I hadn't intended to say anything to anyone.
He persisted, "Is something wrong?"
"I hadn't intended to say anything," I said.
I blurted out everything at that point. It truly seemed the right thing to do.
He looked very disappointed that the elder would do this. They were friends.
"I will take care of this," he said. "This was wrong. It should not have happened."

I heard that Bob and the senior pastor brought the elder in and had a talk. I am not sure what else may or may not have happened. However, Mark (the homeowner), called me at work. He made it clear that when I was in his home that things in his home are to stay there and if that wasn't acceptable then I wasn't welcome. I tried to explain that the elder was there in an official capacity of the church, not just a visit to his home, but he didn't want to hear any of it, logical and true nonetheless.

There were several interesting happenings over the next couple years. I became an observer. Overall, I tried to stay out of the mire.

One afternoon, I called Belinda to chat. When she answered I could tell there was something very wrong. She sounded terrible. I could tell she was depressed and had been crying. She also sounded very tired.

She and her husband had been visiting other churches. They were thinking of leaving the church but had not yet made up their minds. Our services were usually very lengthy. Their children had activities including sports, and thus, practices and games, which required a lot of time. This also meant they couldn't be in church for hours at a time. Their church search was not announced. In fact, they kept a low profile. Regardless, it had gotten back to the Gerald, the Senior Pastor. He wrote them a very nasty letter.

I called Belinda within a couple days after they had received the letter. Both she and her husband were understandably upset. The pastor accused them of all sorts of things that were simply not true. He wrote that they were to have "nothing to do with anyone in the congregation" and that if they tried to "talk with anyone, there would be severe repercussions."

She sobbed, "he told us we are excommunicated."

They tried to meet with this pastor, but he was adamant in his stance. She also made the mistake of calling another elder who she thought she could trust to talk about it, to "fix it" some way. He, of course, supported the senior pastor. She was devastated.

I prayed with her on the phone.

I said, "Belinda you should never have called the elder. You are too trusting. You tell people too much. He is an elder for pete's sake. When you do that, they can come back at you and just hurt you more."

It occurred to me to encourage her to begin a serious study of the Book of Proverbs in the Old Testament. Proverbs had been very helpful to me to gain understanding as to how *things* work. Proverbs is the book of wisdom. My thinking was that if she was able to grasp the precepts, she would no longer be so naïve. She promised she would read it.

She called back within 48 hours. She had done as I recommended. I heard joy and hope in her voice. She was excited.

"Oh, Chérie, thank you so much for all you said. I did what you recommended and I learned so much. God really showed me some things I needed to understand. ..."

She and her husband did leave the church. This was their "true crime," not anything else the Senior Pastor trumped up apparently to soothe his feelings when people chose to leave for whatever reason. It wasn't the first time this sort of thing happened, to women in particular, in that church body. Belinda and her husband both retain scars and battle wounds from this mess, which should never have happened.

A couple months later, I left the church. I didn't leave without talking to Bob about it first.

He said, "I cannot believe this. I certainly didn't expect this."

I said, "I no longer share the same vision as the church. I also disagree with several other things."

It was the truth. I thought that was a very good reason to be looking elsewhere. There was no grudge, nothing that someone had or hadn't done.

He said, "I feel like the church has failed."

I didn't want him to feel responsible. It wasn't because of him I was leaving. He was, in fact, the only reason I stayed for so long.

He continued, "I have only let two women into my life, besides my wife, Janet and you. I simply cannot believe this."

I told him that I was still his friend that he shouldn't in any way feel responsible. I was sincere, and he knew it, but I could tell he was concerned on a larger level perspective; an alarm bigger than my leaving was going off.

We remained friends and when he went into the hospital a month or so later, I visited him. We had a good visit. I had no idea it would be our last visit.

Soon after being released from the hospital, he died due to complications from the surgery. He was only 47 years old.

A couple months later, in a phone conversation I had with the senior pastor, he told me I was to "contact nobody in the church for anything." Apparently, when this "sin" of leaving is committed, you lose your rights as a citizen as well, in his mind.

He probably felt it might have opened doors for others to get the same idea. I had no intention of sowing any discord, though the simple fact of leaving in itself is a message. At least he didn't send me a letter. My only response to him on the phone was, "I am very sorry you feel that way." Our conversation closed on as positive a footing as it could in these circumstances with this man.

Within two years of Bob's death, the elder who had gossiped about Belinda in the home group meeting, left his wife and their grown children, one with a grandchild on the way. He left her for a woman in Texas he had met on the Internet.

This church maintains its size of 300-400 people. They lose some and they gain some. Bob's youngest son is now the Associate Pastor.

I understand that there are books out to help people who have "church wounds." It is so very sad that this is necessary. It should be the opposite. We, as Christians, are supposed to be known to others by our love for each other. Yet, you get blindsided and betrayed by the very ones who are supposed to be supportive. That is why it is so shocking and hurtful. For some, it takes years to recover fully.

We are all a work in progress. I think of churches as hospitals. If we were perfect we wouldn't need church. A person may not get along well with all members of their family either. That doesn't mean we have an excuse for petty, cliquish behavior. The Bible also indicates that we should not be so surprised. His disciples betrayed Jesus as well. Peter denied him three times. He was pained by the betrayal. He loved and forgave them anyway.

Looking back at this time, if I knew then what I know now, I would probably have found some other church much earlier. I would also not likely choose this non-denominational group again. However, the valuable lessons I learned there would probably have then had to be learned somewhere else. That wouldn't have been pleasant either.

The main thing I learned was getting out of my comfort zone. In fact, I was out of my comfort zone so much that I had forgotten what comfortable felt like. I learned to adapt to not ever being very comfortable. I honestly think that God puts us in situations so that *He* becomes our comfort zone. Then, because He is with us, we can deal with just about anything and still think on our feet. It is all about finding joy and contentment while the storms rage around us. It can be done.

A few years later when my friend Janet was near death, her husband wanted to put her into hospice care in the nursing home in which she then lived. A woman who was also Janet's friend, and Janet's husband, argued about putting her into hospice rather than taking measures to improve her health. I was there at the nursing home as well as Belinda and another woman who was presently attending my former church when the argument took place. This latter other woman had a vested interest in Janet's husband as it turned out. However, that was not the time for all that to come out. She reported to the senior pastor about the argument.

A few days later I received a call from the new female pastor, who I had known very well and respected her. She told me that Pastor Gerald had asked her to call. He wanted to know who was present at the nursing home when all this went on. I told her. In spite of Gerald's resentment of my decision to leave, he knew if asked that I would be truthful.

She asked, "Nobody else from here?"

"No," I said.

Then she went on to tell me how hard it is at this time for families and they don't need "outside people intervening in decisions." I told her although I understood that, the woman who had done the "reporting to Gerald" likely had her own *agenda* in the situation. I told her I thought this woman was interested in Janet's husband, or more likely, his assets. I met her previously when I had visited Janet and she was there. Janet's other friend, who was standing up to Janet's husband, was trying to look out for Janet. Her heart was in the right place. I had also met her before at Janet's. What I didn't tell the female pastor was that Janet may have told her friend, this woman, the same thing Janet had told me a few years prior, in confidence.

Janet told me, "If anything ever happens to me, a sudden death or something similar, then have it investigated."

I was shocked and she was serious. She and her husband had had many marriage problems in the past but that had been resolved and she had elected to stay with him. They were married for over forty years. This was the *rest of the story* the church didn't know. I ran into this woman a few years later and asked her if Janet had told her. She was shocked at Janet's request to me and said that Janet had not said anything about this to her. She was just trying to make sure things were not being done too hastily.

The female pastor then asked me what I was doing there. I told her that I was visiting Janet and that we had been friends for 30 years and that I knew her family and had even been to some family events.

She said, "Oh! I didn't realize you had known her so long. Well, I'll be sure to tell Pastor that. You certainly had a long history with her even before you came here."

I think that if I had not known Janet for so long, and had met her in that church, he would possibly have sent me a letter, or some sort of reprimand. It would not have had any impact legally in any way, of course, and emotionally I would have probably been sad for him and that church, for them to think they can reach out and control people in this manner. He probably thought he was being a good *pastor*, a good *shepherd* to his sheepfold.

As a footnote to this story, the woman who had reported the incident to Pastor Gerald went to visit Janet's husband later in the day of Janet's funeral. The husband told me about it at a later time, and he seemed truly embarrassed. His grown children, understandably, had fits over this and his connection to her.

"Dad," they said, "she is after your money and other things you have."

When I met this woman when I stopped to visit Janet while she was still at home, I didn't like her. I suspected her motives the first day I met her. I admit that knowing this, coupled with what Janet had told me about having her death investigated, I had the same concerns as the woman who confronted Janet's husband about hospice. However, I truly do not think he did anything Janet didn't want.

Janet's husband (widower) and the woman who visited him the day of the funeral were "together" until he finally had the will power and courage to rid him of her, several months later. He told me he had asked God to take away the desire for her. Apparently it worked.

Although I never shared much of any of the negatives when I was going to this church with my mom, I did share the positives, such as Pastor Bob and Belinda. Mom used to say she didn't want to get too involved in her church, other than regular attendance. She said if she did, then she always saw things she wished she hadn't seen. She admitted she was not able to get past it and viewed the individuals as not being the people she thought they were from then on and she had a hard time relating to them. It just wasn't worth the deep disappointment to her. This now strikes me as being very ironic, considering the secret she was keeping regarding my conception and parentage. Perhaps this is partially why she kept it to herself. She thought I would not ever be able to "get past it."

On the other hand, if nobody ever got involved, then a church would not survive. Perhaps you are experiencing something similar or witnessing it at your own church. I liken it again to families. We get involved with our families as well, and with friends. Sometimes those relationships get messy, just like our church family. If we turn tail and run at every hardship, nothing would ever be accomplished for good. Again, we are all a work in progress. God help us. The worst thing you can do, however, is to antagonize the situation. Pray about it. Don't borrow trouble. Keep your own backyard clean and use charity in your dealings. Give people a benefit of doubt. Never assume you know everything. Read Proverbs. Let God teach you through these scriptures. There is a time to leave and a time to stay. Be sure you don't get the two confused.

Chapter 38
"Restoration Begins"

"I will restore the relationships which have meant so much to you ..."

"I know that there is good in you Mom. I mean, I turned out well and you raised me," Cara said, as we stood by her back door on one sunny summer day. I was at once confused and shocked. I was unable to respond right then. We had a good relationship, or so I thought. I began to wonder where this was coming from. I always felt that she knew me fairly well. If she did, then from where was this comment originating?

I have since had conversations with all my children at one time or another, to try to clarify choices and decisions I made which had a negative impact on them for a time while they were being raised. I have also asked for and received their forgiveness. Divorce, for example, is not an easy time for anyone. There were also individual events as children that needed to be dealt with and accounted for. Most of it was relatively minor. One may have felt I slighted them in favor of another child, for example.

Sean was possibly the most magnanimous of my grown children. He said, "We all make mistakes, Mom. Parents usually try do the best they can. I know that you did that." One thing my children did seem to be certain of was that I always loved them. I found a measure of comfort in that knowledge.

Ben and I divorced in 1997. None of my children were minors. I figured if the divorce got worse than it already was in and of itself, I didn't want my children to be subjected to the whims of the court. I didn't feel that would be fair to them. So, I made the decision to wait till later. I focused on raising them and other interests, hobbies and attempted to make the best of our situation. Our lives were fairly stable throughout this time, other than the things the children were doing, which was a lot. A person only has so much energy for dealing with things. I believe I made the right decision in waiting.

At the time of the divorce, my sons all seemed to share the opinion that it was long overdue. My daughters were glad that I waited and thought I made the right decision. I have found that there are no decisions that are actually "right" in cases of divorce. All those decisions can be is somehow *less wrong*.

I can understand why a person on the other side (an in-law) of a family may be inclined talk about things that are none of their business when a divorce is in process, for example. It may not be right, but it is understandable. The *best* of divorces can get very messy and emotions are usually fairly raw.

However, when the person who is doing the talking is a member of your own family, it becomes less "understandable." It becomes even less understandable when the divorce and all the things surrounding and compounding it are not the focus after all. It is particularly alarming when you find out that it has been going on for many years, behind your back and to the people who you love the most, your children.

When I first heard the phrase "I will restore the relationships which have meant so much to you …" from Pastor Bob, I had little idea that I had so many relationships that *needed* restoring. I was unaware of the malicious backbiting that had been going on for years, by someone I trusted, but God knew.

"When you are ready, and I am ready, we will deal with some things," one visiting minister at my church had shared with me, something he felt God had shown him for me. Another man, and elder in the church said to me, with an incredulous laugh, "Chérie, you are a Joseph! Even in your own family." And from yet another "prophetic" person who visited the church, this time a female. She spoke "Your storehouses have been looted! …A LOT! …"

Joseph was the young man in the Old Testament Bible story who was favored by his father, and all his brothers were jealous of him, so they sold him into slavery and told their father he'd been killed. I had no idea to what this might refer at the time, nor did I understand how my storehouses were *looted*, so I shelved it. My attitude was that if it was so, then I would learn about it in time and if not, then not. I now know that the "some things" we would *deal with*, mentioned above was a key point. I also now know to what the "Joseph" reference referred. And to the storehouses being looted, yes it is all now *abundantly* clear and on at least three levels, beginning with my birthright and culminating with my sister Dede's actions.

When my children were grade school age, and for the girls even a little younger, they spent a week in the summer at Grandma's in Lima, as I have mentioned before. She managed to show them a very good time and I knew my mother always looked forward to their visits. My sister lived near her and when she wasn't working, she was at Mom's.

I first began to realize Dede's negative feelings about me when I went with her on a trip to Pittsburgh to visit a couple friends of hers. It was just a weekend trip but we had sightseeing planned and it seemed like a good idea at the time. I looked forward to it, not just to the mini vacation but also to spending some quality girl time with my sister. We were in our thirties.

I cannot remember all the details now, but we hadn't been there long when she began to say things, jabs, to me in front of her friends. I am sure we have all experienced this sort of thing, for example, between a married couple where one puts the other down in front of others and if you have experienced this, you know how uncomfortable it is. When you are on the receiving end of it, it is even worse, particularly when you are blindsided with it. At first I simply dismissed it, but it kept happening over and over throughout the weekend, almost on an hour by hour basis. Even one of her friends began to look at me like "what is going on here?" I am sure my face read the same way. It seemed to be one verbal attack after another. When I tried to answer her, she doubled her attack with a vengeance. So, I said nothing in response. I tried to let it be the proverbial water off a ducks back. Her friends were obviously trying to ignore it as well and seemed visibly uncomfortable.

By the time we were on the drive home, she had settled down and acted as if nothing was wrong. I began crying in the car, since we were away from her friends and I could no longer stop the hurt. When she questioned me, she assumed I was just emotional, because I had enjoyed the trip and didn't want it to end. I didn't correct the assumption because I was simply too hurt for any more verbal abuse. I realized in its fullness for the first time, that apparently *my sister hated me.* I had no idea *why* she would hate me, but it was very clear at the time that she did. When we got back to Mom's and we were alone, I told Mom a little about it and that I would never again go anywhere with Dede, ever. Mom just looked at me strangely, but kept silent. I could tell she was not happy about the whole thing. Mom always preferred *peace,* no matter at what cost.

At times Dede would say something so completely off the wall when I was visiting at mom's, again put downs. It was as though she wanted to think I was bereft of any virtue whatsoever, and sought to vilify me at every opportunity.

I remember one time when I reacted defensively (when she was out of earshot), I said to Mom, who had witnessed the whole thing and knew my intent was *not* what Dede said and that, as usual, I was being wrongly accused, "what is *wrong* with her?"

I was baffled.

"I don't know," Mom said with a very worried look on her face.

She really *didn't* know but it was clear that she knew something was indeed wrong. We both did. We stared at each other for several moments, neither one of us knowing what else to say.

Dede was generally on pretty good behavior toward me as long as there was someone neutral around, unless it was Mom, then *all pretensions* on her part were gone. However, she became increasingly overtly critical of me as time passed, even in front of others as she had in Pittsburgh.

When I finally asked her about what was wrong on the Pittsburgh trip, an attempt to get to the bottom of her animosity and to resolve it, she said, "Nothing! It's just that you like to be the center of attention and the one time we are with *my* friends and you aren't being the center of attention, then you think I am picking on you. Get over yourself, Chérie. So much drama!"

My attempt to try to fix whatever it was that was happening was obviously futile. I have learned over and over that a relationship cannot be fixed as long as one of the people involved does not want it fixed.

Mom knew how Dede felt about me. She had to know. It was obvious even to my children. I will never understand how she could she have continued to allow this all through the years. Some things will never have any answers, at least this side of heaven. I can only conclude that she was afraid to rock the boat. She probably *hoped* it would all get better. Unfortunately, not dealing with "sickness," whether it physical or mental or emotional, usually means it just enlarges over time; it escalates. Sometimes we just have no other choice but to let it all go. This is what I did. Some things only God can fix.

If there is a difficult or negative family member or person in your life who has been unfair or told lies about you, you can be resentful if that choice makes you feel better. I can promise you, however, that it won't. It really does come down to something I discovered for myself. Ask yourself, do you really trust God, as you claim? Do you really believe He is in charge? The Word says that, "His arm is not short." Do you believe that? Do you believe that even if it takes a very long time to improve? What do you think the word "longsuffering" means, something the Bible also admonishes us to be, as Christians? It means, dear one, to suffer long if needs be.

I can almost hear you. No, you do *not* have to continue to allow the person who has so wronged you to continue to do this by allowing them access to your life. That would be masochistic and enabling. If it is a family member, this makes it more challenging, but unless the family member is totally disruptive, certainly you can get through family gatherings and still enjoy them. Again, God keeps you in perfect peace, when your mind is stayed or focused on Him. You can also forgive them, pray for them, and let it all go and trust God to deal with the situation. In His good time, He will do so. God is your defender. Rest in this; be at peace. Focus on all His blessings in your life. Focus on your family and good friends and move on. If you don't, it will fester and you will be miserable. It will keep you from enjoying your life. You will have allowed, in essence, the offending person to rob you of actually living your life fully. Nothing is worth this. Nothing. Let it go. He will help you if you ask.

Chapter 39
"Let the games begin …"

Internet-Beware!

Mom knew I was on "Christian" internet singles websites. Not being clued in as to how it all worked, she was very nervous for me to be on the internet in any capacity, although she enjoyed going to the library with Dede and watching her check email and whatever else she did. Dede told me that she was even considering getting her own email address. Unfortunately her health deteriorated to the point where she couldn't make that trip. I always wished that Dede would get her computer set up at Mom's so they could have the convenience there and it would've given Mom something to do, more than just sit, watch TV and the like. A friend of Dede's had given her a computer for free, but Dede procrastinates and it sat there unused for over ten years. It is likely still sitting there.

Mom was right. The internet can be a "bad" place. It can also be a beneficial tool. I now use it for research and email almost exclusively. However, while I was on a singles site I viewed a man's profile that I found to be very interesting and so I pursued it.

His profile headline and commentary:

"Looking for a woman who will be faithful and loyal no matter what. … I am honest and trustworthy. … I command a battalion of 600 men … I am shy. …"

I wrote to him because his profile, listed on this "Christian" website, was so convincing and so real. I was grateful for his service to our country. He seemed so wonderfully sincere and endearing. Certainly a Lt. Colonel in our military could be trusted. Surely Mom would even approve of this one. I got to "know" this man. His name was Don.

"It's strategy, Chérie, being covert. The military used stuff like this during the war to make our enemies think we had weaponry we didn't have. What I do is not any different."

Not any different? Don and I were not talking about war, but about whether it was right for him to lie to women about his age, about the fact that although he told them he was still in the military and active with various things there, including covert maneuvers in far away places, when in fact he was retired from the military for several years, was at home, and was 10 to 12 years or more older than what his various profiles on singles sites indicated. The rest of his profile indicated he was searching for an honest, loving and loyal woman that would stick by him no matter what. I initially felt that I fit these criteria, when I first saw his profile, but perhaps I fit it a little too much.

Sample email notes from him:

Dear Chérie
Much of our platoon suffered heat stroke. I am OK but I still feel the effects. My men are doing pretty good. I am being shipped overseas....
Love, Don

Dear Chérie,
I am in Turkey. Our unit was flown down into Iraq on a covert mission. We watch movements of the Iraqi's with night goggles. We saw a caravan of trucks heading out. Sometimes it looks as though the Iraqi's spotted us somehow. We are covered over with netting and I am emailing from our battleground computer. We take turns manning it and watching while others sleep.
The holidays were good. It was on base and they had the traditional foods, a buffet. ....
I hurt my knee when I was running to get to the chopper. ...All my love,
Don

Dear Chérie

I was wounded but I am OK. I am being sent back to the states. Right now I am in a hopsital in Germany. ...
Love,
Don

Dear Chérie
I am in Greenland, enroute, but here for awhile. I don't know how long and I am staying in BOQ (bachelor officers quarters)...
All my love, Don
Dear Chérie
I am at Ft. Sam Houston.... I should be able to retire soon.

...

Love, Don

Don's emails were always lengthy and filled with the details of his soldier life so far away. I was captivated. He also called from time to time and we had lengthy conversations.

When I thought he was in Iraq, my friend Belinda and I bought several different kinds of candy bars, and toiletries we thought the men in his unit could use. I packed it in a large cardboard box, included a thank you letter to his men and decorated the outside of the box with American flag stickers and other patriotic symbols. I also sent him several cookie packages with a variety of extras in it that a soldier in the field may need. He emailed that the men in his unit came running when they saw him with the big box we sent. He said they particularly liked the chocolate covered raisins we had included. I sent the box to the address he gave me. It was a PO box but he said the postmaster there knew him and knew where he was in the world and would know what APO to forward my mail. I believed him, of course. I know now that I *wanted* to believe him.

All the while, Don was sitting in his own home, at his own computer, lying to me.

When he had finally *gotten himself "home" from the military*, he was too "incapacitated" to visit me or to allow me to come there at that time but promised *that would soon change*. He also said he would retire soon. He told me over time of different medications he was on, including blood pressure medication.

All this happened over a two-year period. How could I have hung in there that long believing him? I don't know. Maybe I knew he was lying deep inside, but couldn't bring myself to admit it. So much time and effort had gone into this "relationship" or potential one.

He told me about Kathy, his adult, mentally developmentally disabled daughter, that he had cared for or had her cared for from the time she was three. Her mother wanted nothing to do with her, and Don and she divorced. Part of the reason for that was because he was gone so much for the military and she found someone else. Viet Nam was a challenging time for many.

His second wife loved horses and he provided horses for her as well as other nice things. Again, he was gone much of the time in the military, so she found someone else and divorced him. Yes, there are always two sides to any story, but there didn't seem to be any reason not to be honest about this. At some point, he also told me of a retired minister friend of his named Paul. He told me the name of the church he and they were currently attending.

When he emailed one day that he quit taking his blood pressure medication because he thought it was making him sick, I was frantic. I knew others who took this medication and what could happen if they didn't. I also knew he was depressed, by his own admission. His emails were filled with constant negativity. I decided to at least *try* to do something to help him although I was 650 miles away. I also knew his daughter could not do anything to help him if he should pass out and be laying there on the floor unconscious.

I called the mega church Don told me about that he and Paul attended. I looked it up online, so I knew it existed. I knew the church would not give out Paul's phone number, but I would give them mine.

A very friendly young woman answered the phone. I explained to her my intent to get hold of the retired minister and why. She told me she thought she knew which man I was talking about. She took my information and said she would contact him and he could decide from there. Later that day, Paul called me.

I asked him if he knew Don and he did. So far, so good. I went on to explain about the blood pressure medication and how worried I was. He said he would try to help. Along with this, he acknowledged that he knew Don pretty well. The time had apparently arrived for me to get some straight answers. I was both relieved to finally have some of those answers and yet terrified of what they would be.

Understandably, Paul was somewhat skeptical since I was a total stranger, when I told him how I knew Don. In order to convince him and his wife that I was indeed who I said I was and also to convince him of Don's stories to me, he gave me their email address and I forwarded three or four of Don's emails. Paul and his wife were then convinced as well as shocked at Don's stories, his lies. Paul set me straight. He also assured me that Don seemed *just fine*, although he knew that he did take medications.

Previously, Don told me a friend of his had died and he was so sad he couldn't be there since he was in Texas in the hospital at Ft. Sam Houston. Paul laughed and told me that Don was at his home and was one of the pallbearers at the friends' funeral. He told me that Don had been at his home the entire time Don was claiming to be in various other parts of the world with the military. Paul told me Don was retired military. So, although he was retired, the part on being in the military was true, as well as the rank he claimed. I have heard that the most believable lie is to mix truth with it so it is harder to discern.

He went on to tell me that he knew Don wrote to many women the world over, likely with similar stories to them. He also said that although Don claimed he was so very ill, that he appeared to be healthy. Giving Don benefit of doubt, he told me that he thought Don did this to assuage loneliness. Paul did admit that Don had seemed to be *dating* a few women from time to time.

Armed with all this now accurate information, although I was in shock, I decided to confront Don in an email. I told him everything, including my initial concerns, which motivated me to attempt to contact Paul. Don was obviously surprised at all the information. He seemed at a loss for words, which was unusual for him.

When I asked him about the care package that Belinda and I had sent to him for his troops, he told me that he had not kept it but had then donated it to the troops himself. Due to the most believable lie theory of mixing truth with the lie, I suspected this might be partly true. In spite of everything, I still wanted to believe in some redeeming quality in this man. He was good, after all, to his adult disabled daughter and cared for her as best he could. He had done this for years. Not many people could or would have chosen to do this. I decided, wisely or not, to accept his apology and to hang in there. I am aware that this flies in the face of common sense and self-preservation. Some would view it as masochistic and neurotic. There are times I have viewed it the same way. I, however, viewed it simply as forgiveness. For some things in life, there really is a fine line. I do believe it is always a good idea to take the high road.

Paul and his wife used their influence to convince Don to allow me to visit. I stayed at Don's home. I got to know Kathy, his daughter. Everything in his life seemed so "normal" *in person*. He was a friendly man who engaged others in intelligent conversation. His education and military background was not a lie. He was a battalion commander before he retired. This is not a lowly position. It is also not a position the US Army would allow someone they considered to be some sort of risk or not stable to occupy. I think this was much of my reasoning for allowing him to continue to be a part of my life, even though this was a painful thing for me. I also developed a close relationship with Paul and his wife. Even though they knew the truth about Don, they did not discard him as a *friend*, or perhaps more as someone they could possibly help in some way. This was also part of my own reasoning.

In 2006, Don asked me to come down to care for Kathy and look after things after his major back surgery. The military and playing college football had taken its toll. I was there from early June through the middle of September. After Don was able to walk better, we went to live variety shows in a nearby city. Kathy loved this. We also went to a buffet regularly, a buffet Don loved since he knew many people there. It was the way he and Kathy socialized and the way they met Paul and his wife. I got to know some of these people as well. Some of them were what most people would call at best eccentric and entertaining, however, at least one man was not only weirdly beyond the norm, but was also engaged in activities that were against the law.

I am departing directly from Don for the moment so I may share the story of

"God's Cell Phone."
(or "An example of WEIRD")

Joe, (aka "weird"), had a full, but cropped-beard, was a 60 something male, 6'2," slender, and 95% bald, but he wore an expensive straight, very long-haired brown wig, and sported nicely manicured acrylic gel nails, (which he had done regularly), and although he had once had a somewhat lucrative marketing job, he didn't do any paid work at the time I met him.

He was somewhat fond of lamenting over his ex-wife and that she divorced him, by saying "what about our vows? Love, honor ... till death do us part, what happened?" He also didn't believe in hell in the hereafter, and that it was all a made up conspiracy, but that heaven was quite real. Those who hold to more traditional beliefs in Joe's estimation were just ignorant and in need of his enlightenment. You could say Joe had a *Christ complex*, with a twist perhaps, like water *drained* of its liquidity and substance, or gravity that no longer holds to you so you may occasionally *float* a little above ground. He had a smooth, mellifluous voice, which had a contrived nice-nice sound to it. Perhaps he ascribed to the adage that to get a person's attention one should "whisper," or in his case use some other unique vocal enticement to gain listeners.

Joe's five grown children turned against him after the divorce, all except for his oldest, Lou Ann. She always had a kindness about her and more tolerance for the bizarre in life. Too bad Tom, her husband, had Joe's number and couldn't stand his father-in-law.

On first glance Joe's appearance was neat enough, other than the wig, and he dressed as though he belonged in GQ, the young, active, senior citizen version. He always had a taste for the finer things. Unfortunately his wallet was not up to the task so Joe was forced to become more inventive to obtain these things.

He apparently decided to become some sort of askew or asymmetrical "Jesus." Perhaps the "twist" was much like the lime one might put in a margarita, except Joe's twist of lime would be tossed in a glass of milk. It may sour some, but it sure would waken the taste buds. To waken others, this was Joe's "mission" or so he expressed and fantasized.

Joe took his mission seriously and perhaps to make his message more real and palatable to the more reticent, he obtained and occasionally donned a white linen robe, complete with a long, white linen cloth draped invitingly over his right arm. He began to call himself, and referred to those he befriended, as "brothers." After attending a mainstream church and managing to offend the church leadership by approaching those for whom he prayed for financial support, he was dismissed from his praying duties. He left this church and after nursing his wounds for a time, he declared himself to be a clergyman, a bonafide minister. He was so convincing to some that Golden Buffet allowed him the minister's discount for their Sunday spread.

Joe also liked to visit known haunts of a variety of people, but in particular those who seemed (in his opinion) to need his message more than others. Armed with his robe, he set out for the little park with the gazebo where drunks and where college students, who liked to debate and flirt liked to hang out. Drunks were simply in need and just soused enough to listen to anyone, while college students liked to fancy themselves as open to all and broadminded, thus, both offering the perfect pawns for Joes purposes. Regardless, most found him totally engaging. More often than not, his conquests would be more mature men down on their luck. He drew them under his wing. They found him comforting. He provided some of their needs for them. Since he gave up gainful employment after his bitter divorce, one might wonder how he was able to provide anything.

Joe held a certain charm for men who had been through a painful time, and who hasn't been through some painful times?

He also held a draw for men who are seemingly and inexplicably mesmerized in almost morbid fascination with the unusual, like those who chase ambulances to see what they can see. Fortunately for Joe, there are more than a few of these men and all he really needs is one (at a time) with money.

All his benefactors are made to feel special and that they are contributing to something "bigger" than themselves, to Joe's version of "God's Kingdom here on earth," or to *Joe* as the case may be, and in his book, they are the same thing. He pocketed much and he gave enough assistance to those he "adopts," or has allowed them to feel as though they had adopted him if this suited his purposes best, to make them feel that he had indeed saved them or they him.

He even helped his benefactors, particularly if he thought they had a little extra cash to "invest." Joe had contacts that provided his benefactors with ironclad *guarantees* that they would not lose money, but may gain them much more money. Some had even been able to recoup at least their initial investment when the dubious "just cannot fail" project failed.

Joe only had one outstanding warrant for his arrest, in a neighboring state. It really was only a *small* felony and since, as in most bureaucracies the right hand doesn't know what the left is doing and nobody had energy to look at their computer, coupled with the fact that Joe kept a "low profile" most of the time, he escaped notice.

Well, he escaped notice except for the close call when the FBI was brought in on an investigation of a couple men who lived in the same housing facility as he. Though they found nothing incriminating to anyone's knowledge regarding Joe, that was a little too close for comfort, and the investigation was still ongoing the last I heard. The man who owned the facility was the one under investigation for allegedly defrauding the elderly out of their homes and property with bogus, realistic looking, official documents, but he allowed Joe to reside there for "free" because (he said) "he would be homeless. I just can't do that." Perhaps there is some irony here, considering the alleged crime. Perhaps this is indicative of the "criminal who has a heart of gold mentality," sort of like Robin Hood.

Joe spent much of his day sleeping since he was usually out all night at the park. When he wasn't sleeping, or eating a meal someone purchased for him, the *only* kind he ate, he was on someone's borrowed cell phone talking with "brothers" who were out of state. Joe cleverly convinced the owner of the cell that perhaps this was "God's cell" and he should feel *privileged* for having provided it, and for being part of something so vast and important.

Joe maintained an even disposition most of the time, unless he was crossed. *Crossed* could be a disagreement over theology or it could mean someone assessed him with a certain amount of accuracy and lacked the temerity of many, to refrain from informing Joe that what he was doing might not be nice, may be against Christian principles, at the least, and is probably even criminal. Most times it was Joe who took the first *swing*. If he perceived someone understood him and his motives more than he would like, and perhaps due to that, threatened his *supply* from a benefactor, he was known to rant, rage, accuse, call for the perpetrator to be "thrown out," ran out of town on a bus, (to the point of calling the bus station to get the schedule and seat availability), called names and all else he would normally preach against. There were simply no holds barred. Most of the time, however, his machinations were quite subtle for most unsuspecting potential "victims" or benefactors, as the case may be.

Since the FBI arrived, Joe moved in with one of his victim benefactors. Joe may have been fine there if he had left well enough alone. This benefactor enjoyed his privacy and didn't like sharing things with Joe's "brothers." Joe had big plans for this house. His intention was to move the brothers in if they needed, and for others simply a nice place to fraternize. All was going according to plan, till the benefactor began to catch on that he was not so important, except as Joe's lackey and the one to provide whatever Joe wanted to do with the "brothers," so the benefactor refused to speak to the "brothers" even when one of them came up to him; if at the buffet, he would say nothing, but just turn and walk away.

Joe then moved to another house with yet another "benefactor." Give Joe a toehold and he would overwhelm you and take over totally.

Some call people like Joe lunatic fringe. They refuse to work. They have a "higher calling" than doing more mundane yet *paying* jobs, after all. Others don't call them anything, but just make a wide berth around them when passing by, perhaps a wise idea. Psychologists may call them narcissists. Whatever you call them, most agree that the term *user* applies.

Unfortunately, Don was one of Joe's benefactors and Joe lived at Don's house for a time. I knew about Joe before my arrival and I knew he was bad news. When I got there, I tried to be open, but it didn't take long for me to realize Joe was exactly the person I thought he was. Paul and his wife agreed with me. They couldn't understand why Don didn't have the backbone to get rid of him.

After Don's surgery, Joe called him several times a day and tried to keep him on the phone for long periods of time, I suspected he did this to exert control over Don. With me there, I think he felt threatened. He was always asking Don for favors. On one occasion, when Joe asked him to come and get him, since his car was being repaired, to get groceries, Don reluctantly said yes but immediately regretted his decision since he had a terrible headache. I offered to go in his place. He seemed grateful. I took Kathy with me. In retrospect, Don should have called Joe back to tell him that I would be coming in his place. However, what was important was that Joe would be able to get his groceries, or so we thought.

When Kathy and I arrived and knocked at his upstairs apartment door, he greeted me with an angry "Where's Don? Why are you here? I was going to have Don take me to the Mud House Lounge to help people tonight." I was surprised at his reaction, but I explained to him about Don's headache and that he'd wanted me to come.

Joe interrupted with "You don't like me. You didn't like me before you even arrived here. You smile and act friendly but you don't mean it." At this point, I told Kathy to go wait for me at the car, since she was beginning to look upset that Joe was yelling at me. She didn't need to see or hear this tirade. She left for the car.

"I'm not going anywhere with you!" Joe screamed. "OK," I answered calmly. "I thought you didn't have any food."

"I have enough to get by."

We exchanged a few more words with him getting angrier and I finally said, "Well, I am done here. You have a big problem."

I went to the car and we drove home.

When we got back Kathy went to her daddy and said "Joe yelled at Mree!" *Mree* was her name for me. I told Don about the whole thing. Don looked surprised. Joe's true colors were just beginning to emerge.

Less than two weeks later while we ate at the buffet, Joe came to the table. He acted as though nothing was amiss, that the prior conversation had not ever taken place. I think he'd hoped I had said nothing to Don so was playing it cool. Finally, I said to him, "I'm sorry, but I find it difficult to make small talk with someone who screamed at me only a few days ago." Don confirmed to him that he had indeed sent me to pick Joe up as I had told him. Joe apologized for thinking otherwise. However, he had said many other things that day. The conversation ended with Joe attempting at first to cajole me and to question my Christianity, my "love for Jesus." I was appalled. I also refused to defend myself. My life was none of his business and I knew his interest was only to gain some foothold so he could exploit it. (The Bible calls this "casting pearls before swine" and that we shouldn't do this.) I ended his efforts when I responded sincerely and bluntly, as I looked directly into his eyes.

"Joe, you are just angry because I am on to you. I know what you are doing. I know who you are. ...

I don't really care what you think of me. For someone to care about another's opinions, they have to respect them. I cannot respect you due to what you do."

Joe stared in shocked silence. I don't think he could quite believe someone, especially a woman, would have the nerve to confront him with total truth and honesty about who he was and what he was up to; he had been uncovered. I admit that I had never before, nor since, been so confrontational with anyone in my life. It shocked me a little, but I knew I did the right thing.

We left and went home. Joe called Don later to tell him to throw me out. He gave him the bus schedule and told him to put me in a cab and send me to the station. "Throw her out Don! She is evil." He ranted. He was beyond even remotely rational.

Don didn't throw me out.

I would like to say that this ended Joe's involvement in Don's life, but that didn't happen fully till a couple years later. By then Don had allowed others in his life who were doing the same thing but in a little lesser way than Joe had done. At least they didn't monopolize as much time as Joe had done. The two of them were also not as controlling and mean spirited as Joe. Paul and his wife and I discussed it on more than one occasion. We concluded that apparently this was just something Don does. Perhaps he had brought home stray puppies as a boy. This was sort of an adult version of that.

A couple other things, which caused me to give Don benefit of doubt, as to his reason for doing some of the things he did, was that not only had he served in Viet Nam as a young soldier and had seen some horrendous things, but also as a small boy he had seen his little three-year-old sister hit and killed by a car. He felt responsible, and thought he should have been able to save her somehow. Then he watched his parents grieving for her. It would have been a horrific thing for any child to go through. He was the oldest of three children and the girl was the youngest. He was also given much responsibility at a young age and didn't seem to have the carefree childhood many have. Perhaps all this entered into his choice, however, to try to "fix" Joe somehow. He was overly patient with Joe's antics.

Don couldn't fix his baby sister and he couldn't fix those he saw killed in Nam. When Paul and his wife and I discussed it, we concluded that Don involved himself in co-dependent relationships both male, and in the past, female. Paul observed that he certainly didn't act like what our perceptions of a man who was once a Lt. Col. would act like. I advised Don that he was only enabling Joe and not doing him any favors by doing this. Paul told him the same thing.

I broke all my "rules" throughout my acquaintanceship with Don, particularly one major one. This was obviously my *weakness*. My rule for *any* relationship, though unwritten, was that if a man lies, he could not be trusted. If he lied about one or more things, he likely has some sort of chronic problem. Drop him immediately. If you cannot trust the other person, you have nothing. If that rule is foremost, then you can move on to lesser rules. That rule was the litmus test, the deal breaker.

My third visit to Don's home was when he asked that I take care of Kathy while he went on a two-week trip to visit his brother in Arizona. Since I didn't charge him anything for this, I probably saved him a couple thousand dollars, which it would have cost him to hire a caregiver at the going rate for that time.

He called every day to check on things while he was away. Kathy and I had a good time when he was gone. I took her to the zoo, to movies, out to eat, to church and she seemed to love it. We were true pals. When Don returned we continued to enjoy outings. Don had asked me a few years prior that if anything happened to him, would I please consider being Kathy's successor guardian. I had agreed, so I looked at this as a way that she could get used to having me around. I thought that she would feel more secure should this transfer take place. Developmentally disabled people adjust very slowly to changes.

Don was in the midst of setting up a trust for her future care. Since he was never one to move swiftly, I thought that if I stayed for awhile he might make better progress, as I could also help him with organization of whatever was needed and take care of other household responsibilities for him. Things did get done while I was there. Don was accustomed to staying up till about 2 or 3:00 AM and sleeping till 10:30, arising to eat cereal and then going back to bed till 2:30 PM. At that time he got up and we got ready to go to the buffet to arrive around 3:30 PM. After dinner, we would go to Walmart, then take his side kick home (one of the men he was currently buying meals), then we went home. Sometimes we went to a movie or to a live show in the nearby city and these activities altered our normal pattern. I usually got up at about 9:00 am and took care of some responsibilities as well as took walks. Kathy was used to Don's schedule and adopted it as her own, although she sometimes got up and spent quality time with me.

The state where Don resides does not have a lot of activities for the developmentally disabled population as some states do. It is sad. She needed so much more to her life than she has. However, that was not my call.

By this time I had long since lost any hope or desire that this "friendship" would go to more than friendship. What I *finally* realized was that the friendship was mostly a one-way friendship. I was *his* friend and did much for him, and he seemed to expect or at least hoped for it. I also knew that Don continued his internet communications with women all over the world, many of whom probably believed his fiction. How many women he has duped, I can only imagine. Some he had met before me, in person. Many were in other countries hoping he would be the one to bring them here. At times he even seemed amused by his own stories. He said the internet is made up of people doing exactly as he was doing, including women who do this to men. I tried to explain that although he was right about some, not all were doing that. Some of these women were probably like me, hopeful, honest and vulnerable.

I knew there had been countless women and Don admitted to this. *All* that he met in person had apparently done some terrible things to him, according to all he shared with me. One of them from another state stayed with him for a few days and after she left he found that one of his guns was missing. He had a large gun collection, an interest developed from being in the military. He said he called the sheriff and reported the stolen items with her as the suspect. I don't recall him ever mentioning that it was ever resolved.

However, while I was there, I reached into the cupboard one day to pull down a cookbook from a kitchen cupboard. He had a number of cooking related *booklets* there as well. I bumped something in the back of the shelf. I pulled out the booklets and looked. I saw a gun. It *unnerved* me a little. I removed it gingerly and took it to him. Lo and behold, it was the very gun he thought this woman had stolen and had reported it stolen and reported her as the "thief." He didn't look all that surprised when I took the gun to him.

All the previous women had either stolen money or he unwisely loaned it and they refused to pay him back by declaring bankruptcy, or some other hardship. Bottom line, they were accused of doing something wrong.

Don and I have now known each other for several years. Not all of it has been unpleasant, obviously, and in fact much of it was truly fun. I have respect for the things that Don did in our military, the sacrifices, as well as sacrifices he has made for his daughter. I have done things in my life for which I am not pleased about also, as we all have. Perhaps I can help Kathy some day. And maybe, if I keep him even a little distracteded, be his friend, he will have less time and less inclination to email, lie, string along, and devastate some other woman or women who have their hopes up, or even to help prevent him, in his own gullibility, to be taken in by agencies or people who are likely illegitimate, as he has been in the past.

I also want him to be well, not just physically, as he has so *many* physical problems, but perhaps more important, spiritually.

I am doing my best not to judge and I am sincerely concerned for him. It grieves me deeply. The state of the world today would indicate this is certainly not the time for any of us to be messing around. He complains about any and everything, most of the time. He doesn't understand why, in such an evil world, that God hasn't acted to stop it by now and why indeed did He create it to begin with knowing it would be so.

Why do any of us do the things, make the choices we make, that seem to fly in the face of common sense? Don and I talk frequently and I believe we have developed a "friendship." I also live my own life and *I am* truly enjoying it.

What is it in your life, beloved? Who is it? What are you getting from this relationship or thing? What do you intend to do about it? Mom always quoted, "To thine own self be true." Are you being *true* to yourself, or are you telling yourself something other than that so that you don't have to deal with what you know you need to deal with? I promise you, it won't go away until you do.

One important and final thing to remember, most people who are actively in "sin" are there because they have been wounded, hurt in some way at some point. They are likely making the wrong choices to escape some of the hurt, the pain and perhaps they have no idea how to make things better. Rather than judge them and/or allow yourself to gossip, search your motivations. True, sin is sin. It is wrong. We have all sinned. Humble compassion, rather than judgment, (which is simply rooted in pride), meeting others where they are is exactly what Jesus has done for you and it is the way for us to respond to others.

Joshua 1:9

New Living Translation (NLT)

[9] This is my command—be strong and courageous! Do not be afraid or discouraged. For the LORD your God is with you wherever you go."

Chapter 40
Letters

Dear Harry Dad,

I know you finally grew to love me. That was all I ever wanted. It would have been nice if you could have been more physically demonstrative of that, but with your rather stoic German upbringing, I know that wouldn't have come natural.

You sacrificed so much for us, especially for Mom. Thank you for being so good to my mother. You always sent her the most flamboyantly romantic cards whatever occasion it was, and you always remembered all those occasions too. Thank you for the pretty cards I got from you as well. It was the closest thing to a hug. You used cards to say what came hard for you to say out loud.

I have wondered at your agreement and participation in the covering of the truth of my natural parentage. I do know you were a wonderful man with impeccable integrity. So, I trust that you thought it was the best thing to do. I accept that.

Thank you for holding on till I got there while you lay in the hospital the last few hours of your life. I am sorry it took me so long. There are so many things I would do over if I could. Oh, and I am so glad you got such a kick out of your grandchildren.

Know this, you are and will forever be, my dad. I love you. It took me till I was in my mid teens to admit it, but I sure hope you knew. I think you did. By for now Dad.

Love,
Your daughter, Chérie

Dear Hubert,

If all I heard is the truth, you knew what Mom wanted when she approached you. Sometimes we make choices we may regret. If what your widow said about you is true, and I believe it is, I know it must have been very painful for you to see me and have to let go. I know you did it because you thought it was the best choice for us all, under these circumstances. My mother could be formidable if and when she thought it was necessary.

For any and all pain my mother's choices probably caused you, I am so very very sorry. Know that I would have loved to know you. There simply are no words to express just how much.

I believe that someday I will get to see you, to know you. Be sure to be there to greet me along with the others upon my arrival, please.

I love you.
Your daughter,
Chérie

Dear Mom,

What a life you had! What a life I have had so far! WOW!

Yes, I know what you did, to what you were referring when we took our walk at my park. I know that you loved me, that you love me. I also know that you didn't intend not telling me to be a betrayal. I know that you didn't intend *anything* to be a betrayal, although this is what it was and you know this is how it felt for me. That is why you came to me that day, to reassure me of your love, no matter what it would begin to look like. Thank you. Thank you so very much.

Do you know how very beautiful I thought you were when I was a very small child? Do you know how much it meant to me that you were my mom? Did I ever tell you that even when I was as old as elementary school, I would look at other children's mothers, their actions, their interactions with their children and I would feel sincerely sorry for the children that they were not as lucky as I because they couldn't have you as their mom? If I didn't ever tell you, then I am now.

I am truly sorry for any hassles I gave you both while growing up and later. I am sorry I wasn't there for you the times I should have been. I am sorry for any selfishness on my part. Mom, I didn't know *how* to talk with you at times. If I had, you may have become upset and I didn't want that, to upset you. Perhaps that is how you felt about not telling me the truth, though my birthright. You likely feared rejection, a normal response. I will probably never know for certain. All that I do know for certain is that you tried to do the best you knew. That is *all* I need to know.

Thank you for being my Mom, for wanting a little girl to be here so very much that you broke the mold to try to achieve it. Here I am! And thank you for doing your best to protect me.

I love you so very, very much. Mom, I always have.

See you!

Love, your girl,

Chérie Ann

And finally:

Dear You,

Do you need to write your own letter to someone? It is time. You may even be able to send or email yours.

Love,

Chérie

Epilogue

I presently live in the same house in which I raised my children.

Mom died in April 2003. Just a few years before her death, I went to Lima to her church to watch her be baptized. What a joyous occasion. She had been a believer for many years, but finally took that final step.

My Aunt Rene lived to the ripe old age of 93, like her dad. She died in early June 2009. She had lived in a nursing facility in my hometown for the last year and a half of her life. She was active and able to stay in her own home till she was 91. My sister held her medical power of attorney and made the decision to move her to the nursing home when she became belligerent about not allowing home care workers into her house. She had Alzheimer's. Basically, true to form, Rene bit off her nose to spite her face as my grandma may have put it. I made every attempt to visit her at least once a month if not more. Most of the time, she recognized me. During one of those visits, she asked me "how old are you now?" I told her and she said, "I don't know how old I am." I told her and she said, "I don't feel like that." I am sure she didn't.

Her skin was as thin as onion paper and it injured easily. The head of the dementia unit always said how pretty she was. For her age, she didn't have many wrinkles.

Ben often accompanied me to go visit her. He knew her a long time as well and liked her husband. It was also enjoyable to watch some of the antics of the other residents in the dementia unit where she lived. They were as children and most were lovable, or at least amusing. She sometimes cried for her mom, I am told. It is sad. I know she would have preferred to be "home." I am sure she is much happier in heaven.

As I look back at my original family, Aunt Rene and Uncle John included, as well as extended members that I have observed, I feel very grateful to have been part of this family. They have and had their faults and foibles as all people and families do, however, they were down to earth and a fun loving group as a whole, who loved life and honestly tried to live it fully with the Golden Rule in mind most of the time. They could be referred to as the "salt of the earth" types of people. Ironically, I learned how to be "real" from them, in spite of their all too human moments of lack in that area. Nobody is perfect. However, overall, they were a true blessing. God knows what He is doing.

My oldest daughter, Becky, is happily married and has three sons. She has kept up her social work license just in case of some emergency, but is presently a stay at home mom. She home schools my grandsons, though also attends public school for a time. Their church has an active home school program so the children have outings and socialization.

My younger daughter Cara continues her job as a middle school history teacher. She is happily married to her high school sweetheart and now has three girls.

Sean earned his bachelor's degree in small business, family and entrepreneurship. During that same time, he served his stint in the Navy Reserve as well as attempting to pay his own way in college, along with working sometimes 70-80 hours a week. Also during this time, he met his wife who worked where he did when he was a shift manager. They are happy together and now own their own franchise in Texas. They also have a very handsome, sweet little son, who I have had the privilege to baby-sit often.

Daniel is working and is happily married to the young woman he met in the church where my old friend Lois, who died, had attended. Their adorable little daughters are growing so fast. The oldest certainly is precocious and a great big sister to her baby sister.

Marc graduated from a private college with a social work degree. He is still in the Air National Guard and he likes it, as well as the extra income it affords. He is now at the sergeant level. He is also Director of Social Work at a nursing home in a nearby suburb. Though he isn't married yet, he hopes to be.

I am a presently a substitute teacher the part of year when I am in my home state, and I like it most days. I love most of all spending whatever time I can with several grandchildren and my grown children and their spouses. We get along quite well and I am very thankful for my life with them.

Though I may have had some challenges particularly in recent years to deal with, though not as many as some people have, I have no regrets other than not spending more time with my children and appreciating them more than I did. I would imagine most moms would say the same.

I shared this with a female friend recently and she wanted to know why. I told her that my time in college was so time consuming and busy. However, I also knew that my children would be more likely to attend college and finish if I achieved this goal before them. It is part of a legacy I wanted for them, a leg up.

My oldest daughter, Becky, summed up a much larger legacy, one for which she is grateful. Though I feel that I haven't always been the best role model in some ways, she told me, "You taught us about Jesus, Mom. I am thankful for that." They, in turn, teach their children about Jesus.

Of course she, Cara, and Sean *also* related how, when I would drop them off for Vacation Bible School at the church I took them to then, they would sneak away after I drove off. They would walk down the street to the store and buy candy with the money I had given each of them for collection time. Cara felt guilty and the reality of it was not lost on her own young daughter, Rose, who, when she learned of it admonished her mom with, *"Mom! You stole Jesus' money!"* Sean simply didn't like the some of the adults at that church who he said "treated us like children." I know exactly how he felt. I never liked adults who did that with me when I was little either. So, I always tried to communicate with my children as young human beings and respected them as such. It seemed to work the best.

Sean confessed that when he was about ten years old, he was the one who threw a stone and it broke the $500.00 windshield on his dad's classic car. At the time he said a neighborhood boy rode past and threw something at it. When we called the police who investigated, he was terrified he would be discovered.

Some things a parent simply doesn't learn about till *much* later. Those are usually things that God takes care of anyway, in His own time.

It is always good to remember that if we are sincere and want to do His will, He will take care of the rest and will cover any mistakes, in the long run. And when you do deviate, don't run from Him. That was one of my biggest lessons. Where are you going to run anyway that He cannot find you? It's just silly.

He will pull you back in line, *always*. He did me, and so He continues.

"Your storehouses have been looted ... A LOT."

BUT, God said...

"And I will restore to you the years that the locust hath eaten, the cankerworm, and the caterpillar, and the palmerworm, my great army which I sent among you. ..." Joel 2: 25

Mom and Dad sure look like nice people, don't they? They were.

Sisters: Aunt Rene and my mother, Mable, taken some time between 2001 and 2003.

This is a picture of my financially secure great grandparents and their family. Grandpa is the young boy, Ira, standing behind his mother. Behind him is Fremont, his elder brother and whose funeral was the first I remember attending. I may have been two years old or perhaps less. Mom carried me in her arms and I remember looking down into the coffin at his body. He was much older than in this picture, of course, but I remember feeling afraid and not liking it there. Beside Fremont, is Grace, their sister. Beside Grandpa is his brother Earl, the one who served time and made great lasagna. It looks like Great Grandpa may have had red hair. Perhaps that is where my red highlights com

The following page is a portrait of my grandparents, Grandpa (Ira Victor, AKA Putter) and Grandma (Sophia Mae) with their children. Beside Grandma is their oldest child, Clifford. Roy is below him. Is it my imagination or does he look like he is full of mischief? Next to Roy is Bonnie, the oldest girl. The sweet little girl with the pretty big bow in her hair is Rene, and the cute tiny blonde girl is Mable, my mother. Those beautiful dresses the girls were wearing were likely homemade ones Grandma sewed.

She also made my mother a doll. The doll had little sewn eyes and nose and a smile. Mom may have been about the age in this picture when she added some material by pinning it to the doll to make it an anatomically correct *boy.* When asked about it she just responded that *he is a boy.* Grandma laughed when she discovered it.

The picture following the family portrait is of Mom, likely taken when she was about fourteen. Notice the way she played with her fingers, exactly the same in both pictures.

This family portrait was probably taken when Mom was in high school although it may have been earlier. With the dark, matronly dresses they wore, it is difficult to tell.

Left to right: bottom-Grandpa, Roy and Clifford. Top: Grandma, Mable (Mom), Rene, and Bonnie.

Rene and Putter on the back porch. This was the house they lived in before Mom and Rene bought the one after they started working at the cigar factory.

The following pictures are a variety taken around the same timeframe, mid 1940's. The first two of Mom, then Rene, were taken at Palisades Park, New Jersey.

Notice the GI getting on the ride behind Rene.

Mom and Rene   Notice the suitcase and the hatbox. I wonder where they were going. This was taken in the back of the house they bought while working at the cigar factory.

This following photo was taken after they moved to this new house, with the enclosed back porch, and the awning in the background. Their good friend Cattie Casey (on left) joined Rene and Mom for this posed backyard picture.

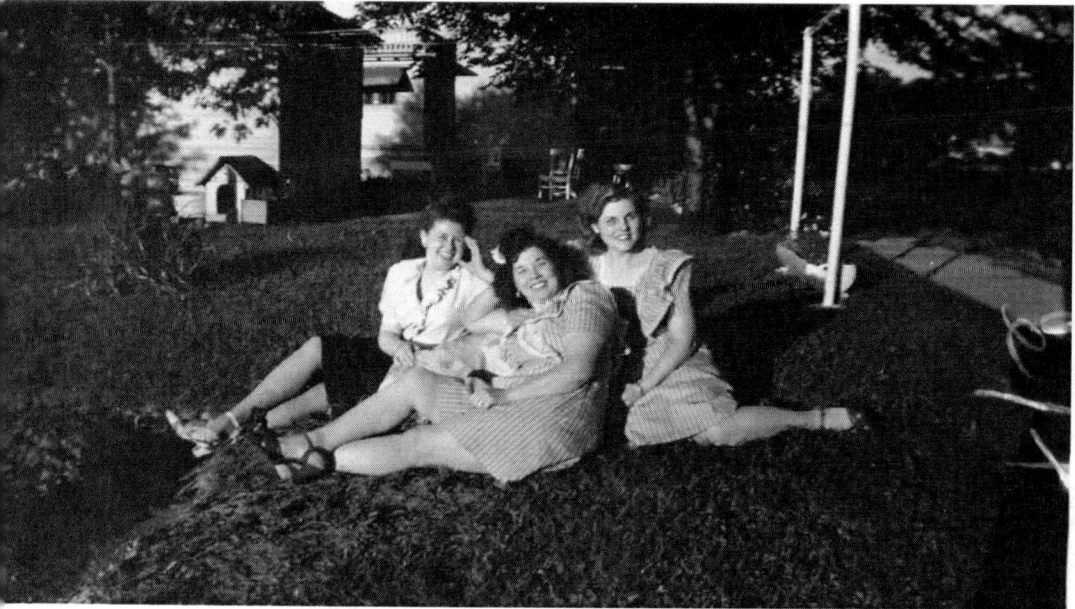

The first of the following two pictures is Mae, (Grandma), taken about the same time as the one above. I remember Mom telling me they had fun that day clowning around. That is their dog behind her. Mom said his name was Jip.

The second picture is my grandpa, Putter, on the job as a switchman at the railroad. Mom took both of these pictures with her Brownie camera.

This is Mom, by their car, which looks, from my research, like a 1939 Ford. See the following picture. Apparently they kept this vehicle for quite some time, as I seem to remember when I was very small, riding in this car on top of a little chair made for children. No car seats back then. The chair was so I could see out.

From the description of this car in the ad, it fits what I scantily remember of the inside of this car. I remember the footrest they mention in the following ad.

DE LUXE FORDOR SEDAN

Many people prefer the Fordor for its fine "town car" appearance, and the convenience of separate doors to front and rear compartments. Seats six comfortably. Generous leg room and head room. Robe cord and ash tray on back of front seat. Foot rest in rear compartment. Big, comfortable arm rests. Pillar lights on both sides. Clear-Vision Ventilation. As in Tudor, spare tire is mounted vertically against inside wall of large luggage compartment.

Mom and Rene, taken behind the house I grew up in.

Mable's "girl," (me at 6 months, I think).

Next page: I was playing in the leaves behind our house. Age about 14 months.

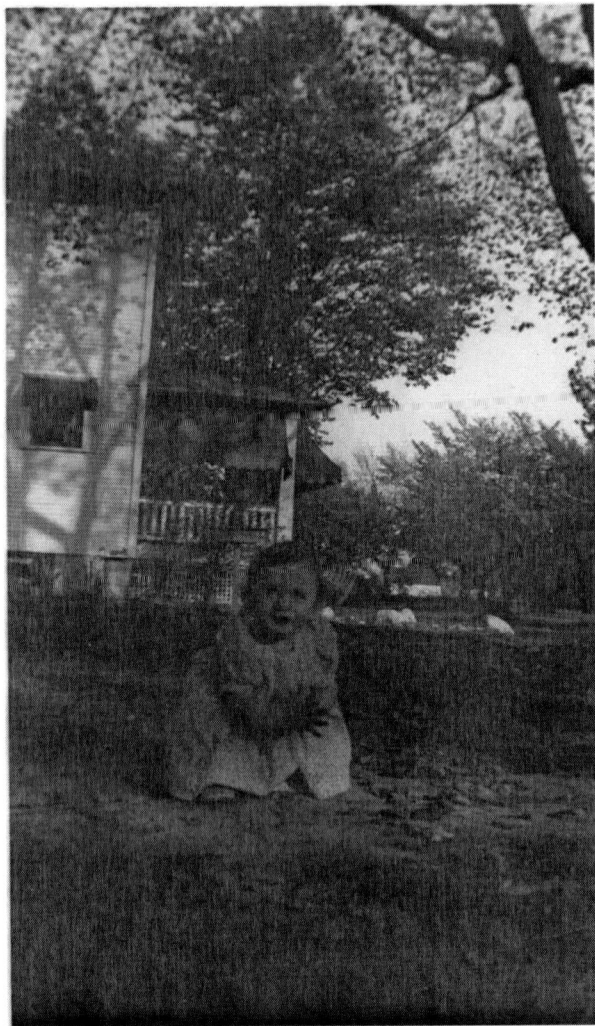

Next-taken in our front yard. That is Hope Street. The caption Mom wrote on the back of this picture is "15 months You know you are a sweetie don't you?"

Next: On the back of this picture she penned, "I had a dollie once too."

Mom had my picture taken a lot back then.

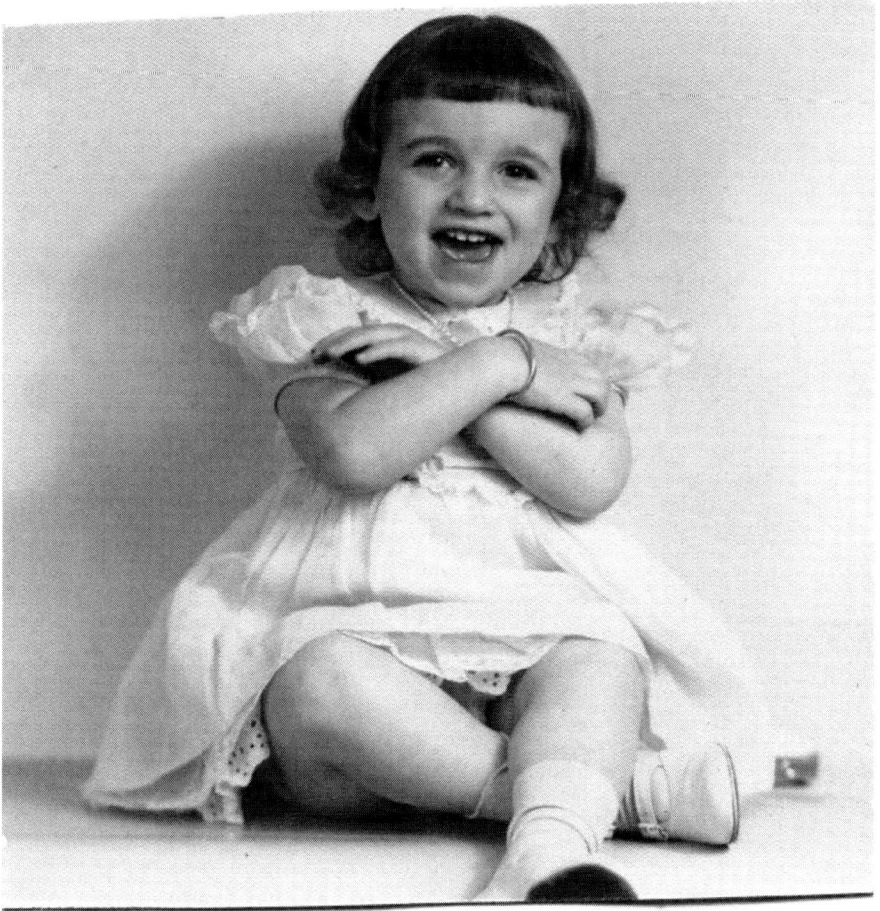

This is the portrait we had taken the day I remember seeing the man who was my father. The dress was from Gregg's Department Store, toddler section. It was a brown and blue plaid, and my socks were brown to match the dress. I wore that little gold bracelet, which was purchased from a jewelry store, for years until I outgrew it and it had to be cut off my arm.

Grandma had a garden. I enjoyed eating the freshly picked strawberries. Mom told me she thought this was cute, but got me off the table right after she took the picture. That's the Lang's house across the street.

Aunt Rene looking very much the way I remember her when I was quite small.

Rene-taken in front of the house I grew up in.

Rene, in her late 80's-early 90's

I was eating a plum while our dog, Patty, watched. This was taken in our backyard not long before we moved to Ewing Avenue.

I remember when this following portrait was taken. The photographer threw the ball to me as if we were playing a game. The ball was soft rubber. After she snapped the picture, she took her ball back. I was upset about it. Mommy told me, "The ball belongs to the photographer. You have balls at home." I remember thinking that it wasn't very nice to give someone something and then take it back from them.

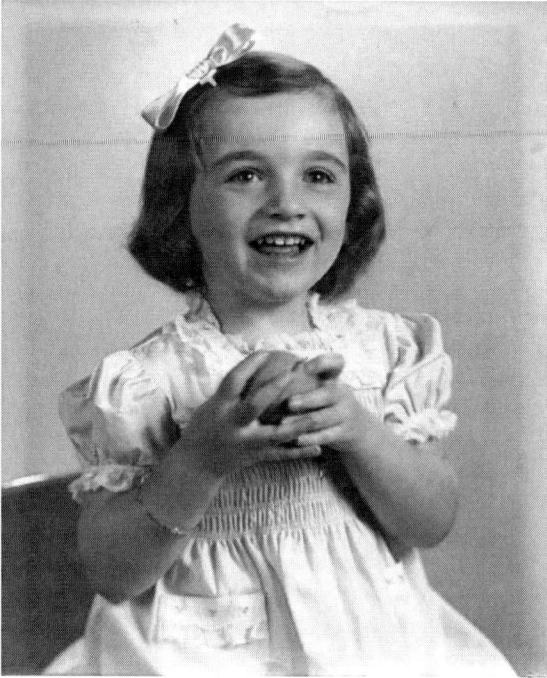

Christmas, mid-50's. Rene and John always joined us. This was also one of those visits where Dad had to go in search of Dede's elf doll, Punky. Rene also always scowled and told Mom how inappropriate it was for Harry to wash all those dishes. Dad's philosophy was that Mom made the meal and he would then wash the dishes.